To Cam

Best wishes!

Great riding with
you on the Cattle Droves!

G. T.

To Helena

WINSTON

Highway 287

Canyon Ferry Highway

ELKHORN MOUNTAINS

CANYON FERRY RESERVOIR

THE BIG BELT MOUNTAINS

Deep Creek Bar

TOWNSEND

Kirk Homestead

Deep Creek Highway

Ross Gulch

To White Sulphur Springs

Sharp Ranch

Greyson Creek

Greyson Creek Subdivision

Hogbacks

Ridge Road

Dry Creek Cabin

Dry Creek Road

Dry Creek Subdivision

Webster Ranch

MONTANA MIRAGE

By

J. T. Flynn

This is a work of fiction. Any resemblance of any of the
characters to persons living or dead is strictly coincidental.

FIRST EDITION

Copyright 1998, by J.T. Flynn
ISBN: 0-9667930-0-5

MOUNTAIN VALLEY PUBLISHING, LLC
Box 971
Three Forks, Montana 59752

DEDICATION

Dedicated to the memory of Lorena Flynn
who taught me the joy of books.

ACKNOWLEDGMENTS

Special thanks to Deborah Whitehurst, Mary Alice Upton, John Ryan, Cheryl Beaty, and Lynne Arensmyer for their input, advice and encouragement.

Part I

Chapter I

September 1st

Banjo saw it first. The ears of the dappled-gray gelding cocked forward. The old pack horse turned and peered into the undergrowth.

William J. Sharp had learned long ago to trust the horse's vision and quickly followed his gaze. The rancher caught flashes of shiny black movement between the duller black and white trunks of the many quaking aspens.

"What is it, Grandpa?" six year old Lane Sharp called from atop the youngster's bay horse which had moved alongside William J.'s own white gelding.

"I don't rightly know," said William J. "But I intend to find out."

William J. wrapped the halter rope of the pack horse around his saddle horn. He forced his own horse to step off the old logging road to the game trail angling below. The rope tightened on his thigh as the gray hesitated but then moved forward in step with the white horse.

"Come on Banjo," said William J. "I know this isn't the way back to the horse trailer, but we'd better check this out."

The three horses, two with saddles and riders and one with panniers for hauling salt blocks, eased through a thick stand of quaking aspen saplings and emerged in the small clearing where they had first glimpsed the flashes of black movement.

A raven, the source of the movement, bounced three times and flew at a steep angle out of the clearing. William J. watched an object drop from the raven's beak as it rose above them. The object sailed slightly as it descended and settled onto the trail. William J. dismounted by the raven's discarded cargo. He placed the calf ear on his leather gloved left palm and examined it closely. The resulting frown added even move wrinkles to the lined and weathered face.

He grabbed the reins and walked further into the clearing. Tufts of black hair formed a large circular pattern near the middle of the clearing. William J. stooped and retrieved a bright yellow ear tag from the center of this clump of hair. He critically examined the plastic tag with the black number "6" clearly etched upon it.

"What is it, Grandpa?" Lane Sharp softly asked again.

"It was a steer calf," said William J. "The sixth one born last winter."

"What happened to it?"

"Mountain lion."

"How can you tell?" asked Lane.

"I've seen the lion kills of many mule deer over the past few years and they've all had this same pattern of hair. A lion must tear at the hide like gangbusters before it eats."

"Have you ever seen a lion kill a deer?"

"I've never even seen a mountain lion. When I was your age, there weren't any lions in this country. Your great grandpa told me that there were a few lions left in his day, but that was well before my time.

"It wasn't until the early 1970s that we started seeing lion tracks again. I remember cutting a track on the backside of Kessler's knob one fall. After that first track, it seemed that every year we would see more and more tracks and then more and more lion kills.

"I've been real close to lions several times—even had one yowl at me one night after dark when I rode down the Flathead Indian Trail, but I've yet to actually see one."

2

"Do they kill many of our calves?"

"This is the first one that I know of," said William J. "We've come up short a few calves each fall and suspected lions, but this is the first one I'm sure a lion killed. Let's dump the rest of this salt and get out of here. I'm sure your daddy will want to know about this calf."

William J. remounted and returned to the old logging road. They rode out of the clump of trees to a flat ridge shelf that overlooked the entire upper Dry Creek basin. They could see each fork of the four small streams that merged at the far end of the vast meadow. A sea of grass tapered from the many beaver ponds in the creek bottom up to the massive quaking aspen grove from which they had just emerged. Here they lifted the fifty pound salt blocks from the panniers on Banjo and dropped them into the two foot depression that had been hollowed from the ground by deer, elk and Black Angus cattle licking the salt block left from the Sharps' last salting trip.

As soon as the blocks were unloaded, they rode toward the pickup and horse trailer parked far below them on the Dry Creek road.

The young mountain lion sat poised and ready. Normally the man and child at the far end of the meadow would have concerned him, but the hunger that burned in his gut focused his attention on the movement in the narrow ravine below. The lion's ears twitched above the tall grass as he cocked his head and tried to determine if this movement were food or foe.

Lately, fortune had not been on his side. A misguided jack rabbit wandering into his path three days before had been his only meal this week. The day before, fate had been doubly cruel to him. He had waited patiently by a well used deer trail until a doe and her fawn had moved from their

3

bedding grounds in the thick timber of Black Butte Gulch toward the water tank used by the Sharp Ranch to water cattle on the ridge above the Ross Gulch corrals.

A quick dash and well-timed leap had placed the fawn in his grasp. The fawn's initial terrorized burst to escape the fangs and claws had pulled both animals off the trail and down a steep ridge.

When the fawn had ducked under a small fir tree, a low-hanging branch had stuck the lion and knocked him from the deer. The fawn had quickly bounded up the ridge and re-joined its mother as the young lion had watched them disappear over the ridge.

He had also encountered the large mature tom that frequented this portion of the Big Belt Mountains on the east side of the Missouri River Valley. A fierce display of teeth and claws followed by two cuffs from the tom's large paws had sent the young lion scurrying in full flight toward his present location on the Greyson Creek drainage.

Now, the young lion's instinct produced mixed signals about the figure moving toward his position. When upright, the human outline registered clearly as danger but the small size of the figure and the frequent bent over position piqued his curiosity and screamed out prey.

Ultimately, the hunger in his gut overrode the danger instinct and he planned his attack. The ravine angled sharply from the meadow and then widened and flattened. The lion focused on a flat grassy opening in the bottom. The trail at this point wound around a small juniper bush which would hide the first few leaps of his approach. The lion anticipated his attack at this site.

The human figure moved intermittently. The young girl stopped and bended frequently. The young lion tensed and waited.

Headwaters County District Attorney Jefferson Kirk stood on the fresh willow cuttings of the beaver dam. He peered across the green meadow. Unaware of the mountain lion stalking her, he watched his eight year old daughter Jenny move into the bottom of a narrow ravine.

Kirk observed with bittersweet feelings. The day was gorgeous. The Montana sky was a canvas of blue with a few cumulus clouds offering interesting shapes of contrast. The slight breeze provided only enough movement to ripple the leaves of the quaking aspen grove that circled the south side of the meadow. The temperature hovered in the seventies. A killing frost hadn't yet hit the Missouri River Valley and the Greyson Creek drainage was resplendently green with all its foliage. His twin daughters, Lisa and Jenny, were enjoying their encounter with nature.

Kirk also enjoyed the relief of knowing that the final legal chapter had ended in the most noteworthy case in the history of Headwaters County. The November before, a serial killer had roamed the mountains randomly killing hunters. The animal rights group, Animals Forever, had created a media event out of the proceedings. The case had also been complicated by the heightened interest caused by the wounding of country western superstar Ray Webster and the murder of another hunter by a copycat killer. The sentencing the preceding Friday of Peter Gable, the copycat killer, had ended months of legal wrangling and media attention.

The only good thing to come out of the entire incident as far as Kirk was concerned, was the relationship that had developed between him and Heidi Singer, a journalist who had covered the shootings and then written a book about the incident. Kirk felt carefree for the first time in many months.

Kirk's feelings were tempered only by his awareness that the girls' summer vacation was now at an end. In the morning, they would be returning to their mother's home in Minnesota. He watched Jenny move into the narrow part of the ravine continually stopping and bending over. Lisa's voice diverted his attention back to the stream.

"Dad I need another fly."

"Here's a 'Crazy Goof,'" said Kirk. He held the gray and yellow fly between his thumb and index finger carefully avoiding the sharp point of the hook. "It's a grasshopper imitation although you'd hardly know it to look at it. A 'Joe's Hopper' looks more like a grasshopper to humans but not to a trout. This is the best hopper imitation I've ever come across."

From beneath a mop of curly blonde hair, eight year old Lisa Kirk rolled her eyes.

"Come on, Dad. Just get the fly on the line. Remember, you're the one who said you can't catch fish unless your line is in the water."

Kirk smiled and ran the tapered leader through the eye of the fly, twisted the line several times and pulled the knot tight. He clipped the excess leader by biting it with his teeth. He gazed up the creek looking for a likely riffle that would hold a rainbow or brook trout.

The location on the Sharp ranch for this fly fishing lesson had been carefully chosen. This section of Greyson Creek meandered through a flat grassy meadow. There was little brush or willow along the stream bank to snare the errant cast of the novice fly fisherman. Every bend in the stream created the calm deep water of a "corner hole" that the trout loved.

Kirk knew from experiences dating back to his child-hood that this meadow stretch of creek was loaded with five to fourteen inch trout.

He continued his instructions as he stripped line from the automatic reel. "The rod tip only goes back to about the one o'clock position and definitely not farther than two o'clock," he said as he stopped the rod just past perpendicular. The ivory fly line arched gracefully behind him and then came back forward after a slight pause. He made several false casts before he shot the line forward and bounced the fly off the cut bank. The fly landed gently in the pool beneath the bank.

The trout responded immediately. Kirk lifted his wrist setting the hook. The motion of his arm accelerated the fish's upward momentum and the rainbow broke the surface flashing briefly in the sunlight before splashing back into the clear water. Kirk raised the rod above his head and the tightening line halted the trout's brief run upstream. The fish fought hard for its size but was quickly landed on the small flat rocks of the narrow gravel bar.

Lisa let out a shriek and grabbed the fat body of the twelve inch rainbow. She held the fish in her palms and examined the bright red and orange stripes on the silver body. "Can we keep him?" she asked.

"No. Put him back and he'll be bigger next time. We're just giving him a little exercise."

Lisa removed the hook and reluctantly eased the fish back into the water. The rainbow swam slowly into the first pool downstream and disappeared under a ceiling of moss.

Lisa smiled broadly. "My turn now." Kirk handed her the rod and she moved along the gravel bar to the next hole. She stripped line from the reel and tried casting. Despite her father's advice, the rod went back within inches of the ground before she whipped it forward much too quickly. The fly landed about five feet short of its target. Two large loops of line lay slack on the water.

Kirk shook his head slowly and moved forward to offer assistance. A brook trout raced several feet from his hiding place along the bank and sucked in the 'goof.' The slack line made setting the hook an ineffective act. Fortunately, beginner's luck prevailed and the brook trout hooked himself as he turned to dart back to the cover along the bank.

Rather than pressing the lever on the automatic reel and feeding the line back onto the spool, Lisa raced across the gravel bar into the meadow carrying the fly rod over her shoulder. She ran until the line tightened and the small brook trout flopped out of the water onto the gravel bar. She dropped the rod in the high grass of the meadow and raced back to capture her prize.

Kirk lay on the bank laughing.

"I got him," she said as she revealed the speckled trout in her grasp.

"I see you do," said Kirk, slightly regaining his composure. "Now, put him back so we can catch some more."

Kirk watched closely as Lisa knelt by the stream and admired the pot bellied brook trout with the deep orange markings on the underside. She slipped it back into the clear water and rubbed the fish slime onto her blue jeans. "Do you want a turn now?"

"No, you go ahead," said Kirk. "You're doing fine. You fish now and I'll give Jenny a turn when she gets back from her rock hunting."

Lisa crossed the gravel bar and climbed a bank that overlooked a deep hole made deeper by the fresh beaver workings at the lower end. She crept to the edge and peeked over the bank. She stripped out several feet of line and extended the graphite rod over the creek. She flicked the rod tip and placed the fly into the calm water in the center of the hole.

She held her breath as the fish rose slowly from the dark water, carefully eying the hopper imitation before darting in for the kill.

At the fish's quick movement, Lisa jerked the rod upward hooking the trout and pulling it several feet out of the water before it dropped straight back into the pool.

She heard a noise behind her. She turned just in time to see Jake, the Australian Shepherd/Border Collie, shooting past her and barreling off the bank into the pool. Jake disappeared below the surface, emerged and shook off on the opposite bank.

Lisa pulled the line and fly from the stream minus the brook trout. "Bad Dog. Bad Jake." she yelled at the dog who now sat innocently looking up at her.

"Dad, call Jake. He made me lose my fish."

Kirk laughed. He called to Jake who splashed down the middle of the stream to meet him. The dog lay on his back with all four feet in the air. Kirk obliged the dog and scratched his belly.

"Jake, you're about as much help fishing as a screen door on a submarine."

Kirk scrambled to his feet and ran into the meadow with Jake racing right behind. He gestured toward the coulee at the far end of the meadow. "Go on, Jake. Go find Jenny." The dog hesitated momentarily then ran across the meadow. Kirk watched briefly but Lisa's distinctive whoop told him that another fish had fallen victim to the Crazy Goof. He turned to observe her next landing technique.

"We're just about there," called Pete Roemer as he pushed back his sweat-stained cowboy hat and waited for Ray Webster to reach his level on the narrow ridge line. Webster gingerly moved up the last stretch of the narrow trail barely keeping ahead of the big appaloosa that scrambled behind him.

"I hope whatever you couldn't wait to show me was worth leaving the best damn party of the year," puffed Webster as the two men stepped out onto the relatively level surface of the sage brush flat.

They led their horses to the sharp edge of the ridge that jutted into the drainage overlooking the ranch headquarters of Webster Enterprises, Inc. Far below, they could see the huge A-framed chalet, the corrals, outbuildings, and the throng of people gathered around the makeshift stage. They heard the sound of country music echoing up the canyon walls.

"I'll admit this is the best seat in the house," Webster said, "but let's go see what's so all fired important so I can get back to entertaining my guests."

Pete Roemer crossed the clearing and motioned for Webster to follow. Roemer tied the horses to two juniper bushes ladened with clumps of purple berries. Roemer, as was his custom, plucked one of the clumps of juniper berries from the tree. He squeezed the berries in the palm of his hand until the tan pulp of the interior was visible and the juice ran through his fingers. Roemer lifted his hand to his nose and sniffed. He wiped the sweet, pungent juice on the legs of his jeans.

He ducked between two of the several junipers that made up the grove. He wound through a narrow alleyway and continued into a natural amphitheater walled by the aromatic cedars.

Roemer walked on by the first circle of deer hair and bones letting Webster make the discovery himself.

"What's this?" asked a startled Ray Webster.

"Lion kill," Roemer said, "And so's that and that and that." He turned and pointed to other circles of mule deer hair and bone fragments scattered around the small clearing.

Webster crisscrossed the clearing several times surveying the carnage. He paused in the center of the opening. The country western singer, obviously shaken, shook his head.

"My God, it looks like we've stumbled into a mountain lion's dining room."

"That's not far from the truth. Lions like to eat on a flat surface if they can. Any animals killed on the slopes above here were dragged or carried to this ridge top to be eaten. I counted seventeen deer and elk carcasses within about three hundred yards of this clearing."

"I guess this explains why we don't have the big herds of mule deer around the chalet anymore," said Webster.

"The old-timers tell me that a mature lion will take two deer a week if given the opportunity. That's a hundred and four deer a year. You get several lions working an area and it doesn't take long to wipe out a deer herd," said Roemer.

"Lions got to make a living, too," Webster said, "But why are we seeing so many more lions all of a sudden? We even allow the lion hunters to take a few. I'd think that'd keep their numbers in check."

"The lion numbers have been building for years," Roemer said, "and lion hunting actually adds to the numbers."

"How?" asked Webster.

"The Fish and Game has a quota. They also have a subquota which further limits the number of females that can be taken. Lion hunters prefer to kill a big tom because they want a trophy they can mount.

"Most all lion hunting is done with dogs. The guide with the dogs searches until he finds a fresh lion track and then he turns the dogs loose on the track. The hunter follows the dogs until the lion climbs a tree. That's always been the downfall of the mountain lion. A lion feels safe from the dogs in a tree. Once treed, a hunter can just walk right up to the tree and shoot the lion.

"Because hunters can get a close up view of the treed lion, they can be real choosy about the lion they take. They can pass up the females and smaller males and shoot only the large toms."

"I still don't see what that has to do with the increase in the number of mountain lions," said Webster.

"In the wild, a large male lion will control his area. If he finds a litter, he'll kill the kittens. When those large toms are hunted and killed, more kittens have the opportunity to reach adulthood."

"I guess that means a mountain lion won't be named 'Father of the Year' anytime soon," said Webster laughing.

"You got it."

"What controls the lion numbers then?"

"If man weren't in the picture, the toms and the overall decline in the deer and elk would eventually reduce the lions' food supply. When the food supply declines, the number of lions and other predators dips back down. When the populations of lions and other predators drop, the deer and elk populations rise again."

"But what happens with man in the picture?" asked Webster.

"This time around I don't think anyone knows for sure," said Roemer. "By the turn of the century, the cattlemen, sheep herders, government trappers and bounty hunters had all but wiped out the mountain lion in Montana. Would've been the best thing, in my opinion, if they had. Now, we're gettin' large numbers of lions in the same parts of Headwaters County where there are large numbers of people and cattle. Something's got to give. When the numbers of lions reaches a certain point and the numbers of deer and elk drop to a certain point, lions are gonna start grabbin' cattle, or worse yet, a kid."

"When's that gonna happen?"

"I don't rightly know, but when it does, all hell's gonna break loose," Roemer said as he nudged a jutting piece of hip bone with his foot.

Webster turned his head and said, "I don't know about that but I do know that all hell's goin' to break loose if I don't get back and play a little for my guests like I promised. Let's get moving. Ever since you said the word 'lion' and showed me these kills, I can't help glancing over my shoulder every few seconds."

They wound back through the maze of junipers. They untied their horses and eased back down the steep slope.

Jenny Kirk winced. The shoulder strap of the bulging fish bag was starting to cut into the side of her neck. She stopped and let the bag slip to the ground. She dumped the contents in a pile next to the trail in the bottom of the ravine. From this pile, she carefully selected three or four essential rocks and placed them back in the fish compartment of the canvas bag. She re-shouldered the bag and again began moving up the small ravine. Jenny rolled over each rock in her path. She was particularly intrigued by any stone containing a band of quartz. The occasional highly polished all white quartz stones equated in her eight year old mind with finding the mother lode.

Where the flat grassy bottom narrowed and the ravine steepened and dropped a few feet, the spring runoff had washed all the topsoil from the surface exposing a cache of stone. She sat sifting intently through the gravel. Jenny found three of the highly coveted quartz pieces which she slipped into the pocket of the fish bag.

Jenny started to step up onto the grassy shelf itself. She paused in midstep at the sound of pounding feet. She felt her pulse quicken and her heart seemed in her throat. She turned and ducked just in time to see Jake coming directly at her. The dog shot past her and disappeared around a tall juniper. The dog barked and growled as he ran up the ridge. She called after him, "Come, Jake. Come, boy." By the time she climbed the drop off and scrambled around the juniper, the dog was just going out of sight over the hill. She ran halfway up the ridge continuously calling to him.

Panting and holding her sides, she stopped and waited. Two minutes later, a winded Jake came running back down the ridge.

"You silly dog," she said. "What in the world were you chasing?"

A distant yell diverted her attention back to the meadow. She turned to see her father motioning for her to come. "Let's go, Jake. I'll race you," she yelled as she bounded down the ridge with Jake running at her side and a fish bag full of rocks beating against her thigh.

They met Lisa and her father at the big beaver dam at the top of the meadow.

"Do you know why this fly is like Dad?" asked Lisa.

"No, why?"

"Because they're both 'crazy goofs,'" giggled Lisa laughing at her own joke.

The young lion trotted briskly along the south rim of the Greyson Creek drainage. The unexpected arrival of the dog and the increased level of human sounds emanating from the meadow had called for the abandonment of the attack and forced a nervous retreat. He paused frequently and looked intently at his back trail for any sign of the dog. As he fled up the drainage, the hungry fire in his gut grew and burned even hotter.

Pete Roemer and Ray Webster led their horses from a wall of thick junipers at the bottom of the ridge that over-looked a grassy meadow. They remounted and rode through the herd of Longhorn cattle congregated in the creek bottom. The cattle scattered in front of the trotting horses.

Ray Webster stopped the big appaloosa and watched the rangy Longhorns enter a clump of willows and then line out as they moved up the coulee across the creek.

"Do you think those cattle are in any danger from lions?" asked Webster.

"No, as tough as those critters are," said Roemer, "a lion'd probably break his teeth and starve to death."

"You still don't like Longhorns much, do you?"

"I don't know what you see in 'em."

Webster swung his arm in an arc that encompassed all the cattle and the meadow and mountain slopes across the creek. "How can you look at that scene and not see and feel the heritage of the American cowboy? I can just picture Charles Goodnight trailing those cattle up from Texas. Can't you just picture Gil Favor or Rowdy Yates a ridin' up and yellin', 'Head 'em up and move 'em out?'"

"All I can see is a bunch of mangy cows that raise calves the cattle buyers don't want," Roemer said.

"I think you're being too hard on the breed myself. Since we got 'em, I've been doin' some reading about the Longhorn. Said that Longhorns are great for 'calving ease.' Also, if you cross them with several other breeds, you can eventually create a cow that has the best traits of each breed."

"That's already been done," Roemer said.

"Really?"

"Yeah, and do you know what they call the result?"

"No, what?"

"A 'Hereford'." Roemer laughed.

"Say what you will, but the lions better leave these long-horned beauties alone. They're the best of their breed that money can buy."

"If they'd put me in charge, I'd take care of the lions," Pete said.

"And just what'd you do?"

"I'd get rid of the quotas and the lion hunting season and then I'd put a $1,000 bounty on them until they were all wiped out."

"That's not what I'd call politically or environmentally correct," Webster said.

"I'm so sick of political correctness that I could spit," Pete said. "And you talk about environmental correctness. The only problem with our environment I can see is that there's just too damn many people. Everyone's talking about and wanting a natural environment but raw nature is pretty damn cold and harsh and demands that the old, weak and unfit die. But humans are too damn soft hearted to really let nature work. If you want the true balance of nature, then just put the mountain lions in Central Park or downtown LA. That oughta take care of the homeless problem."

"I can see that you'll get the 'Humanitarian of the Year' award just about the same time that a mountain lion wins 'Father of the Year,'" said Webster. "Lighten up a little. What'd a mountain lion ever do to you?"

"More than you'd think," Roemer said. "My grandfather had a place in the Shields Valley at the base of the Crazy Mountains. He bought the neighbor place on credit and tried to pay for it running sheep. The coyotes and lions were a getting their share but he was making a go of it until a female lion with two half grown kittens ran a big flock right off a cliff. He lost that place and almost the home place too."

"That was all before your time," Webster said.

"I still feel the effects, though. My Dad eventually took over the home place where I grew up. My older brother stayed and then he took over. When I was ready, there just wasn't any room for me. If we'd still had the neighbor place, that'd been my spot. I'd be callin' my own shots today on my own spread if not for mountain lions."

"And the fox would've caught the rabbit if he hadn't of stopped to take a shit. If it'd all gone down that a way, you wouldn't have danced with some of the best lookin' women in Nashville. I saw a couple of them eying you before we left. You should grab one of those ladies and make her Mrs. Pete Roemer."

"Not a chance."

"How is it that you never married?"

"I may not have married, but I've done my share of honeymoonin'," said Roemer with a grin. "I was always waiting to get a place of my own and settle down. Kept thinking that it was gonna happen and then land prices went sky high and somehow life just slipped away. But I think you're right about a couple of those gals. They've done decided that they'd like themselves a cowboy."

"Let's not keep them waitin' then," said Ray Webster. "Let's gallop in and make a dramatic entrance."

"You think you're up to it?" asked Roemer.

"No problem," said Webster. "One of the great things about gettin' shot in the ass is that you get so much scar tissue that it's just like having a leather butt. I may never get saddle sore again. Hi Oh Silver away," yelled Webster as he firmly grabbed the saddlehorn with his left hand and kicked the appaloosa into a gallop.

They raced across the meadow and entered the court-yard at Webster Enterprises headquarters with the flourish of pounding hooves and a cloud of dust. Webster rode to the base of the stage. He dismounted and climbed the stairs. He grabbed the mike and shouted to the crowd,"Y'all havin' a good time?" The resounding applause and whoops indicated that the crowd he had flown in from Nashville in the char-tered jet were enjoying themselves.

Webster launched into his latest hit, "Rattlesnakes Won't Bite You When It's Cold." The crowd danced and sang along. When he finished, he ad libbed a new line, "Rattlesnakes won't bite you when it's cold but if you still want a thrill a mountain lion will."

When the crowd finally quieted down, Webster said, "Ladies and gentlemen, I've just come from a mountain lion killing grounds. There are probably mountain lions watching us even as I speak. Pete Roemer has told me that he has never heard of a mountain lion attacking two people together. As a safety precaution, I want you to find someone to snuggle up with while I sing you a love song."

As the voice of Ray Webster bounced up the canyon walls, a large lion tom stretched and looked curiously down on the commotion far below.

The small fishing boat bobbed gently on the glass like surface of Canyon Ferry Lake. "Old Baldy" peak loomed above the lake on the east side of the Missouri River Valley and the bright sunlight illuminated the many promontories of the Elkhorn range to the west.

Headwaters County Sheriff, Ben Green, would have appreciated the view if his chin had not been resting on his chest along with his black felt cowboy hat. The only visible portions of his face were the ends of the handle bar mustache that curled around each side of the hat brim like two small antennae.

The sheriff reclined in a lawn chair with a casting rod propped loosely between his legs. A jerk dislodged the fishing pole and sent it careening toward the rear of the boat. Ben scrambled to his feet and lurched to the back of the boat. He caught the casting rod in one hand and his cowboy hat in the other just as they were going over the side.

"Nice save," called Deputy Tucker from the driver's seat.

"This'd better be a good trout," Ben said as he set the drag and began playing the fish. "When this fish hit, I had just shot a six point bull elk and was on my way back to a hunting lodge filled with hot tubs and long legged women."

The fish made two long runs into the lake. Ben cranked the handle on the reel while Tucker stood ready with the landing net. The fish quickly tired and the sheriff worked it toward the boat.

"What is it?" asked Tucker.

"A carp," said Ben disgustedly as the golden scaled fish turned sideways on the surface. Tucker netted the fish and took out the hook. After the trash fish was unceremoniously released back into the lake with an underhanded high looping toss, the sheriff sat back down in the lawn chair.

"Damn fish," exclaimed Ben. "I think I'll take the bait off the hook. That's about as relaxed as I've felt in a long time. You know, Tuck, I think all of the hoopla over the shootings is finally over and we'll be able to get back to business as usual."

"I think you're right," Tucker said.

"I thought we'd have a trial for sure," said Ben.

"Yeah, me too. But once that blonde journalist hinted at some link between Animals Forever and Gable, they dropped him like a hot rock."

"They certainly did leave him twisting in the wind,"

Ben said. "Once that happened, I thought he'd squeal like a stuck pig. Kirk even offered him a favorable sentencing recommendation for his cooperation, but he wouldn't say 'boo'."

"Hell, I even hear Ray Webster's ass is healed up," Tucker said. "He's probably back in the saddle again."

"In more ways than one," said Ben. "I hear he flew in a whole plane load of people for the long weekend. From what the boys at the Mini Mart told me, I understand that there were a lot of mighty fine lookin' women among 'em."

"Must be a tough life having to fight off all them groupies," said Tucker. "What's he doing back in Montana anyway?"

"The boys at the Mini Mart said he's up to chase his Longhorns around the pasture some and do a little bow hunting."

"When does the archery season open?"

"This coming Saturday," Ben said, "along with the grouse season. And with everything quieted back down again, I'm gonna head into my old camp in the Elkhorns for a few days and see if my dog'll point up a bird or two."

"Sounds like pretty tough duty."

"It's thankless dirty work but somebody has to do it," said Ben as he leaned back in the lawn chair and repositioned the hat over his face.

William J. held a platter while his wife Mary placed one last drumstick on the mound of fried chicken. He carefully crossed the floor and placed the plate in the center of the kitchen table.

William J. took his chair and gazed out the picture window at the view of the horse pasture and pole corrals. As he waited for grandsons Lane and Cody to finish washing up, he watched his white gelding amble out of the row of cottonwood trees that lined Deep Creek. The horse flopped down on a bare spot on the creek bank and rolled on its back several times.

"Sends a shiver up my spine every time I see a horse roll that way," said William J. "Always afraid they'll twist a gut."

"Old Snowball must have got a workout," John Sharp said as he followed William J.'s gaze.

"He did," said William J. "He made three trips in and back, but that ought to keep the cattle in salt until it's time to wean."

"Did you see any elk in the quakies?"

"Not a one, but I did find this," said William J. sliding the yellow calf tag across the table.

"Dead?"

"Yup, Had all the markings of a lion kill. Lots of hide and hair."

"With all the deer and elk kills we've been seeing, I thought this was gonna happen," John said, tossing the tag back across the table. "It was just a matter of time. I'm surprised that it took this long. I figure that a lion must look at a calf as just another entree in the smorgasbord of life."

"I hope the lions don't start thinking of calves as a daily entree choice," said William J. glumly. "I'm afraid that once a lion gets a taste for beef, it'll just keep on killin' cattle. A calf has to be a lot easier to catch than a deer or elk."

"Without a doubt," John said. "So what's our course of action? Do we want to report it? If so, to whom—the Sheriff? The Fish and Game?

William J. grinned. "Pete Roemer always said that if you have trouble with lions, grizzlies or wolves to apply the three S's: shoot, shovel and shut up."

"Pete used to say the same thing about women." John laughed. "That option may be a little too drastic at this point, but I don't think we ought to report this right away. This is the kind of story that the media can blow way out of proportion."

"We certainly don't want that kind of attention," William J said. "Especially if this is an isolated killing."

"Maybe the first thing I ought to do," said John, "is take a ride and see if we've lost any other cattle. Tomorrow I'll park the horse trailer on the ridge road and ride through the Dry Creek Basin. Then, I can drop into Upper Greyson Creek and ride through the cattle above Greyson Creek Lakes and circle back to the trailer."

"Can I come with you and ride the new gray horse?" asked Lane as he slid into the chair next to William J.

"The only thing you're riding tomorrow, young man, is a yellow school bus," his mother said as she placed a platter filled with steaming corn on the cob next to the platter of chicken. "Did you forget that tomorrow is your first day of school?"

"Oh yeah, but I'd still like to ride the new horse."

"You'd better stick with your old 'Toots,'" William J. said. "That gray'd drop you on your head for sure."

Misty and four-year-old Cody took their seats. Seventy-year-old Mary Sharp stood while her family dished up their plates. She made certain that her grandsons had the appropriate vegetables and the desired pieces of chicken. Only after everyone had their food did Mary Sharp take her place at the table.

"I'm going to have to start raising four-legged chickens to meet the demand for drumsticks," Mary said. "Personally, I find this lion business a little scary. John, I think you'd better keep an eye on the boys when you're out in the mountains."

"Statistically these boys are probably safer in the mountains than they are sitting at your kitchen table right now."

"The food's not that bad." William J. grinned.

"They say there are three categories of lies, 'lies' 'damn lies' and 'statistics,'" Mary Sharp said glaring at both her son and husband. "An ounce of prevention is worth a pound of cure. You don't want Lane and Cody ending up being a statistic."

22

"Oh, before I forget," said William J. "Mort Chappel flagged me down this morning. He's finally decided to retire. He asked if we'd be interested in buying his two sections of mountain pasture."

"What's he want for it?" asked John. "Those sections would be perfect for running heifers."

"Mort said that he'd a lot rather see us have them than a developer or some high-dollared out-of-stater. Says he'd let it go for $100 an acre and he'd carry the paper."

"That's still $128,000," said John, whistling softly. "How would we pay for it? We're just barely making our payments now. There's no way to pay for $100 an acre pasture with cattle. It'd be overpriced at $50 an acre if you've got to make the payments raisin' cows."

"That's the rub," said William J. "But it sure as hell beats shelling out the $500 to $1000 an acre the developers and celebrities are payin'. Mort's giving us a bargain."

"I can't believe you're even thinking about buying more land," interjected Mary. "Don't you have enough already?"

"If we put it on a thirty-year contract, I'll only be 103 when we get it paid off," said William J. with a smile. "If Mort sells that ground to someone else, we'll never have another chance at it. It's not often that something comes up for sale right next to you. The way the fool people are buyin' up Montana, I'm afraid the time's comin' when a rancher isn't ever again gonna be able to buy a piece of mountain ground. I can't believe people will pay ten to twenty times what property will produce. At $100 an acre, this looks to me like the opportunity of a lifetime."

"You must be into your fourth or fifth lifetime then," said Mary. "Did it ever occur to you that we might ought to be selling land at those prices instead of buying?"

William J. and John shot her an astonished look.

"Sell land—What for?" asked William J. "Craziest thing I ever heard of."

"Well, I guess I'd better get some more chickens," said Mary. "It looks like we're going to keep needing my egg money."

"It's going to take a lot more than egg money," Misty said. "If cattle can only pay for $50 an acre land, you need to come up with another source for the other $50 an acre. It looks like I'll have to keep teaching too."

"Misty's right," said John. "But I really think this may be the last chance we have to pick up any property adjoining the ranch. On two sides we're hemmed in by the National Forest and Ray Webster. The Greyson Creek and Dry Creek subdivisions rule out any expansion in that direction. Mort's property is the only way we can go."

"That Greyson Creek subdivision still gravels me," said William J. "Old Harp Kirby leased me that property for twenty-five years and then sold it right out from under me. Never even had a chance at it. Can't believe people actually want to live up in that country. If we ever get winter again, they'll wish they had a place in the valley."

"It's gone full cycle," said Misty. "That country used to be carved into small homesteads. Over the years, those homesteads have all been consolidated into just a few large ranches—ours included. Now it's slowly being divided up once again. This time into twenty-acre ranchettes."

"Only this time, the settlers don't need the land to support them," said William J. "And they can't wait to move here, but as soon as they come they can't wait to make it just like where they came from. Seems like the first words out their mouths are 'that's not the way we did it.'"

John nodded. "They say they're coming here for the lifestyle, but the first thing they want to do is change things. I don't think they have a clue what we're about. I had the pickup and horse trailer stopped on the steep grade where the Ridge Road drops into Dry Creek. The bulls'd been fightin' and had about fifty yards of fence tore out. I was

24

pounding steel posts when I see the retired doctor that bought the first lot in the Dry Creek subdivision driving down the ridge. I quit work and walked over to the trailer to make sure that he could get by. Well, I see that there's plenty of room—at least a ten foot wide strip with one grapefruit sized rock sticking up on one side. He's got a $30,000 new four wheel drive so I figure that there's no problem. I go back to pounding posts. The next thing I know he's right behind me indignant as all get out and wantin' me to move my truck and trailer so he can get by."

"What'd you do?" asked Misty.

"I backed the pickup and trailer right up on the bank. Parked the truck at such an angle that I had to crawl out the passenger side."

"Do you think he got the point?" asked Misty.

"Not at all. I think it went right by him."

"It's going to get worse before it gets better," said William J. "People want to move into the mountains, but they fail to realize that by moving up there, they're destroying the very things that made them move here. It doesn't make any sense to me."

"I think that's why we got to buy Mort's land," said John. "If a developer gets a hold of it, we'll have a subdivision and all its problems on that side too."

"You still have to figure out how to make the payments," said Mary.

"Can you guide more hunters?" asked Misty.

"Between our local hunting association and guided nonresidents, the rifle season's pretty well maxed out," John said.

"What about guiding during the archery season?" Misty asked.

"That's a possibility," said John. "Except, I don't know a blooming thing about hunting with a bow and arrow."

"You're never too old to learn," said Mary.

"But where do you go to sign up for Bow Hunting 101?" asked John.

"Kirk could always show you the ropes," William J. said.

"That's a thought," said John. "But considering all the static I've given him over the years about his face paint and camouflage, I'm not sure I want to ask. But if that's what it takes to swing the deal, I guess I can swallow my pride and ask him. I hate having to admit that I could learn something from him though. After dinner, I'll ride up the creek and see if I can tag along with him this season. We'd have to book hunters for next fall when Mort's payment would come due."

"Things will be a little lean around here for awhile," William J. said. "We're kinda betting on the come, but it's not like this opportunity's gonna come along again—once it's gone, it's gone. If there's no objection, I'll call Mort tomorrow and tell him to get the paperwork started."

"Can I go with you to see Kirk?" asked Lane.

"You're not going any place this evening, but to bed," John said. "You want to be well rested for your first day of school."

Mary Sharp shook her head. "If it weren't for these boys, I wouldn't go along with this land buying nonsense. But it just seems like yesterday that Lanie here was born and now he's starting first grade. In no more than the blink of an eye, these boys will be out of school. If they are both foolish enough to want to come back and ranch, we're going to need more land. So as much as I don't like the idea of going even further in debt, you may as well call Mort."

The oven timer rang. Mary rose and crossed the kitchen. She opened the oven door and removed a chocolate pie with a meringue topping. The smell of the hot pie filled the room as she placed it on a cooling rack.

"This has to cool," said Mary. "If you want dessert, you'll just have to wait."

"In that case, I think I'll ride up and see Kirk while the pie is cooling," said John as he retrieved his silver Stetson from the oak bureau next to the door. "But if I know Kirk, he'll probably follow me home once he learns there's a piece of homemade chocolate pie on the premises."

John hurried down the front steps of the ranch house and strode briskly across the courtyard. He squeezed his six-foot five-inch frame between two of the pole rails and quickly caught the roan gelding standing by the galvanized water tank.

Jefferson Kirk stood by the pole corral across from his log house trimming the mane of Nugget, his palomino gelding and intermittently tossing a willow stick for Jake to fetch. A horse and rider trotted up the cottonwood lined driveway and Jake bounded to meet them. The dog quivered at the prospect of visitors.

"Hello, Jake, I'm glad to see you too," called John Sharp as he dismounted and scratched the dog's belly as it lay on the toe of his cowboy boot with all four feet in the air.

"Whadda ya know?" called Kirk.

"Takes a big dog to weigh a ton," said Sharp.

"Yeah, I know and 'a bigger dog to whip him.'"

"I always thought it wasn't 'the size of the dog in the fight but the size of the fight in the dog,'" Sharp said.

"I guess it just goes to show that pithy sayings sometimes conflict."

"That may be true," said Sharp pushing back the brim of his cowboy hat, "but you don't have to be crude about it."

"I said, 'pithy', you imbecile. "P-I-T-H-Y."

"Whatever, it still sounds dirty to me," said Sharp with a grin. "I know what you mean about those sayings though. Like, what is it? 'out of sight/out of mind,' or 'absence makes the heart grow fonder?'"

"In my case definitely 'absence makes the heart grow fonder,'" said Kirk.

"Not missing a certain blonde, are we?"

"You know it," Kirk said.

"How is her book tour going anyway?"

"Heidi thinks it's going great. The publicity given the shootings by the animal rights activists and Ray Webster's celebrity status gave the promotion tour a jump start. I think it'd be selling better if she'd taken my advice and called it, 'The Shootings of Headwaters County' instead of 'Montana Pursuit.'"

"I leaned toward 'A River Runs By It' myself," said Sharp.

"Let's face it. Women historically have resisted our suggestions," Kirk said.

"I don't understand it either." John laughed. "Especially when we've had such good ones like these. Maybe she'll rename it for the movie."

"That's always a possibility but I wouldn't hold my breath if I were you. The book tour's only about half over so I'm going to be missing her for quite awhile longer.

And she's not the only blonde I'll be missing. Lisa and Jenny have to fly back to their mother's tomorrow. Except for the start of bow season, there's not much to look forward to around here."

"That's what I'm here to talk to you about," said Sharp who explained the plans to buy the Chappel property." I was thinking that maybe you could bring me up to snuff on bow hunting so I'd be able to guide the archery hunters without looking like a total idiot. Do you think you could do that?"

"I've always enjoyed a challenge," said Kirk. "Makin' a bow hunter out of you is possible, but makin' you not look like a complete idiot may be beyond me."

"Just cut the BS and tell me what you think I should do first."

Kirk eyed the lanky frame of the rancher and said, "You aren't going to find camouflage clothes on the rack at WalMart. The first thing you do is go down to Montana XL in Townsend and have them measure you up for some camo to fit. They have a 'rockaflauge' pattern that blends well in this country."

"What other gear am I going to need?"

"There are calls, scents and enough gadgets and gizmos to turn your bow into a rifle. Archery hunting added a complete line of merchandise to the sporting goods industry. What do you have in the way of elk calls?"

"I have one of those curly-qued copper tubes," Sharp said.

"Those are dinosaurs. The diaphragm calls that fit right in your mouth have made your call obsolete. To guide bow hunters you're going to need to learn to call elk. I'll tell you what. Why don't I pick up all the gear that you'll need and then you can pay me back."

"Sounds good to me," Sharp said. "When do you want to go out?"

"The sooner the better," said Kirk. "The season opens Saturday. How about we stay at your cabin on Upper Greyson Creek and go out at first light Saturday morning."

"That works for me," said Sharp. "I'll get down and get

fitted for those camoed duds as soon as I get back from riding tomorrow."

When he finished trimming Nugget's tail, Kirk turned the palomino back into the corral. "Want to come in for a beer?"

"No, I think I'd better start on back," said Sharp who related William J.'s discovery of the dead calf and his plans for the following morning.

After Sharp disappeared around the bend in the drive-way, Kirk climbed the stairs to the spacious porch of the log house. He leaned against a supporting beam and watched the sun dip behind the Elkhorn Mountains to the west.

Kirk reflected joyously on the days events and dreaded the inevitable events of the coming day. His melancholy mood dissolved instantly upon entering the house. As soon as he reached the foot of the stairs, he heard the pounding of feet and excited screams. He looked up just in time to see his daughters launching themselves into space. He caught a giggling girl in each arm. Their momentum carried them backward into the living room and they tumbled to the carpet.

"Don't do that," yelled Kirk. "If I'd missed you, you'd both be flatter than a coupla tortillas."

"Daddy, you'll never miss us," Jenny said as she scrambled to her feet.

"That's where you're wrong. I'm going to miss you guys the instant the plane leaves the ground."

"We're going to miss you too," said Lisa. "I wish that we could all live together again."

"We've had this discussion before," said Kirk. "You know that's just not going to happen. But I sure am going to miss having you guys around. Now let's get you up to bed. If we're going to hike back into Greyson Creek before we go to the airport, we've got to get up plenty early. While Jenny fetches her stash of rocks, Lisa and I'll see if we can catch one last fish."

With a girl under each arm, Kirk trudged up the stairs to their room. After tucking them in, he resumed his position on the porch against the beam.

He stood there watching the horizon until all streaks of light faded in the west and myriad stars glistened forth in the black sky.

Chapter II

Tuesday September 2nd

The streams of the Big Belt Mountains flow westerly to their confluence with the Missouri River. A long broad ridge separates the Dry Creek drainage from the Greyson Creek drainage. Appropriately named, "The Ridge Road" follows this ridge line east into the mountains.

John Sharp felt twinges of trepidation as he drove the flatbed truck, pulling the goose necked trailer up the steep grade of the Ridge Road. The many Black Angus cattle scattered throughout the mountains this time of year were his security blanket. His livelihood and the economic viability of the entire fourth generation Sharp Ranch, depended on the continued well being of this herd of cows.

The advent of a new variable, the mountain lion, in the many roadblocks encountered between the birth of a calf in the spring and its sale in the fall was troubling. "It's tough enough already." he said out loud.

The sight of the first few cows and calves grazing in a grassy swale eased his fears somewhat.

He parked the horse trailer on a wide flat red-shaled shelf. Sharp unloaded Strawberry, re-tightened the cinch and then returned to the cab of the pickup for a lined denim jacket. The chill of the clear mountain air foretold the changing of the seasons.

Sharp rode south toward the upper Dry Creek basin. He detoured from the main trail to ride to the top of one sparsely timbered knob. This promontory offered a view unique to any point in Montana. From this location in the Big Belt Mountains, Sharp could see six different mountain ranges: the Elkhorns to the west; the Tobacco Roots to the southwest; the Bridgers to the southeast; the Spanish Peaks to the south; the Crazies to the east; and the remainder of the Big Belts to

32

the north. This site also offered a birds-eye view of much of the Sharp's mountain pasture.

Sharp dismounted and removed a spotting scope from his saddle bags. He glassed the open parks and finger ridges visible below him. While it was reassuring to see many cattle dispersed throughout the Sharp summer range, the primary focus of his spotting was birds not cattle.

He scanned the slopes and coulees looking for the congregation of magpies, turkey buzzards or ravens indicating the presence of a dead carcass.

The howl of coyotes diverted his attention momentarily. He swung the spotting scope in the direction of the crescendo of yowls and yips. Two mature coyotes and two half-grown pups sat with their heads pointed skyward.

Sharp pivoted slowly on the high promontory scanning methodically with the aide of the high-tech optics. A group of elk emerged from the dark timber on one of the finger ridges which protruded beneath Berberet's Knob. The spotting scope clearly revealed the antlerless heads of fifteen animals. The rut had apparently not yet started. Sharp filed this observation into his memory bank for future reference.

Sharp failed to detect any scavenger birds. He remounted and dropped off the knob to the trail leading into the basin itself. His spirits rose and warmed with the morning sun. Sharp rode past many groups of cow/calf pairs. To his trained eye, the calves appeared in excellent shape. Another six weeks of water, grass and mama's milk would add the "bloom" the cattle buyers wanted to see.

An insolent black baldie steer with a blade of grass still hanging from its mouth advanced toward the horse and rider. The calf shook its head menacingly. Sharp couldn't resist calling the young animal's bluff. He spurred Strawberry and charged toward the calf until its resolve melted with the impending arrival of horse and rider. The calf scrambled down the slope with its bawling mother in pursuit. Sharp grinned broadly at this small victory.

33

He continued on through the pockets of pine, sagebrush and quaking aspen. On a bench overlooking the beaver dams in the meadow, the horse detoured around a steep rock outcropping. A pair of Camp Robbers rose out of the bottom of the steep ravine. This sighting and a raven's call convinced Sharp to step from the horse and scramble down the red shaled slope.

The foul smell of death alerted his senses and directed his path. As he moved, the stench grew stronger and the walls of the ravine narrowed. Beneath the brushy canopy, he discovered tufts of deer hair leading to the scattered remains of a mule deer carcass. "At least it's not a calf," he said as he surveyed the carnage.

An eerie feeling came over Sharp as he eyed the steep rock ledges that rose above him. He shivered slightly in spite of himself. "You're gettin' to be an old woman, John Sharp," he said, but he still warily watched the rock ledges, half expecting a lion to peek over the edge at him.

He pulled himself out of the ravine using the branches of juniper for support. He paused briefly on the edge of the rim and caught his breath before remounting.

When he completed his search of the Dry Creek basin, Sharp pointed the gelding north and followed a narrow sliver of timber to the top of the ridge and dropped into the Greyson Creek drainage. An intense midday sun bore down. He shucked his jacket and secured it to the back of his saddle with rawhide strips.

The horse assumed an easy traveling gait. As he scanned the landscape, the rancher's mind wandered, acting as a comfortable companion. No topic was too mundane or beyond consideration. One moment he mentally debated free will versus predestination, and the next happily recalled the obscene parrot joke overheard at the barber shop last Tuesday.

He thought about the dead deer and the killer lion. He pondered the similarities between the lion and himself. They were both making a living from the grass-eating animals that wandered this territory. They were both predators. They were competitors. Was this territory big enough to support both of them? While he understood and respected the survival abilities of the big cats, he felt the ruthlessness of a competitor. Without a doubt, he concluded, he would defend "his territory" with the same tenacity that the lion defended "his."

As he crossed onto the Greyson Creek side of the ridge, Sharp rode through a swarm of juvenile lodge pole pines in a series of old clearcuts. He angled down the slope through this mass of trees. The horse slogged through the soft creek bottom. He crossed the creek just above a vast beaver dam below one of the Sharp Ranch hunting cabins.

A white lather oozed around Strawberry's breast collar as they climbed the steep slope on the north side of the creek. Sharp allowed the horse a breather and a drink at the two potholes known as the Greyson Creek Lakes. A knot of black cattle lay on plateau next to the lakes. Sharp eased the horse through the herd checking ear tag numbers against those in the small notebook he always packed with him.

The absence of any lion activity in the entire upper Greyson Creek drainage relieved most of Sharp's fears. By the time he circled back to the creek and entered the roadway that wound through the Greyson Creek subdivision, the twinges of insecurity he had felt that morning had all but dissipated.

A bead of sweat formed under Grover Arlen's toupee and ran down his cheek. The president of Animals Forever had maneuvered to delay this meeting with the board of directors. But the day had finally arrived and the confrontation over his involvement in the shooting incident in Montana could not be put off any longer.

Since Arlen had founded the animal rights organization,

the directors' positions had been largely ceremonial in nature and the board had routinely rubber stamped his decisions and expenditures. Arlen had handpicked most of the board members. Today's meeting had been different from the outset.

For the last forty-five minutes, members of the board had vehemently castigated his judgment for thrusting the organization into the hunter shooting incident. Arlen had expected some fallout, but the adamant demands by several of the board members came as a surprise.

By the time Grover Arlen rose to respond to the many accusations, he knew his position was in jeopardy. Arlen walked slowly to the front of the conference room. He paused dramatically at the broad expanse of glass and looked out through the morning smog to the Los Angeles traffic some forty floors below.

Turning back to face the board, he began to speak softly and slowly, "Ladies and gentlemen, I have listened carefully to the charges against me. To those charges, let me simply say, I plead guilty. I plead guilty to caring too much about animals. I plead guilty to having too much faith in humans. I plead guilty to being ahead of my time. I plead guilty to placing animals' interests ahead of my own.

"I'm not telling you that mistakes weren't made. Frankly, I underestimated the level of consciousness of the American public. The public is not yet ready to accept justifiable use of force in the defense of animals. I had hoped the human species had evolved to that point. Sadly, I was mistaken.

"But, ladies and gentlemen of the board, all is not lost. The memory of the public is surprisingly short. We did suffer through some negative publicity and a brief decline in donations. Recently however, both memberships and contributions have returned to their former levels.

"I can't help but remember when this organization was

nothing more than a dream operating out of the basement of my movie studio. Now, we are an international organization.

"I will apologize for my actions, but not for my motives. No man is bigger than the organization and if this board feels that my resignation would further the cause of animals then I would humbly abide by your wishes. But ladies and gentlemen," said Arlen his voice rising. "I submit to you that my only sins have been caused by caring too much about the defenseless creatures of the animal kingdom."

Arlen walked back to his seat at the highly polished oak table. Katherine Pareaux, the fashion designer and one of the major contributors, was the first to speak. "I think the last thing this organization ought to do at this time is to make a dramatic and rash change of leadership," she said as she pushed back her chair and crossed her internationally renowned legs. "I, too, am appalled at the thinking of the American public. Why or how anyone can stomach wearing the fur of dead animals totally escapes me. I thought my line of fake fur products would be an overnight success. So, I can understand Grover's premature advocation of an extension of animal rights. Maybe this effort in Montana was not totally in vain. As a result of those very efforts, perhaps the level of consciousness of the public has been raised a millimeter. It's only with many stops and starts that we make advances. Maybe fifty years from now the incident in Montana will be seen as the first small but pivotal step in banning sport hunting and in gaining recognition for the use of force in defense of animals.

"I think we should never forget that this organization was the brain child of Mr. Grover Arlen. We should not be hasty in our judgments. For the time being, I believe we need to operate as we have in the past. Mr. Chairman, I move that any discussion or decision regarding a change of leadership be deferred until our regularly scheduled membership and board of directors meeting in February. We will have a better sense of the public's mood at that time."

The motion passed with only two members abstaining. The chairman then returned to the more mundane topics on the agenda.

After the meeting, Grover Arlen sat in his corner office dictating thank you letters to the board members who had supported him.

"Ronald, I thought I was in trouble for a minute there," he said to his secretary. "Katherine Pareaux really saved my ass. She bought me the time I need. By the time the board meets again, I'll make the Montana incident seem but ancient history."

"What do you have in mind?" asked Ronald.

"I'm not quite sure," said Arlen. "But I'll need an issue that captures the public's interest and refocuses their attention. I'll just bide my time. Something will develop."

"Or you'll develop it," Ronald said.

"Que sera, sera," said Arlen allowing himself a smile for the first time that morning.

"Was that a party or was that a party?" asked Ray Webster as he drew back the compound bow and released an arrow toward a target hung on a stack of straw bales.

"It was a party," said Roemer.

"Weren't those some of the finest lookin' women you ever did see?"

"They were a little scrawny if you ask me," Roemer said. "I've always liked those 'hug and chalk' girls myself."

"Hug and chalk girls?"

"Yeah, you know the kind that you hug and you chalk and you hug and you chalk until you get all the way around 'em."

"I see," Webster said and laughed. "Well, I guess fat girls need loving too."

"Without a doubt." Roemer smiled. "But don't get me wrong, I'm not complainin' any 'bout them Nashville ladies. They were sure soft on the eyes."

"And other places too," Webster said.

"It doesn't hurt my feelings any that they're gone though," said Roemer.

"It is nice to finally regain the peace and quiet around here," Webster said as they reached the target.

Roemer pulled out the three arrows and then placed his palm flat against the target covering three holes.

"I think you've finally got the hang of this bow and arrow business," Roemer said. "But I still don't know why you want to chase around the woods with makeup on your face dressed like you're on national guard maneuvers trying to stick an elk with an arrow. Especially when if you'd just wait a month you could shoot 'em with a rifle."

"You just don't get it, do you? Just think about it. Walking the same forests and hills as the Indians. Using the same weapon. Stalking the descendants of the very elk they stalked. Living from the fruits of the land. How can you ignore the appeal of recapturing that way of life?"

"I wonder what sporting goods store the Indians got one of these compound bows from?" Roemer asked with a slight grin.

"I'm getting excited just thinking about bugling in a big bull," Webster said. "When you first told me that some kid had killed the big bull, I didn't even want to hunt elk again. But when I got to thinking about arrowing a bull that's fifteen yards away snortin' and pawin', the elk hunting batteries got plum recharged."

"If you shoot like this," said Roemer pointing at the

39

target. "A bull elk's in big trouble. And I wouldn't worry about the big bull being killed. After a big storm last winter, I counted over fifty branch bulls with the elk herd. Five or six of them were dandies. And they'll be bigger this fall. Any one of them could be in the same category as the big one."

"Do you really think so?" asked Webster.

"It's sure within the realm of possibility," Roemer said. "One of the advantages to owning 25,000 acres in the mountains is that you're always going to have big elk. It's just a matter of finding the right one."

"Maybe we ought to think about doing some scouting to find that right one," Webster said. "Why don't you catch the horses while I practice a little more?"

Roemer crossed the grounds of the ranch headquarters of Webster Enterprises. He lured the horses into the corral with the aide of a bucket of oats and saddled Webster's appaloosa and his own bay.

From the ranch, Webster and Roemer rode up a winding gulch that slowly climbed the northeast ridge and emptied onto a sagebrush-covered plateau. They paused here so that Roemer could glass the many elk grounds that surrounded this natural crossing point. At the far end of the plateau, their ascent ended at a sheer rock ledge. Here they angled off the plateau and entered a thick pocket of Douglas fir.

Their eyes had barely adjusted to the darkness of the shaded slope when Roemer reined in his horse and pointed into the undergrowth above the game trail. At first, Webster couldn't see anything, but then a flash of movement revealed an ivory tipped antler protruding above a row of jack pines.

As Webster turned his horse in the direction of the elk, he heard the loud crack of a branch breaking. The antler disappeared and they heard the sound of brush popping and breaking as the animal retreated.

The two riders urged their horses through the timber

and up the opposite slope. When they reached the brow of the hill, the bull elk was scrambling up through the scattered timber across the ravine.

"That's a pretty decent bull," said Roemer. Webster nodded. They watched until the bull disappeared over the horizon and then continued the spotting expedition as they rode further to the north.

As the late afternoon shadows lengthened, they reached a bare knoll which overlooked the broad grassy meadow where the Webster property cornered with the adjacent Sharp Ranch and National Forest Service lands. Scattered throughout the relative flat of this high mountain saddle, several hundred elk grazed and frolicked. The decidedly lighter and tanner bodies revealed the location of the bull elk. Webster eagerly took the spotting scope from Roemer and sat admiring the wildlife display before them. After several minutes, Roemer tapped Webster on the shoulder.

"We need to head back if we don't want to ride in the dark." Reluctantly, Webster agreed. They eased back down the slope and crossed onto the long slope which would take them back to the chalet.

"What an impressive sight," Webster said. "But most of those elk are on the Forest and the Sharp Ranch."

"They are for now," Roemer said. "But at the first hint of hunting pressure, most of 'em will high tail it right back onto your property."

"I certainly hope so, but I still don't like the elk making side trips. I remember all too well what happened to that monster bull last year. I'd like it better if we had a little more property for the elk to roam. Do you think I could buy some more ground from the Sharps or the government?"

"Fat chance. The Forest Service doesn't sell property anymore. They'll exchange parcels if they feel it's in the public's interest but never an outright sale. A sale by the

Sharp Ranch seems even less likely. I don't think the word sell is even in William J.'s vocabulary."

"Isn't there anything next to us that we might be able to pick up?"

"There's Mor Chappel's two sections," Roemer said. "Mort's getting up in years and doesn't have any kids. I think he might sell."

"Do you know this Mort?"

"I spent two winters feeding his cows and calvin' out his heifers."

"That's great," Webster said. "When you get some time, why don't you feel him out about selling. Price isn't an object. Just have to sell some more CD's. It would be nice to have a little more control of the elk. Besides the last thing I'd want is to have some developer buy those two sections and put a subdivision right next to us. I think we'd better have them."

They continued their descent down the long slope. As they cleared the obstruction of the shorter parallel ridge, the chalet and corrals came into sight in the meadow far below.

The sight of several magpies fluttering on one of the timbered fingers that branched off the main connecting ridge, focused their attention. They directed their horses toward the flock of black and white birds. The scavengers noisily scattered as the horses and riders approached.

Clearly visible in the circle of brown and white hair was the bloody skull of a Longhorn steer. Three feet of shiny horn protruded from each side of the dead animal's head. The steer appeared to smile grotesquely up at them because the lion had completely stripped the fleshy lips from the skull.

"What the hell?" Webster asked.

"I guess I was wrong," said Roemer grimly. "Apparently these Longhorns ain't as tough as I thought."

John Sharp dismounted and walked up the narrow path to the porch steps of the new log home. A middle aged man stood on the porch. He held a large hand carved sign in his outstretched arms. The sign proclaimed "The Bensons" in large letters. The man eyed the ten penny nail he had driven into a log and tried to center the hanging wire which he had attached to the back of the sign.

"The lower right hand corner needs to be about an inch higher," boomed John Sharp's deep voice.

The man jumped and turned to see Sharp smiling broadly.

"You startled me," said Roger Benson as he wiped the sweat from his bald head and readjusted the wire rimmed glasses. "We don't get many visitors here on Greyson Creek."

Sharp thrust a large hand in Benson's direction. "I'm John Sharp. We own the property on both sides of the subdivision."

Benson flinched slightly at the steel-like grip and introduced himself.

Sharp surveyed the new construction. "It sure didn't take you long to put this home up. The last time I was through here, this was nothing more than a foundation."

"We bought a log home kit," Benson said. "It only took the work crew three weeks to put this up."

"Where are you from?" asked Sharp.

"We moved here from New Orleans. I worked ten years for an investment firm. I finally got tired of the crime and traffic. We sold our house in the suburbs and moved up here. Saw a classified ad in USA Today."

"How you gonna make a living?" asked Sharp.

"Well, I banked a pretty good chunk of change when I sold the house and I withdrew all my profit sharing funds. I hope to do some investment counseling right from here."

"You'd better not plan on gettin' in and out of here in the winter," said Sharp. "The road into here gets plugged shut a lot of the time."

"I think you locals exaggerate about the bad winters," said Benson as he recentered the wooden sign. "Besides, I've got a four wheel drive and two snowmobiles if the weather gets tough. Let her snow."

A small girl peeked around the edge of the porch.

"Faith, come here and meet Mr. Sharp," called Benson.

The girl came forward shyly. Sharp knelt and shook the girl's hand.

"Would you like to meet my horse?" asked Sharp. A broad smile signaled her answer. Sharp led her to the horse.

"Just reach out your hand and let Strawberry smell you," said Sharp.

Faith complied and the horse placed his soft pink nose against her outstretched palm.

"Give him this," said Sharp handing her an alfalfa pellet.

Faith held one end of the two inch pellet and extended it tentatively toward the animal. The horse eagerly sucked in the pellet with one swipe of his coarse grained tongue. The girl giggled and pulled her arm back quickly.

"I think he likes you," said Sharp, grinning. Strawberry nuzzled against her seeking more treats.

"Go get your mother," said Benson. "I want her to meet Mr. Sharp."

"Please call me John. I always look over my shoulder when someone says 'mister.' Your daughter's a cutie. How old is she?"

"Six going on thirty," Benson said.

"I have a son the same age. School started today. Maybe they're in the same class."

"We're going to home school Faith," said Benson earnestly. "One of the other reasons we moved here was to get her beyond the influence of the secular school system. We believe strongly that God chose this spot for us and it's His plan that we live here."

"You'll be glad you don't have to drive her to the school bus everyday. That's for sure," said Sharp.

Emma Benson was a stern looking woman in a long gingham dress.

"Won't you come in for some coffee and pie," Emma said.

"I rarely pass up homemade pie," said Sharp with regret, "but I'll have to take a rain check. My pickup and horse trailer are parked quite a ways up Ridge Road. If I want out of the hills before dark, I'd better get a move on, but thanks anyway."

"I'd better get to movin' too," said Benson. "I've more fence poles to cut. I've been cutting them two at a time from a patch up the coulee and dragging 'em down by hand. It's hard work, but it feels really good after sitting in an office for ten years."

Sharp remounted and tipped his hat goodbye. When he reached the bend in the road, he looked back and saw Faith still standing on the porch watching him. He waved and she waved back.

The muscles in her long trim legs burned. Heidi Singer strained as the stair stepper entered the "steep climb" phase of the program. She closed her eyes and gutted her way through this phase of the workout.

When the program entered the "cool down" segment, she glanced around the fitness room of the Denver Marriott.

All workout rooms looked the same she thought. All contained the rudimentary number of stationary bikes, Nordic tracks, weight machines and related equipment. The fitness rooms were always adjacent to saunas that were too cold and to hot tubs that were always filled with foam and fat men with white pasty skin. Maybe she was just being overly cynical, but even the ringing of the bell on the stair stepper alerting her to the end of the program sounded the same.

She wiped the sweat from her brow, moved from the stair stepper and stretched out on a floor mat. A fold of flesh puckered slightly at the waist of her black Spandex body suit. She frowned. The fold was hardly noticeable but she reluctantly admitted to herself that the small bulge had not been present the week before.

The book tour was now taking a physical toll. For some time, she had felt the mental strain caused by the same motel rooms, restaurant food, airports, bookstores and the same shallow conversations about her book.

She felt particularly disturbed because the publication of the book and the resulting promotional tour had been the fulfillment of a childhood dream. The failure to find the expected satisfaction upon accomplishing this long held goal added greatly to her feeling of discontent.

Heidi thought about Jefferson Kirk. She recalled his touch and the sound of his voice when he said her name. If only he could make a commitment.

She thought almost as often about Mary Sharp's home cooking and the blueness of the vast Montana sky and the majesty of the mountains.

She had also become painfully aware that she missed the journalistic adrenaline rush of covering a late breaking news story. The events of the preceding months seemed almost surreal. The journalistic call to Montana to cover the shooting death of Jason Hodges, the resulting murders and the wounding of Ray Webster spiced by the involvement of Animals

Forever and her relationship with the Headwaters County district attorney all seemed a blur.

She squeezed the offending fold of flesh between her thumb and index finger and ran her hands along the firm buttocks that filled the bodysuit. She forced a smile and pulled back her honey blonde hair.

She shook herself as if her state of mind were a physical thing. Enough self-pity, she thought. She was making good money. She was certainly better off than a lot of people. Some people live their entire lives without achieving their dreams. No one said life was fair or perfect. A person could only control a finite number of things. But an extra fold of flesh was something she could control. Heidi returned to the stair stepper and set the timer for an additional ten minutes. As she placed her workout shoes in the foot pads of the machine, Jefferson Kirk's face with its broad smile and characteristic wink flashed before her and she shivered.

Kirk didn't want to go home. He didn't want to face the big empty log house alone. He lingered at the District Attorney's office. Kirk undertook all the disagreeable chores he normally avoided. He dictated a brief in a misdemeanor drug case. He replaced the books he had taken from the law library and neglected to return. He refiled the numerous file folders cluttering his desk.

When Kirk finally glanced out the single window of his small corner office, he was surprised to see that it was dark. He scanned the last draft of his brief and tossed the text back onto the desk next to the picture of Lisa and Jenny. He locked up the office and took the outside fire escape to his Chevy Blazer. He drove five miles east from Townsend to the forty acre parcel that constituted all that remained of the original Kirk Homestead.

The golden dog burst down the porch steps to meet the

familiar white Blazer. "Good ol' Jake," said Kirk. "At least you're always glad to see me."

Kirk slipped into the log home and changed into sweat pants and running shoes. With Jake at his side, Kirk ran the steepest hill rising above the Deep Creek residence. At the top of the slope, he stopped to catch his breath and scanned the night sky.

Here, far from the lights of town, a million stars studded the black canvas of sky. The Milky Way splashed boldly from horizon to horizon. He found the Big Dipper in the northern sky. He recalled following the line of the stars in the side of the "dipper" until his arm had pointed to the North Star and also draped loosely around Heidi Singer's shoulders. She had laughed gaily at being duped by the school boy trick. He had pulled her to him and they had kissed deeply.

Kirk regained his breath and jogged the more gradual incline to the horse pasture in the creek bottom. He sprinted to the house and went to the phone. He stretched leisurely as he waited for the connection to clear.

A twinge of excitement pulsed through him as he heard the distinctive tone of her voice saying "Hello" without pronouncing the "H".

"Hi ya, gorgeous," he said. "How about taking pity on a poor lonely attorney in Montana. What would it take to get you to come visit?"

"Mr. 'C,'" Heidi said. "Or else an exciting story like the one that first got me there."

"Well, we can rule out Mr. 'C.' It's been too soon after meeting up with the big 'D' and as the song goes that don't stand for Dallas. I'll just have to come up with another story of a lifetime."

"Please hurry," Heidi said. "I'm tired of living out of a suitcase and eating at the Holiday Inns of the world. You won't believe this, but the other night I even dreamed of Mary Sharp's fried chicken."

"I've been having dreams about breasts and thighs myself," Kirk said.

"You'd just better dream about cold showers, big fella. I'm starting to think my mother was right. A man won't buy the cow if he gets the milk for free."

"I wouldn't mind buyin' the cow if the cow didn't want to take half the ranch with her when you sell her."

"That line is growing old," she said. "Besides, you're probably just waiting for the movie rights from the book to sell and then you'll marry me for my money."

"Sounds good to me." Kirk laughed. "Why don't you periodically send me and my accountant a financial statement so that we can determine the fiscally appropriate time to pop the question?"

"I think I'll do just that, but if I were you, I wouldn't hold my breath waiting for it to get there."

Tired of the familiar theme, Kirk maneuvered to change the subject. "I really do miss you. Where's your next stop?"

"Seattle."

"That's almost on the way."

"Not exactly. But I'm serious, if you come up with a good story, let me know. I've got several publications that would buy a good freelance piece. It certainly would feel good to work on a challenging story again."

"I'm racking my brain, but I'm drawing a complete blank. Good or bad, I think Headwaters County has finally returned to normal. But if I think of something, you'll be the first to know."

Ben Green leaned back in the recliner with the television remote control gripped firmly in his right hand. He flipped randomly through the channels.

49

"Would you pick a channel and leave it there," Beth said.

"That's the trouble with you women," Ben said. "You think a person can only watch one program at a time."

The phone rang. "I'll be right there," he said and hung up.

"What is it?" asked Beth.

"A Mrs. Benson is at the office. She lives in the Greyson Creek subdivision and their six year old daughter's missing. They don't have any phone service up there so she drove all the way into town to make the report."

"Lost?"

"Maybe."

"How long's she been missing?"

"There's a little confusion about that," Ben said. "Apparently the mother needed a few things in town. Mr. Benson was cutting poles above the home site. Mom made a picnic lunch, sent the girl out to meet him, and left. Mr. Benson worked until dark and hiked home. When no one was there, he just assumed the girl was with Mom. They didn't know the girl was missing until Mrs. Benson got back."

"The poor little thing. She must be terrified out of her wits."

"The family's from the South so there ain't a whole lot of mountain savvy to draw on. She probably got turned around and went the wrong direction."

"What are you gonna do?" asked Beth.

"I had the dispatcher call out Tucker, Deputy Woods and four or five of the Search and Rescue unit. We'll go up and see if we can find her."

When Ben Green arrived at the Headwaters County Sheriff's office, he was met by a frantic Emma Benson.

"Where have you looked so far?" asked Ben.

"It was totally dark by the time I got home. Roger and I climbed the hill above the house and called for her and then cut across to the patch of timber where we've been cutting poles. It really isn't very far. I'd have never let her go if I thought there was any chance she'd get lost."

"Kids can get turned around real easily in that country," said Ben. "They get absorbed in their thoughts and just wander. Once they lose their bearings, there's no way to get re-oriented. Fortunately, the nights are fairly warm now. With any luck, we should have her rounded up in no time at all."

"I hope so," said Emma.

"Where's your husband?" asked Ben.

"He was going to climb to the top of the ridge and make a big circle back to the creek above the house. He thought he'd be back at the house by the time we get there."

"Maybe they'll both be there to meet us," said Ben squeezing the woman's hand.

The two deputies and the members of the Search and Rescue team gathered outside the squat brick sheriff's office.

"Why don't you drive Mrs. Benson's vehicle, Tuck?" Ben asked. "I'll put her in with me and Woods."

Ben helped Emma Benson into the passenger seat of the Jeep Wagoneer that served as his patrol car. With the Search and Rescue Suburban and Tucker following, Ben drove east on the Deep Creek highway toward the intersection with the less traveled mountain road leading to the Greyson Creek subdivision.

Emma Benson sat erect, looking intently ahead and clutching a small stuffed dog.

"We moved here because we worried so about keeping Faith safe from the gangs and drugs, but I've never been as worried as I am now," Emma said.

"Worrying don't change a thing. Besides," said Ben, "your husband will probably be tucking her into bed by the time we get there."

"I hope you're right," Emma said weakly.

Roger Benson was waiting in the driveway when the sheriff pulled across the bridge spanning Greyson Creek. Ben rolled down his window and the worried man recounted his futile search efforts.

Ben gathered the searchers around the vehicle and barked out directions.

"Let's send the Search and Rescue unit up on top to the Ridge Road. You can cover about a six mile section of the road. She hasn't had time to get a whole lot farther. She may be walking on the road itself, but she might still be going the wrong direction. Walk out on some of those ridges that overlook Greyson Creek and yell for her. You should be able to hear a cry for help a far piece from up there. Tucker and I can cover the trail in the bottom of the ravine back to the pole patch. Mr. Benson and Woods will walk up the west ridge above us. We'll regroup at the top and compare notes. Mrs. Benson you stay home just in case your daughter wanders back. Are there any questions? Good, let's get going."

Tucker and Ben waited at the bottom of the ravine and watched the light of Woods' lantern as the deputy and Benson climbed through the scattered timber to the ridge above them. When the light reached the ridge top and began moving to the south, they began moving up the well defined game trail in the bottom. They paused periodically and shouted "Faith."

They focused their own flashlights above and below the trail. The faint light created eerie figures as the shadows of the trees and rocks danced across the opposite slope of the narrow canyon.

Something glistened at the outer edge of this corridor of light. Ben stopped and peered above the trail.

52

"What?" asked Tucker.

"I thought I caught the reflection of something," said Ben as he followed the beam of light up the slope. "Shine your light this way."

Tucker focused his light on the area in front Ben.

"What is it?" Tucker asked.

"A sandwich," Ben said as he picked up a clear plastic baggie and examined it closely. "Peanut butter and jelly if I don't miss my guess."

Tucker climbed up and joined Ben. Ben flashed his light around the grassy bench. Another object several feet away caught his eye. He moved forward and shined his light down on a canvas tote bag. He knelt to retrieve the bag. The underside of the bag was wet and sticky to the touch. He pulled his hand back quickly. He directed the light beam toward his hand revealing a palm and fingers covered with red streaks of blood.

Tucker cast the light further up the hill. He saw what looked like a clump of grass but upon closer inspection revealed itself as a hank of human hair. Tucker shined his light. He bent forward and retched.

Chapter III

Wednesday, September 3rd

Pink morning light filtered into the Wagoneer as Ben sat in front of the sheriff's office. He remained behind the steering wheel for several minutes not having the energy to pull himself from the seat.

He had felt completely inadequate in trying to comfort the grieving couple. How do you explain such a tragedy? He had tried to lessen the guilt the couple felt. No one could be blamed. It was just so damn tragic.

His thoughts turned from reflection on the grisly details of the long evening to the immediate concerns of the sheriff's office. Deputy Tucker and Deputy Woods had left for Great Falls with the body bag containing Faith Benson's remains. Dr. Hanning, the pathologist, would perform the autopsy to confirm what they already knew. His mind fast-forwarded through a kaleidoscope of thoughts. What to do about the lion, the press and the traffic court bench trials set for that morning.

With great effort, he pulled himself from the vehicle and entered the sheriff's office. He spoke briefly with Fish and Game Warden Dave Berg and then called Jefferson Kirk.

Kirk listened in horror as Ben recounted the grim details. He felt a chill run through him. Kirk frequently dealt with the details of bloody, grisly crimes, but this affected him unlike any other. He thought about his own daughters hiking in the same drainage just a few miles downstream from the Benson residence. By the time Ben Green finished his briefing, Kirk was covered with sweat.

"Is there anything I can do?" Kirk asked.

"Well for starters you can cancel the traffic court cases set for this morning."

"No problem. I'm sure the judge will be agreeable to a continuance under the circumstances. What's on your agenda?"

"I talked with Warden Berg and we're going to go after the lion as soon as we can round up some dogs."

"Where you going to get lion hounds?" asked Kirk.

"Berg and I are gonna run down Slats Smith and see if we can use his dogs."

"You and Slats aren't exactly on the best of terms, are you?"

"He and I get along just fine when he's not drinkin'. Slats thinks because he's six foot three that he's a fighter. He forgets he's thinner than the 'slats' of the chicken house roof he's named after, especially when he's been in the fire water. He gets on the fight and ends up as our guest in the 'crow bar hotel.' He's sorry as all get out when he finally sobers up. Besides, he's got the best lion dogs in the county and there isn't anything like a regular job interfering with his availability."

"You're absolutely sure it's a lion?"

"No doubt. There were clear paw prints in the black mud in the bottom of the ravine. And the wounds—it was a lion alright."

"Well, good luck. I hope you get him. Is there anything else you need from me?"

"The press will be sniffing around wanting all the gory details," Ben said. "I'd appreciate if you'd make a press release and handle all the questions until we get back."

"I got you covered," Kirk said. "But you'd better give me a little more information."

Kirk shuffled through the telephone table for a note pad and a pencil and the sheriff gave him all the "who, what, where, when and how" information necessary for dissemination of the details of the tragedy.

Kirk drafted a short press release. He changed into his running clothes and ran the hill overlooking Deep Creek. A giant orange ball of sun poked above the Big Belt Mountains as he reached the top of the steep incline. He coasted down the long gradual slope to the horse pasture mulling over the tragedy and mentally proofing the press release.

He called Heidi Singer in Denver. "Wake up, gorgeous. I think I got a story for you."

Kirk read her the press release and shared the other information provided by Ben Green.

"It is newsworthy," said Heidi. "What a human interest angle. A family uproots from the city to flee the dangers of crime. They relocate to a remote mountain cabin in Montana and their only child is attacked and killed by a mountain lion. Who has this story so far?"

"Right now only you. I'll give the press release to the dispatcher at the sheriff's office on my way to work. The string reporter will pick it up sometime during the day."

"Great," Heidi said. "That should give me more than enough lead time. I've already got enough material. I think the AP will pick it up. If I can put off my book signings for a couple days, I'll fly in and do a follow up on the pursuit of the lion."

"Don't you feel guilty advancing your career and lining your own pockets because of the misfortunes of others?" Kirk asked.

"I could accept that if it came from anyone other than an attorney," said Heidi with a slight edge to her voice. "If it weren't for thefts, rapes and murders, you'd probably be sleeping in the streets."

"It'd never happen," Kirk said. "If crime were eliminated, I'd just find some rich spinster author and marry her for her money."

"Oh, give me a break. Don't you have to go to work or something?"

"As a matter of fact I do."

"Well, I'll make some phone calls. If everything falls into place, I'll crank out the story this morning and catch a flight to Helena this afternoon."

Kirk sat for a few minutes staring at the receiver. He had run a full gamut of emotions since he awoke. He at once felt sadness and compassion for the Benson family, but also the flush of excitement at the prospect of Heidi's arrival.

Ben turned the Wagoneer off the highway onto a graveled secondary road. He and Fish and Game Warden Berg traveled west toward Canyon Ferry Lake on a deeply rutted road. They crept from pothole to pothole.

The road ended at an old homestead shaded by many giant golden willows. An old chicken house with no windows and a sagging roof leaned almost onto the roadway. Farther back in the trees stood a two story frame house with weathered gray siding. A row of dog houses constructed from plywood sheets sat to the right of the house. On the top of each of these structures stood one of the various and sundry breeds of dog used for chasing mountain lions. Each hound was attached to its house with a long piece of metal chain.

The dogs bayed and barked at the arrival of the sheriff and warden. The sound of the slack pieces of metal chain banging against the roofs of the dog houses and the howling of the dogs made it evident that no one would ever sneak up on the residence.

The door of the house flung open and Slats Smith stepped onto the narrow porch.

"Shadup you mangy mutts." he yelled. The hounds jumped from the roofs and ducked into their houses.

Slats strode across the cluttered lawn to meet his visitors. A lazy left eye and a nose which at one time had been placed against his left cheek by a drunken cowboy gave Slats the appearance of looking two directions at once. Flaming red hair curled out from under a grease stained cowboy hat, and a ragged, full beard showed streaks of gray.

"Well hello, Warden Berg and Sheriff Green. Is this a social call or did I forget to make my traffic court payments again?"

"We're here because we need your help," Ben said.

Ben again recounted the events of the lion attack and explained the need to chase and kill the lion responsible.

"That's all well and good," said Smith. "But you've forgotten to mention the most important detail."

"What's that?"

"What's in the deal for Ol' Slats?"

"The county'd pay you $150 a day plus expenses. Also, if we can get the lion within three days, there's a $500 bonus in it for you."

"When do we start?" asked Slats with a grin.

"We'll take our cue from you," said Berg. "You know lions and dogs better than anybody."

Slats nodded at the acknowledgment of his expertise by the wildlife official and began to warm to the venture.

"What's the terrain around the area look like?" asked Slats.

"I have a map here," said Berg, spreading the rolled up document across the hood of the Wagoneer.

"We need to find a fresh track," said Slats. "During the December lion season, we constantly drive the roads trying to find a fresh track in the snow. It's a waste of time puttin' the dogs on too old a trail. Do you have any idea which way the lion went from the kill site?"

Ben shook his head. "There were a few tracks in the mud, but once he got out of the bottom, there just weren't anymore."

"There's some old loggin' roads running on both sides of that area," said Slats pointing to several thin lines on the map. "I have a huge piece of carpet that I drag behind my truck. It makes a nice tracking bed. I'd suggest we sweep all of those roads late this afternoon and at daylight go back with the dogs and see if there's any new tracks."

"Sounds like a plan to me," said Ben. "Most of those old logging roads are on the Sharp Ranch property. I'll have to get permission and a key for their gates."

"You take care of that if you think it's necessary," Slats said. "I'll get my gear loaded and meet you at the Deep Creek Bar at four o'clock."

"It's a date." Ben ducked back into the Wagoneer.

At the starting of the engine, the black and tan dogs re-emerged from their shelters and jumped back onto the roofs. The hounds resumed their baying and howling and the metal chains again clattered beneath their feet.

"That's a pretty cushy little bonus you offered Slats," said the Warden as he rolled up the window.

"I'm afraid if I didn't hold out some kind of carrot for a quick capture, that come Christmas Slats would still be chasin' lion."

"I just hope Slats is as good at this as everyone says," Berg said.

A sound resembling the quack of a tortured duck reverberated through the living room of John and Misty Sharp's house. Sharp readjusted the reed and again forced air against the diaphragm elk call.

This time the melodious notes of a bull elk's bugle floated from his mouth. He repeated the procedure producing the same result.

Misty rushed into the living room and placed her hands on her hips. "Must you make that noise in here?"

"Just practicin'," John said. "I don't know if I'm ready to call in elk, but it's good to know I can call in women."

"About two more squawks from you and there'll be just about as many women in this house as there are elk."

"I can take a hint," said John heading for the door.

He continued his elk calling efforts on the front porch. He became so absorbed in his success that he failed to notice the Headwaters County vehicle pull into the driveway in front of the house.

"That's a mighty fine bugle," said Ben. "But I think you'd have better luck a bringing in a bull if you'd go up country a piece."

"I'm tryin' a new technique," said Sharp. "I'm going to hook this elk call to an amplifier and hunt elk right from the porch."

"Let me know if you get it perfected," said Ben. I'm gettin' to the age where huntin' elk from a rockin' chair don't sound all that bad."

"You'll be the first to know. But what brings you out our way?"

Ben told Sharp about the death of Faith Benson.

"I can't believe it," said Sharp sadly. "I just met the Benson family yesterday. She was a beautiful little girl. Damn

60

the mountain lions anyway. Looks to me like we were gettin' along just fine with out 'em. Dad found a calf killed by a lion just the other day and now the Benson girl."

"That's interesting," said Ben. "The dispatcher just radioed that Pete Roemer reported a lion killed one of Webster's prize Longhorns. They wanted something done right away but until we get the lion responsible for killing the girl, their lion problem will have to take a backseat."

"Maybe it's the same lion," Sharp said.

"Do you think so"?

"Could be. I've heard a lion will work an area anywhere between thirty to seventy square miles."

"The Benson residence, your ranch and the Webster property are certainly within that radius. We'll have to keep that possibility in mind."

"What are you going to do about the lion?" asked Sharp.

"That's what I'm here to see you about. I've lined up Slats Smith and his hounds and we're goin' after the lion as soon as possible. We'd like to get your permission and a gate key to get on your property."

"No problem," Sharp said. "Probably be the first time that Slats has ever been there legally."

"You've caught Slats on there before?"

"A time or two and there's been three or four other times I just missed him. I don't think boundary lines mean much to Slats."

"I reckon you're right, but he sure can find mountain lions."

"So rumor has it," Sharp said.

"I'd better git," said Ben. "I've been up all night and I'd like to catch a coupla hours sleep before I meet Slats this afternoon."

"I wish you luck. But don't let the fact that the lion has calf blood on his whiskers keep you from pulling the trigger."

"I hear ya," said Ben with a slight nod.

As soon as the Sheriff drove away, Sharp relayed the news to Misty who began preparing food to take to the Bensons. Sharp drove to the shop to tell William J.

The old man pulled himself from under the hay baler upon hearing of the tragedy.

"It's sad, damn sad," said William J. "But you know those people kinda asked for it if you ask me. They move into the woods to get close to nature and then act surprised when nature up and bites 'em in the ass. In some ways you can't blame the lion for killing the girl or our cattle. He's just doing what he does naturally."

"The only problem," Sharp said, "is what a lion does naturally doesn't always mesh with humans or cattle."

"Sad as it may be, this incident may be what it takes to mobilize people into action to get rid of some lions," William J. said.

"It certainly has the sheriff mobilized," Sharp said. "But if we want to bale hay yet today, we'd better get mobilized ourselves and finish this repair job."

The small commuter plane which had been described to Heidi Singer as a "culvert with wings" began its final descent into the Helena airport. Heidi took a deep breath and held it until the small plane touched down. The safe landing of the plane seemed yet another little miracle in a day where everything had gone right.

The book stores in Seattle had been most accommodating in rescheduling the book signings. One had even divulged that they weren't quite ready for her and were relieved to have the delay.

The article on the mountain lion attack itself had "flowed like butter." She had written the copy in one sitting. Her own experience of coming to Montana as a novice totally unfamiliar with the mountains or its wildlife had given her the right perspective and understanding of her subject. For the first time in her journalistic memory, she had not changed a word or punctuation mark.

Marketing the piece had also gone surprisingly well. The Associated Press had agreed to run the short piece in the following morning's dailies and two other publications had picked up the longer version to run as a feature.

But for as perfect as the day seemed, she felt anxious as she thought of her relationship with Jefferson Kirk and the course of action she had decided to follow.

She peered through the small oval window as the plane taxied to the terminal. As the plane stopped, a man and yellow dog ran onto the tarmac. She felt a rush of excitement as she recognized the tall figure with the tousled hair and crooked grin. She grabbed her carry on luggage and scrambled down the steps into the arms of Jefferson Kirk.

The trip from Helena to Townsend passed quickly as Heidi and Kirk reacquainted. She told Kirk about her and day including her success in placing the story of the mountain lion attack.

Kirk advised her of Ben's plans for chasing and killing the lion. He enthralled her further with a description of the life and times of Slats Smith.

"Slats sounds perfect for a character sketch," Heidi said, "or at the very least, he ought to be the centerpiece of my follow-up story. Do you think he'll give me an interview?"

"If I know Slats, he'll tell you more than you'll ever want to know,"

When they entered Townsend, Heidi pointed toward the large motel sign visible in the distance.

"Pull in at the Mustang Motel. I'll get a room there."

"You're joking."

"No, I'm dead serious," she said. "I've been thinking a lot about our relationship and I know you're still not over the divorce and not sure about making another commitment. I just think it would be better if we didn't stay together while you're sorting things out."

"Can't we discuss this over a drink?" asked Kirk.

"That's fine by me. But you're not going to try to get me drunk and take advantage of me, are you?"

"Candy's dandy, but liquor is quicker," Kirk said and smiled.

Ben pushed further down on the accelerator of the Wagoneer in an effort to keep up with Slats Smith's truck. The flatbed disappeared around a sharp corner in the bottom of Ross Gulch. Ben and Warden Berg followed as best they could. They drove out of the bottom and reached the three-mile stretch of the Ross Gulch Road which crossed the grassy benches north of Greyson Creek. By this time, a trail of dust was the only visible evidence of Smith's vehicle.

"You'd think the bonus you offered Slats expires today," Berg said.

"You wouldn't think that old wreck of a truck could move that fast," Ben said.

"He'll slow up when he hits the steep grade into Greyson Creek."

"I wouldn't bet on it," said Ben peering through the dust.

They dropped into the Greyson Creek drainage themselves and drove up the creek past several of the homes in the remote subdivision. A sobering sight greeted them when they reached the Benson residence. Numerous trucks and cars lined both sides of the roadway. Two long narrow tables on the lawn offered a buffet of dishes prepared by the visitors. Small groups of people stood outside the log home.

Ben maneuvered the Wagoneer through the parked vehicles and stopped just out of sight above the Benson's twenty-acre tract. Slats Smith stood in the middle of the road waiting for them.

"Let's take a look at the kill site," Slats said. "I'd like to get an idea about the cat we're lookin' for."

The three men crossed the main stream and followed the small tributary of Greyson Creek to a point just below the lion attack. Ben thought the location not nearly as eerie or sinister in the stark light of the late afternoon sun as it had appeared in the artificial glow of their flashlights the previous evening. Ben climbed to the bench where Faith Benson's body had been discovered. He oriented himself with the blood stains still visible on the pine grass and returned to the spot where the lion had crossed the soft bottom.

There in the stiff black mud, were the tracks of the lion. Slats knelt and ran his fingers around the interior of each of the paw prints.

"Ain't much of a lion if you ask me," Slats said. "Probably nothing more than a yearling. It's really not very big."

"It was more than big enough," Ben said grimly. "Do you think you'll recognize the track if you see it again?"

"The tracks are pretty small and the cat's got all its toes so there ain't much other than size to set it apart from any other track. We'll just have to rely on the feelin' in Ol' Slats' gut."

They returned to the vehicles and drove further up the

graveled road through a locked gate onto Sharp Ranch property. Smith parked his truck in the middle of the hard packed roadway.

Under Slats' direction, Ben and Berg, with much effort, removed a section of harrow from the bed of the truck. Slats attached this section of the old piece of farm equipment to the heavy metal bumper of the truck with a large gauged length of log chain. He adjusted the metal spikes of the harrow so the sharp points touched the road surface. For additional weight he added a section of railroad tie to the top of the harrow and lashed it down with a rusty length of barbed wire.

The men unrolled a large remnant of carpet and attached it to the back of the harrow section with several lengths of nylon rope.

"This rug looks awfully familiar," said Ben.

"It oughta," Slats said and laughed. "I got it from out of the courtroom when they remodeled the courthouse."

"It don't look a damn bit better behind your truck than it did in the courtroom," Ben said.

With all the attachments completed, Slats drove his truck forward a short distance to demonstrate the effectiveness of the equipment. The sharp metal spikes of the harrow section bit into and loosened the hard packed roadway. The large square of carpeting then smoothed the disturbed surface. Slats stopped the truck and quickly ran back beyond the section of carpet and stepped onto the roadway. He pointed to the distinct boot print left in the freshly disturbed surface.

"A lion'll never cross the road without me findin' out," Slats said.

"Let's hope so," said Berg, "but we need to get going before it gets dark."

Ben and Berg joined Slats in the cab of the flatbed. Slats put the truck in low gear and slowly proceeded up the road.

A mile up the creek an old logging road switch-backed up the steep slope to the south. This area consisted of twenty year old clear cuts filled with a thick regrowth of lodge pole pine just tall enough that it was impossible to see across the clear cuts.

The sweep job proceeded steadily as Ben and Berg adjusted the harrow and carpet around each corner of the switchback road. They drove a network of logging and county roads until they completed a large circle and arrived back at the Wagoneer just before dark. They unhooked the harrow and carpeting and left them next to the road in the event a repeat of the sweeping process would be necessary.

"I'll meet you right here at daylight," said Slats as he drove off.

Ben and Berg joined the grieving people gathered at the Benson residence and briefly explained the plans for the following morning.

Part II

Chapter IV

Thursday September 4th

In the penthouse suite of the Manhattan high-rise, Grover Arlen stood up so quickly that he spilled his cup of espresso on the morning edition of the *New York Times*. He sopped up the coffee from the paper with a terry cloth towel and re-read Heidi Singer's story. He quickly knew that this, his first day in New York, would also be his last.

"This is perfect," he said as he waved the paper back and forth to dry it.

Even though it was still five in the morning in Los Angeles, Arlen called Ronald Bates, his personal secretary.

"I'm going to dictate a press release. I want you to type and distribute it to the media as soon as possible."

"Just a minute, Grover," said Ronald. "Let me get out of bed and get a pen and some paper. What's up anyway?"

"I've found our issue." Arlen said. "You won't believe this but Sheriff Ben Green is once again in the center of the controversy."

"Or you'll put him in the center of the controversy," Ronald said.

"You're awfully suspicious first thing in the morning, aren't you?"

While Ronald gathered the items necessary to record the dictation, Arlen folded the paper isolating Heidi Singer's article. When Ronald indicated he was ready, Arlen held the phone in one hand, the article in the other and began speaking into the receiver: "While Animals Forever extends its utmost sympathy to the family and friends of Faith Benson, we cannot sit idly by while Headwaters County officials arbitrarily take the life of a mountain lion. Animals Forever

68

believes an animal should not be destroyed merely because it engages in natural conduct in its natural environment.

"We believe that Headwaters County Sheriff Ben Green is currently engaging in a search and destroy mission without lawful authority. He is attempting to pursue and kill this lion with dogs. This is not only inhumane treatment of the lion, but also unfairly and needlessly places the dogs in jeopardy of death or serious injury. Also, because dogs cannot discriminate between the mountain lion responsible and an innocent lion in the vicinity, it is imperative that this vengeful course of action be abandoned immediately.

"Animals Forever hereby implores Headwaters County Sheriff Ben Green to voluntarily cease his effort to chase and kill this mountain lion. In the event the sheriff chooses to ignore this request and continue his efforts, Animals Forever will initiate the appropriate legal action to enjoin this activity."

"You really don't think the sheriff's going to pay any attention to this request, do you?" asked Ronald.

"Not on your life," said Arlen. "That's why I'm calling Tanner Trent the minute I get off the phone with you."

After several tries, Arlen reached the renowned attorney at Trent's beach house.

"It's not even six o'clock yet," said Trent.

"It does come twice a day," said Arlen.

"Tell me what's so urgent that you had to track me down at this ungodly hour," said Trent.

Arlen read the newspaper article in its entirety to the attorney.

"An interesting development indeed," Trent said. "But what do you want from me?"

"I want you to get an injunction stopping the Headwaters County Sheriff from killing the mountain lion."

"An injunction? When?"

"Yesterday!"

"Getting an injunction isn't exactly like getting a Big Mac. Assuming I had the appropriate petition and affidavits drafted, I'd still have to corner a Federal District judge. And you're in New York. The judge with jurisdiction is in Helena, Montana. It's not something that can be accomplished immediately."

"That's why they invented phones and faxes," said Arlen. "Contact Greg what's his name—the attorney in Helena you associated with on the criminal cases last year. This opportunity is too good to be true. If we do this right, we can refocus the public's interest away from our ill-advised endeavor last year. By involving the same players and portraying them in an unfavorable light, we can show the public that just maybe we weren't really the bad guys after all."

"I'll see what I can do," said Trent. "But what are you going to do while I'm scrambling around? I may need to have you sign an affidavit in support of the temporary restraining order."

"I'm catching the first plane back to LA. I'll call you as soon as I get back."

"Mule deer," Slats Smith said matter-of-factly. "Looks like a doe with a coupla fawns."

Smith pushed himself back onto the hood of his flatbed truck. He grasped the ram shaped hood ornament with one hand and motioned Ben forward with the other.

Ben ground the gears of the transmission slightly as he forced the unfamiliar shift into position. He eased up on the clutch and held Slats' truck to the far right of the roadway. He drove next to the smooth surface they had created the previous day.

70

Slats concentrated on the roadway looking for any new indentation or disturbance. Every time he sighted any disruption, no matter how slight, he signaled Ben to stop so he could examine the roadway more closely.

The six lion hounds rode on the back of the flatbed in crude kennels cobbled together from grocery carts.

"Where do you think Slats got the grocery carts?" asked Warden Berg.

"I don't even want to know," said Ben. "But I wouldn't be surprised if I went back through the sheriff's log that I'd find a complaint from Bob's Grocery reporting the mysterious disappearance of several carts."

They reversed the route they had followed the previous day. They moved steadily except for a stretch of road upon which several head of Sharp Ranch cattle had walked. In this section of road, Slats Smith walked in front of the vehicle moving methodically from side to side focusing intently on the checkered patches of undisturbed soil. He watched for any tracks overlayed on the hoof prints of the Black Angus cattle.

As they climbed the steep slope out of the Greyson Creek drainage, Slats easily sorted through the numerous deer, elk, and coyote tracks crossing the soft surface.

At a point near the top of the main ridge above the Greyson Creek subdivision, the track of a mountain lion grabbed Smith's attention and he bounded off the hood of the truck before it came to a stop. He knelt in the roadway over the paw prints. He removed a folding knife from the leather case at his side. He locked the blade open and flicked some dirt into the prints.

"This kitty's goin' into Greyson Creek," said Slats.

"Do you think it's the same lion?" asked Ben.

"I don't think so," Slats said. "This cat's not big by any means, but I think the paws are a hair bigger than the tracks we saw in the mud. Let's drive some more road. We can always come back."

"This process is more art than science," Ben said to Berg as they climbed back into the truck.

"I sure hope we're not wasting our time," Berg said. "That lion could be fifteen miles from here by now."

"Do you have any better ideas?"

"No."

"I guess we just keep going then," said Ben. "If this is a young lion with a full belly, he may not have wandered far."

They followed the well maintained county road three more miles to the east. The tracking bed then angled to the north on an old logging road through a pocket of mature Douglas fir. The temperature dropped several degrees as they escaped the mid-morning sun.

At the far edge of the timber, a wide grassy swale intersected the road as it graded around the top of the drainage. They found another lion track coming out of the bottom and traveling to the southeast.

"This is your lion," Slats said.

"Are you sure?" asked Berg.

"I'd bet you my bonus on it."

"Then let's go get him," said Ben pulling the high powered rifle from the gun rack in the back window.

Slats opened the door of one of the dog carriers.

"Heater's the best dog I've ever owned," said Slats proudly. "He's strong and fast and he's got a voice you can't mistake from two miles away. Some dogs'll bark only when they're on the chase. Some'll only bay when the lion's treed. Not Heater. He barks nonstop until the lion's dead. He's an independent cuss though. Heater don't trust no nose but his own. He'll always work out the trail himself. Won't follow the other dogs unless he's actually smelled the scent himself."

Slats led Heater to the lion track. Heater bayed deeply and strained against the nylon tether which restrained him. Slats unclasped the leash snap and the dog scaled the road bank barking in the same deep voice. The other dogs joined in the crescendo as they clamored against the metal doors of the homemade kennels. Slats quickly released the other dogs and they followed Heater up the swale. Spike, the young black hound with a shrill voice, raced ahead of the other dogs and overtook Heater just before the horizon.

"That's a good sign," said Slats. "Spike'll chase a fresh track, but he tends to lag behind on an old trail and will eventually quit and come back. The other dogs don't pay him any mind though. They'll come to Heater's bark on the dead run, but don't give poor Spike any heed whatsoever."

"How long do you think it'll take them to tree the lion?" asked Berg.

"Hard to tell."

"More art than science," said Berg giving Ben a knowing look.

"Every lion's different," Slats said. "A lion on an empty belly will travel a lot further and faster than one that's just ate."

"This lion ate not long ago," Ben said grimly as the three man scrambled up the slope.

The young lion lay sleeping on a narrow rock outcropping tucked deep in a pocket of lodge pole pine. His neck fur bristled and ears immediately cocked forward at the distant sound of the baying hound. He pressed his tawny body full length against the cool pine grass. The long tail swung nervously from side to side and he hissed involuntarily.

73

Except for the tail, the lion remained motionless, the large yellow eyes peering intently down the slope. The barking followed the narrow swale out of the bottom of Greyson Creek through a deep canyon and onto the timbered incline where he lay.

The instinctive knowledge that the hounds were on his back trail heightened his consciousness. At the first flash of the black coat of the lead dog, the young lion whirled and bounded straight up the rocky incline.

Spike, the first dog to reach the lion's bedding area, ran helter skelter across the limestone shelf. The smell of lion permeated the still midmorning air and the young hound's voice became shriller in recognition of the fresh scent. Heater, the veteran of many lion chases, moved more deliberately onto the outcropping. He pressed his nose against the pine grass flattened by the prone body of the sleeping cougar. The hound ferreted through the conflicting scent trails and followed up the slope on the tracks of the retreating lion. The other hounds upon hearing the new tones raced through the bedding area without any hesitation and fell in behind Heater and Spike adding their own voices to the chorus.

Ben felt the familiar adrenaline rush of the excitement of the hunt. The three men hurried along the route taken by the dogs at a pace humanly impossible to sustain. Ben felt his heart pounding in his chest and each sinew and muscle of his legs.

He was about to acknowledge the twenty year age difference between himself and his younger cohorts when Slats called back to him, "Sheriff, if the goin's too tough, you could go back for the truck and drive around to the top of the ridge." The condescending tone of voice struck a chord with the veteran outdoors man who lifted the black felt cowboy hat from his head and wiped the accumulated sweat from his brow and determinedly kept his legs pumping up the incline.

Slats stopped short when he detected the changing pitch of the dogs' collective voice.

"They've hit fresh scent," Slats said.

"Let's grade the drainage," Ben said as he lined the direction of the baying dogs with their current position. "Maybe we can take a big loop out of the trail and avoid this hole."

"Sound's good to me," said Berg. "We're at least forty-five minutes behind right now and falling farther behind by the minute."

The men altered their course and adopted a more direct and less physically demanding route. They listened, over the sound of their own heavy breathing, to the dogs distant baying. "The lion's treed," said Slats twenty minutes later as he detected a change of the hounds' collective voice. "We might as well take our time. He ain't going nowhere."

But the three men picked up their pace. They scrambled down a steep slope covered with scattered timber and fields of large algae covered boulders. The footing was treacherous. Each man fell at least once. At the bottom, they entered a long narrow park edged by a dozen quaking aspens and then crossed the Ridge Road onto the Dry Creek side of the drainage.

When they cleared the first stand of trees, they were greeted by the sight of the lion perched on the single branch of an enormous dead Ponderosa pine jutting from a rocky knob above the Dry Creek Canyon. The lion stood silhouetted against the deep blue sky.

A lightning strike had shattered the top thirty feet of the tree. Hundreds of pieces of wood, some bleached by the sun and others blackened by the strike, lay scattered at the base of the old snag. The lion paced on the remaining limb which towered thirty feet above the ground on the downhill side but stood a mere fifteen feet in the air on the uphill side. The hounds bayed and yelped at the hissing, growling cat as they alternated between leaping up the trunk and running directly under the lion on the overhanging limb.

Ben removed the rifle slung across his shoulder and jacked a cartridge into the chamber.

"I hope one of those stumbles didn't knock off my scope," Ben said as he pushed on the safety and re-shouldered the rifle. They eased the last three hundred yards across the bare ridge to the tree never talking and never taking their eyes from the cougar.

When they came abreast of the dead snag, Ben brought the rifle to his shoulder and focused the cross hairs of the scope on the chest of the pacing lion. The lion moved closer to the trunk blocking the angle for a shot from the uphill side of the tree. Ben moved to the side and slightly down the slope. He steadied the rifle and squeezed the trigger. The rifle cracked above the din of the snarling lion and the barking dogs. The cougar stood motionless and then toppled from the limb to the ground below. Spike piled onto the fallen animal. The lion clamped his jaws onto one of Spike's front feet piercing a paw with an incisor. Spike jerked his foot from the lion's mouth yelping shrilly. He hopped several yards up the slope never touching the injured foot to the ground.

Ben quickly worked the bolt of the 30.06 ejecting the empty shell casing and inserting another cartridge into the chamber. He sighted again on the lion but this time the cat remained still.

Slats, wielding a dead limb from the fallen tree top, prevented the other dogs from getting to the fallen cougar.

"Why don't you take the dogs outa here and go get the truck," Ben yelled to Slats. "Dave and I'll pack the cat up to the road and meet you."

Slats nodded and set to lashing the hounds together with a long length of yellow nylon rope. Slats, with the help of the warden, pulled the reluctant hounds several yards up the slope before they acknowledged Slats' loud and obscene commands and lined out in the direction of the truck. Spike still packed his left front foot.

Berg returned to the tree and photographed the lion and then rolled the animal over on its back. He cautiously felt the pulse at the neck confirming the death. Ben lowered the rifle and both men sat silently for several minutes. Ben felt a sense of sadness despite the carnage suspected of the dead animal.

Ben climbed to his feet with some difficulty and snapped a long dead branch from the fallen snag. He placed the makeshift game pole along the length of the lion's body and lashed the front and back legs to the limb. With one man in front and one behind, they hoisted the lion between them, each man balancing an end of the branch across his shoulders. They slowly plodded up the grade to the Ridge Road. They lay the lion on a bank above the roadway. With the excitement over, Ben felt both an emotional letdown and physical fatigue.

"Ya think we got the right lion?" asked Berg as he leaned back against the road bank.

"Slats thinks so, but we'll let the forensic boys tell us for sure."

"I hope this is it," Berg said. "I don't have many hikes like that left in me."

"If you'd follow that route every day for a month, you'd get in shape." Ben laughed.

"If it didn't kill me first."

When Slats arrived, they stretched the lion across the hood of the truck and secured it with the same nylon rope they had used to restrain the dogs. They drove down the ridge and turned back into the Greyson Creek drainage. When they crossed the creek, Ben told Slats to turn up the creek to the Greyson Creek subdivision.

"Stop here," Ben said when they pulled parallel to the Benson residence. "Seeing this lion may be the last thing in the world that the Bensons want to do, but I'm gonna give them the opportunity anyway."

Slats and Berg waited in the cab as Ben walked across the bridge and rapped on the front door of the log home. He disappeared inside for a few minutes and returned followed by a grim faced Emma Benson.

Emma walked slowly to the truck and examined the mountain lion.

"This can't be the lion," she said. "He seems so small—so pitiful looking. There must be some mistake."

"We'll send the body to the pathologist as soon as we get back to town," Ben said trying to avoid any confrontation. "He'll be able to tell us for sure. I left my vehicle at the Deep Creek Bar. I'll call in and make the arrangements as soon as we get out to the highway. I'll let you know his findings as soon as he calls me."

Emma took one long last look at the body of the lion and then turned quickly and trudged slowly back to the house with her head in her hands.

The three men drove out of the Greyson Creek canyon and followed Ross Gulch Road to its intersection with the highway just above the Deep Creek Bar. Slats dropped off Ben and Berg at the sheriff's vehicle and headed into Townsend ahead of them. Ben radioed the dispatcher and directed her to contact the pathologist to advise him of the impending arrival of the lion. He then drove the ten miles down Deep Creek Canyon to Townsend.

As Ben pulled in and parked behind the sheriff's office, he saw Slats standing with one foot on the front bumper of his truck. Before Slats stood a large group of media and passerbys. Slats was describing the chase in great detail to those assembled around the vehicle.

Ben edged next to Jefferson Kirk who stood on the fringe of the crowd.

"Where'd this mob come from?" asked Ben.

"Scanner land's at work," Kirk said. "When you radioed in about the forensic examination of the lion, the word spread quickly. Also, Slats cruised Main Street from end to end before you got here."

"He's in all his glory, isn't he?" said Ben nodding toward Slats who was pacing back and forth in front of the truck snarling like the treed lion.

"He does seem to be enjoying himself," Kirk said. "The press is eating this up."

Amongst those assembled in front of Smith were the reporter from the local paper, *The Townsend Star*, Heidi Singer and a camera crew from NBC.

"The NBC people didn't get here because they had their police scanners tuned into the Headwaters County Sheriff's office," said Ben. "How in the hell did they find out?"

"Coincidence." said Kirk. "They were in West Yellowstone finishing up a story about the bison in Yellowstone Park. They read Heidi Singer's story in the morning paper and headed this way."

"It looks like they're getting an earful," said Ben.

As the action described by Slats expanded to include the actions of the sheriff and warden, the circle of people also expanded to include the two officers. Ben and Dave Berg reluctantly fielded questions. Ben disliked the media attention immensely. Eventually, a well-dressed, middle-aged man stepped forward and asked, "Are you Headwaters County Sheriff Ben Green?"

"At least that's one question I can answer," said Ben with a slight laugh. "Yes, I am."

The man then handed several papers to the sheriff saying, "I'm Gene Baker from the U.S. Marshall's office. Consider yourself served."

Ben paged quickly through the legal documents and then handed them to Kirk. Kirk skimmed past the summons and introductory materials and read the meat of the complaint.

"What's up?" asked Heidi Singer.

"Grover Arlen and Animals Forever have struck again," said Kirk. "The Federal District Court has issued a temporary restraining order enjoining the sheriff and the warden or anyone on their behalf from chasing and killing the lion responsible for the death of Faith Benson."

"Well, they're too damn late," said Slats. "The cat's already in the bag, so to speak."

"What's the basis for the complaint?" asked Heidi.

"The gist of it is that the sheriff acted without legal authority, that the use of dogs doesn't guarantee the killing of the lion responsible thereby threatening innocent lions and, finally, that chasing lions with dogs places the dogs in needless jeopardy."

"Is there any merit to the allegations?" asked Heidi. "Sheriff, what was your authority for killing the lion?"

Ben looked at Kirk and stammered, "I'm the sheriff and a little girl had been killed by a lion. It just seemed the right thing to do. I called Warden Berg and he agreed with me."

"Are you sure this is the lion?" asked the NBC correspondent as the camera zoomed in on Ben and then panned over to the lion.

"Not for sure," said Ben.

"Isn't it true that a dog was injured during the incident?" asked the NBC reporter.

"A dog did get a foot bitten," said Ben.

"So you're pretty much agreeing with the allegations of Animals Forever, aren't you?" asked the correspondent.

"The sheriff won't be making any further comments about the allegations in the complaint until he's had the opportunity to review them fully with his legal advisor," said Kirk stepping forward. "If Mr. Smith is correct in his assessment that this is the lion responsible for the death of Faith Benson, then allegations or no allegations, the issue is moot. I'm sure Mr. Smith would be glad to tell you the basis for his conclusions about the identity of the lion."

Slats returned to the dead lion and held up one of the paws for the camera. He explained in great deal how he had compared the paw print of this lion with the print in the mud at the kill sight.

Ben and Kirk slipped away from the crowd.

Once they were out of ear shot, Ben whispered, "What in the hell is this BS about my legal authority to kill the lion? Don't I have a duty to protect and serve?"

"Calm down," said Kirk. "Sometimes you just have to consider the source."

"That's easy for you to say, but I feel like I've just been handed my head on a platter."

"It certainly wasn't the ideal time to be served," Kirk said.

"No legal authority, my ass. What about the theory that says a person has the right to use force in defense of others? It's the same legal doctrine Animals Forever argued gave someone the right to shoot a hunter in order to save a game animal. They've turned it around and now I have to claim the same right to justify my actions."

"Ironic, isn't it?" said Kirk with a smile.

When the TV crew finished with Slats, Heidi Singer latched onto him and led him by the hand toward Ben and Kirk.

"Slats sure looks broke to lead," whispered Ben to Kirk as the two approached across the parking lot.

"Sheriff, can I get a picture of you and Mr. Smith?" asked Heidi.

Heidi positioned the two men together. As Slats draped his arm around the sheriff's neck, Heidi snapped the picture.

"Great shot," Heidi said. "I've just about got all the material I need. Ben, could you answer just one more question for me?"

"Oh, why not?"

"When will the pathologist give you his opinion as to whether this is the lion that did the killing?" asked Heidi.

"Dr. Hanning told the dispatcher that he has another examination to perform first thing in the morning but that he'll try to get to it tomorrow afternoon. If not, he indicated that he'd come in over the weekend, so we should have the results no later than Monday."

"In light of the restraining order obtained by Animals Forever, what do you plan to do if this isn't the right lion?"

"That's two questions," said Ben. "I only agreed to one. I'll answer the second one if and when the time comes."

"Turnabout seems fair play," Kirk said. "How's about if the reporter answers a question of her own?"

"What do you want to know?" asked Heidi.

"Would the lady be interested in having dinner with a poor lonely district attorney?"

"She would, but it'll have to be late. I've got a lot of work ahead of me. Also, it's on the condition that the same poor lonely District Attorney give me a ride to the airport after dinner. I was able to book a 10:30 flight to Seattle."

"I can live with those conditions," said Kirk.

When Heidi left, Slats turned to Ben with his arm extended and his palm out.

"What?" asked Ben.

"I'm ready for my pay and bonus," said Slats.

"Eight hundred dollars for a day and a half of work plus expenses ain't bad wages."

"I'm afraid the county don't quite work that way," said Ben. "You'll have to come into my office and sign a claim form. You won't get paid until the first of the month. And I'm sure not agreeing to pay the bonus until I'm sure we got the right lion."

"Damn, I worked up a considerable thirst, too," said Slats.

"Here's twenty-five bucks," said Ben handing it to Slats. "I'll borrow it from petty cash until the first of the month. Also, I'll have one of the deputies take you to the county shop and he'll fill your truck with gas."

"You agreed to pay expenses," said Slats. "Will you cover the veterinary bill for Spike?"

"Yeah. Why don't you take him out to the vet clinic and have them send the bill to the county."

"I'll do that right away," said Slats. "Ya know, sheriff, back in Missouri the veterinarian is also the taxidermist."

"Really?"

"Yeah, one way or the other you always get your dog back."

"You're a sick man." Ben laughed.

The two men left Kirk in the parking lot and entered Ben's office.

"You know, sheriff," whispered Slats, even though no one else was around, "we've still got time today to go after the other lion track we saw this morning. Heck, the dogs barely worked up a sweat on the last one."

"With the restraining order in effect, I don't think that'd

be a good idea," said Ben. "Besides, you already told the national news that we've got the right lion. Have you ever been wrong?"

"I thought I was wrong once, but I was mistaken," said Slats laughing loudly at his own joke.

"Sign this claim form and get out of here," said Ben shaking his head. "I've got work to do."

Kirk settled behind his desk and prepared to undertake the mundane legal work represented by the many file folders which cluttered his desk.

"John Sharp was here to see you, but I seem to have lost him," said a smiling Marge Johns from the doorway.

"What's this all about?" asked Kirk immediately becoming suspicious and on guard.

Kirk rose and looked out into the reception area. John Sharp stood pressed against the wall of law books in new camouflage clothing.

"What are you doing?" Kirk asked.

"I'm taking these new duds back," said Sharp. "They obviously don't work. You saw me right off."

"You've just got the wrong style," said Kirk, "if you want to hide in law libraries, you'll need Pacific Reporter tan in a law book pattern."

"Maybe you're right. I'm just in the wrong environment. These'll probably blend right into the mountain once we get into the woods."

"Blend in hell. You can be your own damn mountain," said Kirk, eying Sharp's 6'5" frame. "Come on in before the paying customers think the courthouse is under attack by some para-military organization."

Kirk told Sharp about the legal action of Animals Forever and the issuance of the restraining order.

"If they can stop the sheriff from killing a lion that murdered a sweet little girl, what chance do we have of getting rid of a lion killing our cattle?" asked Sharp.

"Nothing's easy anymore," Kirk said. "I'm just glad they got the lion before we were served with the restraining order."

"I also see that Heidi's back in town. I suppose that means I won't be hunting with you this weekend."

"Not at all. I'm putting her on a plane this evening. As soon as the funeral is over tomorrow, I'll be ready to head up country. Do you still think we ought to go to upper Greyson Creek where you saw the sign the other day?"

"Those elk will always be there," said Sharp. "I heard through the grapevine that there's a big herd holding in the wide saddle where we corner with Webster and the Forest. Once those elk get a little pressure, they'll move onto Webster's and stay there until we get some weather. We might as well hunt them while we got a chance."

"I just hope you can hit what I call in," said Sharp.

"How's your calling coming along?" asked Kirk.

Sharp fumbled in a front pocket and pulled out the black plastic case containing his diaphragm elk call. He placed the call on his tongue and cupping his hands to his mouth produced the shrill bugle of a mature bull elk. Marge Johns burst through the door.

"I haven't called in an elk yet," said Sharp, "but I'm two for two on good looking women."

"I didn't realize an elk call had such an effect on the female of the human species," said Kirk. "Maybe I should give it a try on Heidi."

"I swear the only difference between men and boys is

the cost of their toys," said Marge as she shut the office door tightly behind her.

"How are things going between you and the lovely Ms. Singer?" asked Sharp.

"I'm getting the big push to make a commitment."

"What's wrong with that?" asked Sharp. "It's about time you settled down again. Besides, I thought you believed her to be the greatest thing since stick matches."

"I guess I still do," said Kirk. "I wouldn't hesitate a minute if I hadn't felt the same way the first time around. I just really want to be sure this time."

"You don't want to fool around until you let a good thing completely pass you by," said Sharp.

"I've thought about that too," Kirk said. "I probably need to reflect on the whole issue on the top of some mountain hopefully with a bull elk within bow range."

"That can be arranged," said Sharp. "I'll pick you up tomorrow right after the funeral."

Sharp left through the reception area blowing the elk call as he passed Marge John's desk, laughing heartily at her obscene response.

"That was wonderful," said Heidi savoring the last morsel of fish.

"There's nothing like fresh trout," said Kirk as he removed one last fish from the gas barbecue.

After dinner Kirk moved to the edge of the redwood deck and pointed to the willows lining the creek bank. Two whitetail deer danced through a narrow opening and moved into the meadow. Heidi pressed against him from behind, slipping her arms around his waist.

"A person could get used to a view like that," she said. "I wish I could stay longer, but if you're going to get me to the airport on time, we'd better get moving. But before I go, I've got to say goodbye to Nugget. Come with me."

Before Kirk could respond or turn and get her within his grasp, she had skipped down the stairs of the deck and disappeared around the corner of the house. By the time he caught up, she was dipping a coffee can into the wooden oat bin next to the pole corral.

As he watched her pour the oats onto her palm letting Nugget retrieve the grains with vigorous movements of his lips and tongue, he couldn't help but recall her hesitation to approach the large animal on her first visit.

"You be good, Nugget," she said as she poured the remainder of the oats into a metal feed barrel in the corral and ran her hand along his neck.

They walked arm in arm along the footpath by the creek and then angled back across the meadow to Kirk's Blazer for the trip to the Helena airport.

"The NBC crew kind of upstaged you and stole your thunder today, didn't they?" asked Kirk.

"They certainly changed the thrust of my piece," Heidi said. "They took all the freshness out of the story of the lion kill itself, but they did reach a national audience. They created a market for the side bar stories. I wrote a feature on Slats and his lion chasing methods. It's a good piece and will get excellent exposure because of NBC's presence. I'll also be able to do a follow up story. If the sheriff killed the right lion, that's one angle. If he didn't, then the real lion is still on the loose and the sheriff is enjoined by Animals Forever from pursuing. That's also a newsworthy angle."

"You can't lose either way," said Kirk.

Chapter V

Friday, September 5th

"We can't lose either way," said a delighted Grover Arlen to his secretary. Arlen pointed to the morning paper lying on his desk. The divided picture on the page below the headline, "HUNTERS and HUNTED," displayed on one half a smiling Slats Smith with an arm flung around the shoulders of Ben Green and on the other half revealed the image of the dead lion stretched across the hood of a truck.

"If the lion killed by Ben Green is determined to be the mountain lion that killed the girl, we merely emphasize that the lion was in its natural environment. Its actions were controlled solely by its instinctive drive to survive."

The short, squat man rose from his chair, the pitch of his voice rising with him, "But if on the other hand, it's determined that he in fact killed the wrong lion, we can declare 'I told you so' in letters six feet high. We'll demand the resignation of the good sheriff and ask for some kind of civil damages on behalf of wildlife. It's a win/win situation either way."

"What do we do until there is a determination?" asked Ronald.

"In the interim, we keep the pressure on," said Arlen.

"How?"

"We issue the following press release," said Arlen as he reached for the small dictaphone on the edge of the large oak desk. Once Ronald had gathered a notepad, he began to speak slowly and deliberately, "Ego. Ego is a dangerous thing particularly if you are an animal in Headwaters County, Montana. The ego of Headwaters County Sheriff Ben Green has caused him to pursue a course of action that is unwise and harmful to animals. Yesterday, we at Animals Forever warned that this course of action, if followed, would place both dogs and innocent mountain lions at risk. We, to the best of our abilities, tried to prevent the sheriff from proceeding with this action, but alas, a lion was killed and a dog seriously injured before legal proceedings could enjoin his actions.

"Was the lion murdered by Sheriff Green responsible for the tragic death of Faith Benson? No one knows. The sheriff himself has admitted that he doesn't know. The mother of Faith Benson has clearly stated that she doesn't think it's the right lion. Even if it is, the present uncertainty underscores Animals Forever's position. Even if it is the lion, who gave the sheriff the right to take the life of a lion obeying its own instincts in its own environment? Why did the sheriff so quickly take this action? We think we know. Ego. We can only assume that the sheriff's fifteen minutes of fame resulting from the past year's shooting incidents has passed. He now needs some other grandiose and high profile action to propel himself back into the public consciousness so he can receive the attention he so obviously craves. It is a sad day for animals. A sad day indeed."

"Pretty harsh stuff, isn't it?" asked Ronald.

"This'll seem mild if the pathologist determines the lion killed by Ben Green wasn't responsible for Faith Benson's death," said Arlen.

When Ronald left to prepare the press release, Arlen placed a call to Tanner Trent.

"Great job." said Arlen. "Tell me, how'd you manage to get Ben Green served on national television?"

"That was a nice touch," Trent said. "But I have to admit that the timing of the process server's arrival was merely coincidental with the presence of the TV cameras."

"Luck is the residue of preparation," said Arlen.

"You may be right," said Trent. "We certainly had to bust our butts and pull some strings to get the restraining order issued in such short order. It looks though like we may have won the battle but lost the war. They still killed a lion."

"No matter, we still made our point," Arlen said. "But if the lion they killed turns out to be the wrong one, I'll be back in touch and we can discuss further legal proceedings against Headwaters County and the good Sheriff Green."

"Please give me a little more advance notice," said Trent. "I hate throwing actions together without doing the requisite amount of research and thoroughly reviewing the documents. That's how mistakes get made."

"I'll try my best," said Arlen "But sometimes you just have to go with the flow and react. Besides, you're being far too modest. You're just like the Sundance Kid. You shoot better on the move."

"Maybe so, but if they got the lion that did the killing, the issue is moot. You've made a point, but I don't think you'll get anymore mileage out of the situation."

"Don't underestimate the ability of Grover Arlen to milk the publicity from a story, especially since we've now had national exposure. I'm sure I can think of a dozen different ways to keep this issue from dying."

William J. Sharp waited at the top of one side of the high school gymnasium. He leaned against the "B" of the word "BULLDOGS" which had been painted in large blue letters on the concrete block wall. The heat at this level was stifling.

The bleachers on both sides of the basketball court, as well as the rows of folding chairs on the floor itself, were filled with people. And still people came. The funeral service itself had to be delayed while the high school administrator commandeered several high school students to set up more folding chairs.

The Benson family had initially planned to hold the service at the small funeral home on Main Street. Ben had urged them to reconsider and move the service to the local high school gym.

William J. saw Mary Sharp sitting on the opposite side of the gymnasium. He noticed other husbands and wives seated apart. People apparently had felt the need to come and obviously had not mentioned their intentions to their spouses.

Misty played the piano to begin the service. The minister of the small evangelical church which the Bensons attended had never spoken before such a large audience. He spoke of "God's will" and "thanking the Lord in all things."

William J. listened skeptically. While he believed in God, he believed generally that God helped those who helped themselves. He, for one, wasn't going to thank the Lord for mountain lions or the death of a small child. He had faith. It just didn't extend that far. If slaughtering a little girl were in God's plan, he promised himself to ask the Lord about it the minute he walked through the pearly gates.

Mary Sharp looked across the gymnasium and smiled slightly when she spied William J. He was a softie she thought, definitely all bark and no bite. For all of his ranting about the stupidity of the Bensons for moving into the mountains, he still was at the funeral.

Mary sobbed slightly as the funeral progressed. God must have needed Faith Benson badly. She felt twinges of guilt that it was Faith Benson and not her grandsons, Lane or Cody.

Jefferson Kirk carried the same thought without the guilt. He all too clearly recalled the hikes and fishing trips into the hills and meadows adjacent to the Benson tract. The reason for Faith Benson being the victim rather than one of the twins whether fate, luck or God's will made no difference to Kirk. He was just glad if it had to happen, it hadn't happened to Lisa or Jenny.

The service ended with the recitation of the Lord's Prayer. After the very audible "Amen", the crowd filtered from the school building. The mourners lingered in the courtyard outside the school rather than going directly to their cars for the procession to the cemetery.

After visiting with several neighboring ranchers and other friends, William J. drove to the real estate office on Main Street.

Mort Chappel was already seated in the realtor's office when William J. arrived. The real estate agent handed William J. the buy/sell agreement. He quickly perused the filled in blanks of the pre-printed form. The structure of the agreement seemed fairly standard. Five thousand dollars earnest money would be held in the realtor's trust account until the closing date on the first of December. At that time, the Sharps would pay an additional twenty-five thousand dollars to Mort Chappel. The balance of the purchase price would be paid to the escrow agent in annual installments on or before the first day of December for the next thirty years.

"Looks good to me," said William J. as he scrawled his name on the bottom of the agreement.

William J. and Chappel left the real estate office together.

"How 'bout a drink to cement the deal?" asked Chappel.

"Fine by me," William J. said. "But since you've got all my money, you'll have to buy."

"I'll buy the first one."

The two men angled across Main Street to the rock faced front of the Mint Bar. William J.'s eyes adjusted quickly from the bright sunlight to the dim interior. He strode to the long hardwood bar and called for two ditchwaters.

The bartender placed the glasses in front of them. William J. raised his glass and tipped it slightly toward Chappel saying, "You left that range in better shape than you found it. You did right by it."

This simple acknowledgment and tribute to his stewardship by William J. pleased Chappel and confirmed for him that he'd made the right decision. Each man slowly drained his glass and felt the bite of the bourbon. They sat silently while the bartender refilled their glasses.

"You know, I could have got a lot more for those two sections," Chappel said.

"I know you could." said William J.

"Just yesterday, Pete Roemer called me and told me that Ray Webster wanted to buy them. Told me to just set my price. But I'd rather see you have 'em."

"What'd ya tell Pete?" asked William J.

"I told him I already had a deal with you, but if it fell through I'd get back to him. I guess I'd rather see Webster have 'em than see some developer carve 'em up into twenty acre tracts."

"You know though," said William J., "at $100 an acre those two sections will never pay for themselves."

"I know. I've penciled it out a dozen different ways myself. I've figured it running yearlings or cow/calf pairs, leases with the hunting rights, leases without the hunting rights. It don't matter. There's no way that property will produce enough income to service that kind of debt. You'll have to rob the income from other parts of your operation to make up the difference."

"That's how I read it too," said William J. "What in the hell's gonna happen to the cattlemen when the land is worth ten times what a cow will pay for?"

"I don't know," Chappel said, "but I don't think it's going to be good. Sooner or later the country will all be sold to the highest bidder. The only consolation is that you and I won't be around to see it happen, unless you plan on living forever."

"We both know that ain't goin' to happen," William J. said. "You only have to look around this bar to know our days are numbered. At this time of day ten years ago, we'd have been sitting in the company of Charlie Masola, Bill Flynn, Chet Scoffield, Frank McArthur and half a dozen others—all sittin' here like birds on a wire. You could've fired one bullet and killed the whole lot of us. But they're all dead. Seems like you, me and Pete Cartwright are the only ones left."

"You're just a pup compared to me," said Chappel. "If I was your age, I'd still be planting trees fully expecting to sit in their shade. Hell, at my age, I don't even buy green bananas anymore."

"How old are you?" asked William J.

"I'll be eighty-four this spring."

"You don't look it."

"Looks don't fool a steep flight of stairs," Chappel said. "I hate to give it up, but those are young man hills and I've cheated time quite a bit as it is. But I don't think either of us is going to like the changes that are comin'."

"I wouldn't worry about it so much," said William J., "if I didn't have a coupla grandsons. I'd like to think that a hundred years from now some fella named Sharp will still be calving in the spring, pasturing the cattle in the Big Belts for the summer and shipping calves in the fall."

"There's no use worrying about it," said Chappel. "What's going to happen is going to happen."

"You're probably right," William J. said. "They say if you want to hear God laugh, just tell Him your plans."

"Let's plan on another drink then," said Chappel motioning for the bartender.

The funeral service left Kirk feeling the absence of his own daughters. The large log home on Deep Creek had never seemed emptier. He interrupted the task of gathering his hunting equipment to call the twins. Sarah, his ex-wife,

94

answered the phone. The sound of her voice still touched some nerve deep within his psyche. He mentally chastised himself for letting her still get to him.

"I'd like to visit with the girls," he said flatly.

"They're not here. They had a birthday party and sleep over at a friend's house."

Sarah related that she and the girls had learned the details of the mountain lion kill on the evening news.

"The news made it sound like the sheriff killed the wrong lion and suggested that Ben Green was nothing more than a publicity hound engaging in dramatic and unnecessary theatrics to regain public attention for himself." said Sarah.

"Really." said Kirk. "Who said that?"

"I think an animal rights group was making the charges. Anyway, it was part of the piece that was on the six o'clock news."

"Ben will be fit to be tied when he hears that," said Kirk."

"It doesn't matter what is true so much as what people think is true," said Sarah.

"You're probably right. Ben still isn't going to be happy though. But enough of that. How are things going with you?"

"The glamour of the job has definitely worn off," Sarah said. "I'm tired of showing the same houses to the same people, but it still beats living out in the middle of nowhere in a cold Montana winter. But then I guess you know how I feel in that regard."

"To ad nauseam."

"I do have to run," said Sarah. "I'll tell the girls you called and have them call you Sunday night."

Kirk hung up the phone admitting that the conversation

was the most civil they had been to each other in the two years since the divorce.

Kirk finished assembling his bow hunting equipment and groceries just as John Sharp's flat bed truck drove up the driveway. He heard the diesel engine die followed immediately by the squeal of an elk bugle.

Kirk carried his gear to the truck, and as they had done on many occasions dating back to their childhood, the two men embarked on a hunting trip. They drove up the creek and turned south onto a secondary road that wound into the Dry Creek drainage. They drove past the new homes of the Dry Creek subdivision and then through a narrow canyon with rock walls rising two hundred feet above the roadway. Aging cottonwood trees with massive gnarly trunks lined the creek bottom as the road wound above the narrow canyon. The leaves of the cottonwoods contained hints of yellow revealing at least a few nights of frost.

John Sharp stopped his truck in the roadway across from the Dry Creek cabin. The log cabin with the high gabled roof stood alone in a small clearing surrounded by fir trees. Dry Creek flowed over a waterfall into a wide deep pool below and to the immediate east of the structure.

A long narrow footbridge spanned between the cabin and the parking lot across the creek. The late afternoon sun reflected off the cascade of water and illuminated the frothy white clumps of foam that circled the perimeter of the pool at the base of the falls. A water ouzel sat perched on a rock at the edge of the pool dipping several times in its characteristic fashion before diving beneath the surface of the stream and disappearing entirely.

The sight of the cabin with its associated memories produced a rush of excitement and Kirk felt the return of "hunting fever." After a few minutes of reflection, John Sharp put the truck in gear, drove another hundred yards up the road and turned into the parking lot.

Two trucks were already parked there. Two men and two teenage boys were gathered on the far side of the lot. They were closely examining a life-size fiberglass elk target.

Kirk recognized the group as Doc Adams, Garth Hart and their two sons. The men were part of the group that annually paid a fee to the Sharp Ranch's hunting association to access the lands owned or leased by the Sharps. However, Kirk's and Sharp's association with the two men predated the creation of the hunting club. All were part of an informal group that for years had passed through the Dry Creek cabin during hunting season.

Doc Adams looked up from a kneeling position and called to John Sharp.

"Hey Sharpie, did you up and join the National Guard or what?"

"No, I actually came up here to see what I could learn about bow hunting," Sharp said. "I figured I'd just watch you."

"Came to learn at the feet of the master, did you?"

"Something like that, Doc, but more in line with the thinking that says 'no matter how inadequate or inferior one may be, one can always assist the betterment of mankind by serving as a bad example.'"

"Well, here's a tip for you then," said Adams. "If you get lost in the woods while bow hunting, shoot three times into the air and then sit down and wait for me."

"I'll take that advice in the same spirit that it was given," said Sharp.

Kirk eyed the three well-grouped arrows sticking from the fatal area of the elk target.

"Someone's got their bow well tuned," said Kirk pulling the arrows from the target.

"Karl's been practicing for two months," said Doc

Adams nodding toward his son. "He can shoot the bullseye out of a target when he knows the distance, but we'll see tomorrow what he can do when a big bull comes in and he has to guess the yardage."

The doctor pulled a small bottle from one of his pockets and tossed it to Sharp.

"What's this?"

"Grade A number one cow elk urine," said Adams. "Guaranteed to cover your scent and lure in the biggest bull on the mountain."

"I wonder how they collect it," Sharp said as he unscrewed the cap.

"If you ever start thinking your own job sucks," said Adams, "just remember that there's some poor schmuck out there collecting elk pee."

"This label says $10.95," said Sharp. "The fellow chasin' the elk around with a Dixie cup may be a schmuck but he sure as hell ain't poor and it sure has to beat the job of collecting grizzly urine. Do you think this stuff really works?"

"Wouldn't be caught in the woods without it," Adams said.

John finished removing the cap and tentatively smelled the contents. "It's definitely elk urine. Kirk, do you use this?"

"I used to but not anymore."

"How come?"

"Couple reasons," said Kirk. "First, I think that the sense of smell of an elk is so refined that if an elk winds a hunter covered with elk urine, the elk just thinks 'Ah, I smell a human being covered with elk urine'. The bottled elk scent also covers the scent of real elk. If you use the scent yourself, you lose the availability of one of your own senses. The bottom line is that if you don't want an elk to smell you, the best advice is to stay down wind."

Sharp screwed the cap back on the bottle and tossed it back to Doc Adams. "Thanks anyway, Doc, but for once in his life Kirk actually made sense."

"Suit yourself," said Adams, "but when that big bull walks right up to me like a love sick pup, and I shoot him at point blank range, don't come crying to me."

"I'm a little disappointed in you and Garth," said Kirk. "I guessed you'd be out spotting us up some elk or at the very least fixing dinner."

"Don't need to go spotting," said Mark Hart. "We already know where the elk are."

"Don't be blabbing our secrets now," said Doc Adams.

"The elk that come out of the Hogbacks into the hay meadows on Deep Creek ain't much of a secret," said the boy. "Everybody in the county's been watchin' them from the Deep Creek Highway."

"I guess we know where you're going in the morning," said Kirk. "Sounds like the Hogbacks are on the itinerary."

"That's right," said Garth. "The elk herd's followed the exact same route out of the juniper pockets on the north Hogback to the hay meadows for the last three days. There are several bodacious ambush points along that trail. If they come that way in the morning, one of us will have a point blank shot. You ought to come in with us. We'd be able to cover some of the alternate routes."

"I think we'll pass," said Sharp. "There's supposed to be a big herd of elk in the saddle between us and Webster. We'd better hunt 'em there while we have the chance."

"You're in luck on the dinner score, though," said Garth Hart. "Doc roasted up a turkey yesterday. It's heating in the oven as we speak."

"Now that is good news," Kirk said. "When do we eat?"

"Just as soon as I can whip up a batch of my world

famous stuffing," said Adams. "The first two steps of the recipe call for pouring two cold beers into the cook."

"Sounds a lot like your recipe for barbecued ribs," said Sharp. "But I'm not going to argue with success. Those ribs are always pretty damn good."

"Even when he burns 'em," said Kirk. "Which is most of the time."

The men and boys crossed the narrow footbridge above the waterfalls to the log cabin. An old discolored washtub sat on the front porch, filled with an equal amount of ice and water. Several cans of beer floated in the watery slush.

Kirk fished a can of Coors Light from the tub. He popped the top, took a long sip and felt the incredibly cold beer slide easily down his throat.

"I'd better have another," he said as he extracted a second beer from the washtub on his way up the porch steps. "Doc may need an assistant cook."

The smell of roast turkey greeted the hunters as they entered the one-room cabin. Doc Adams removed the foil covered bird from the antique "Monarch" range. He poured the turkey drippings into a pan on the top of the woodburner and returned the turkey to the oven.

Sharp rummaged through a bureau drawer and produced a deck of cards. While Doc Adams fixed gravy and stuffing, the other hunters engaged in an intense, spirited game of pitch.

Doc Adams' announcement, "Dinner is served," immediately suspended the card game. On large platters, the men piled slices of fresh baked bread, turkey and stuffing and covered the steaming accumulation with gravy.

"Doc, I take back every bad thing I ever said about you," said Sharp. "This dinner's great."

Their mouths full, the other hunters nodded.

After dinner, the card game and hunting camp banter resumed beneath the propane lanterns. Doc Adams replaced Garth Hart at the card table and Garth, "the Budweiser jukebox," broke out his guitar and sang a repertoire of songs ranging from folk ballads to contemporary country western.

The conversation of the card players drifted easily across a wide spectrum of topics covering the serious, the absurd and the profane as well as the subjects of the moment: bow hunting and mountain lions.

"Do you think the elk are in the rut yet?" asked Adams.

"It's still pretty early." said Kirk. "As hot as it's been, I don't think the bulls will be very active."

"I'm afraid you may be right," said Adams. "Sometimes though early's the best time. If you can be out there when the bulls first start to travel looking for cows, they'll come to a bugle on a dead run without even paying any attention to the wind."

"That'd be nice," said Kirk, "but I'm not going to get my hopes up. What do you think, Mark?"

"You old guys can worry about the elk," said Mark. "I already got a trophy bull hanging on my bedroom wall. I just want to find a big mossy-horned mule deer buck to hang across from him. I just hope the mountain lions don't beat me to him."

"Listen to him, would you?" said Adams. "He shoots one big elk and he's leaving the rest of 'em to us. That big bull's spoiled him for life. But I do share his concern about the mountain lions. If half of what I've been reading and hearing is true, I'm afraid deer hunting may become a thing of the past. You boys think the sportsmen are just crying wolf so to speak or are the lions really hurting the deer population?"

"I think its more than hype," said Sharp. "You can't believe how many lion kills I've ridden across when I've been checking cattle. The fact that we've finally lost a calf to a lion tells me that the deer numbers are way down."

"It may just be my imagination," said Kirk, "but I think deer habits have changed the last few years because of lions. I first thought that mule deer were just getting dumber. They seemed to stay exposed in the open longer than ever before. I've finally concluded that they now feel less threatened if they can see you. They'll stay out in the open rather than go into a thicket or a narrow coulee where a lion might be hiding. They've almost developed an antelope mentality. It's a subtle change, but just watch the doe/fawn groups you see this fall and see if you don't agree."

"Maybe the death of the girl will spur some action to get rid of a few lions," said Adams.

"Don't count on it," said Kirk. "Animals Forever will fight any such action tooth and nail. I just hope Ben Green and Slats Smith got the right lion yesterday."

After several games of pitch, the hunters played one game of hearts which, in accordance with hunting camp ritual, signaled the last game of the evening. Kirk laid back on a two inch foam pad rolled out on the cabin floor. He pulled his sleeping bag over himself without getting into the bag itself.

The discussion, jokes and jibes continued long after the light faded from the propane lanterns. Finally, Kirk heard Doc Adams ask Sharp if he knew what you got when you crossed a donkey with an onion, but he was asleep before he heard the answer.

Chapter VI

Saturday, September 6th

Breakfast at the Dry Creek cabin on the opening morning of archery season was a simple affair, far different from the more elaborate traditional breakfasts preceding the opening of rifle season. The early advent of daylight this time of year forced the dispension of any meal of significance.

Between arranging hunting equipment and applying camouflage makeup to their faces, the hunters hurriedly munched breakfast bars and gulped glasses of milk and orange juice. It was still completely dark when the group left the cabin. Using a flashlight to find their way back across the footbridge, the men and boys loaded their gear and themselves into the four wheel drive vehicles.

Doc Adams, Garth Hart, and sons drove down the creek en route to the predetermined ambush points in the Hogback Mountains. Kirk and Sharp drove up the creek for their assault on the saddle where the Webster, Sharp and Forest Service properties came together. Each group faced a long hike in the dark to get to where they intended to be at daylight.

A short distance above the cabin, Kirk and Sharp noticed a blue Honda Civic with a California license plate parked by the road.

"It doesn't matter how early you get out," said Sharp. "Someone is always ahead of you."

"And a nonresident no less," Kirk said. "I wonder which way they went."

"It shouldn't make any difference," said Sharp. "If they went north, they're completely out of our hair and if they did go south, they've so much altitude to gain that we'll beat 'em to the top easily. If they went south, they obviously don't know much about the area. It's pure foolishness to try to climb out of this hole from here."

"We have a pretty good hole to crawl out of ourselves," said Kirk. "And I'm sure there are those who would question our sanity for climbing around these mountains in the dark."

A few miles further up the road, Sharp parked the pickup in a small pullout next to the stream. They quickly began the ascent out of the bottom of the drainage.

Twenty minutes of steady exertion, slogging up through the undergrowth, placed them atop a finger ridge that paralleled the Dry Creek drainage and then turned and angled to the top of the south side of the rugged canyon.

They caught their breath and began following the narrow rocky spine toward the top. The grade here was also steep, but in comparison to the first leg of their climb, the terrain seemed almost flat.

They felt their way along the narrow trail which clung to the ridge top pausing periodically, listening, hoping to hear an elk bugle across some distant canyon. Each foot of elevation on their climb out of the drainage broadened the horizon, revealing another expanse of stars.

Kirk felt the sweat pouring off of him and he frequently held open the neck of his T-shirt to vent his body warmth into the cool night air.

By the time they reached the ridge top overlooking the location of the reported elk sightings, streaks of light filled the eastern sky. With their backs against a rock ledge, they sat waiting for daylight, listening intently for the sounds of elk.

"It's quiet," whispered Kirk finally.

"Too quiet," said Sharp. "The bulls are either not buglin' or there just aren't any elk in the area. We ought to have heard something by now."

Almost immediately, the silence was shattered by a high pitched noise. The first note of this sound instantly raised their hopes of an elk bugle and dashed the same hopes with the next note as they distinguished the familiar howl of a distant coyote. The coyote's salute to the dawning of a new day was greeted by several answering howls and then the woods went silent again.

Kirk rested his head against the rock ledge and dozed slightly. As he was about to drift off, he felt a tug on his pant leg. He looked up to see Sharp pointing into the timber below them.

A dark form moved through the shadows and once on the skyline revealed itself as a cow elk. The cow ambled down the ridge and crossed out of the timber into the open and again disappeared into the gray morning light.

Kirk peered into the saddle. First, he saw what he thought were juniper bushes scattered throughout the broad sagebrush covered swale. But the increasing light revealed the bushes to be elk feeding in the open.

"This'd be a piece of cake, if it were rifle season," whispered Sharp. "You could just set your gun barrel over the edge of the ridge and pick out your elk."

"That's the frustrating thing about bow hunting," Kirk said. "The elk seem so close, yet they are too far to shoot."

"Look at 'em all," said Sharp.

With each passing moment, more elk became visible and greater detail could be observed.

"There's a nice bull," said Kirk pointing to a light colored body next to the timber. "At least a six point."

As it became fully light, it became apparent that the elk were slowly but steadily moving into a large pocket of timber across the Sharp's boundary fence on the Forest Service lands.

"What's the plan?" asked Sharp.

"It looks like the elk are going to bed down for the day in that thicket on the Forest. They sure aren't doing any bugling. I don't usually like to bugle myself until I hear a bull. Let's get downwind of that pocket and sneak in close. We can use the cow call and maybe suck in a bull."

"Let's get movin' then," whispered Sharp. "We're burnin' daylight."

"We'll have to take it easy," Kirk said. "We don't want to blunder into some elk on our side of the coulee and spook them right through the big herd."

They dropped back off the ridge top enough that their forms wouldn't be silhouetted on the skyline. Fortunately, a well traveled game trail paralleled the ridge line providing easy footing and allowing quiet movement.

When they were well beyond the pocket of timber on the parallel ridge, Kirk and Sharp eased back to the top and peeked across the swale. The last two elk entered the tree line and disappeared. Kirk removed a disposable lighter from the large front pocket of his camouflage pants. He flicked the lighter and held it aloft for several seconds observing which direction the slight morning breeze would point the flame. The flame gently tilted and pointed straight toward the thick timber that the elk had entered.

"Damn it anyway," said Kirk. "Sometimes I think these lighters are just elk detectors. It seems like the wind's always at my back. We'll have to go a ways further and quarter back to them. It's not a great wind but it'll work if we get around 'em."

"No matter," said Sharp smiling. "It'll change again by the time we get there."

They made a wide loop and came at the elk bedding area with a cross wind. Their pace slowed as they neared the location of the herd.

"How much further do you want to go?" asked Sharp.

Kirk shrugged. "We could jump elk anytime. Let's find a good location and set up."

At the top of the next rise, Kirk found two small jack pines about five feet apart. He crouched between them. When he stood up, his head just showed above each tree. He held out his bow and drew the string back from both a standing and a kneeling position.

"This looks like a good spot," whispered Kirk. "I've got cover in front and back of me and there are good shooting lanes on either side of the trees."

"Where do you want me?" asked Sharp.

"Why don't you go about thirty yards down the ridge and use your cow call. Hopefully a bull will wander right by me on his way to check you out."

From the quiver attached to his bow, Kirk removed a razor sharp broad head. He nocked the arrow on the string and set the bow on the pine grass. He watched while Sharp stepped off thirty paces down the narrow ridge and crouched behind two small spreading junipers by a steep drop off. Soon the mewing of a cow elk followed by the squeak of an answering calf emanated from Sharp's hiding place.

Pete Roemer tightened the cinch on Ray Webster's appaloosa and then checked the cinch on his bay.

"This slope's steep as hell," said Roemer, "but it'll sure save us a lot of time if we climb out of this bottom now."

"It's probably a good thing it's dark," said Webster. "You'd probably never get me to ride up here in the daylight."

Roemer gave the bay horse his head and let him set his own pace and route up the grade. Webster's appaloosa whinnied and followed.

"I hope you don't ride off a cliff," said Webster. "I'm afraid this appie would follow right behind you."

The horses angled back and forth up the slope until they were within about twenty yards of the top and then lunged straight up the last stretch almost unseating Webster. The riders dismounted under a Douglas fir.

"Let's tie the horses here," said Roemer. "We can walk the rest of the way."

Roemer removed two halters from his saddle bags and slipped the bridles off each horse. He clipped a nylon halter rope to each halter and secured the horses to an isolated lodge pole pine. Webster untied his compound bow from behind the saddle, and in the dark, the two men gingerly felt their way down the ridge to an open park.

Roemer twisted the head from a strand of Timothy grass. He dried his hand and worked the seed head between his thumb and index finger dislodging the powdery grains of seed onto his palm. With the eastern sky as a backdrop, he tossed the seed into the air and watched the drift of the grains.

"A perfect wind," said Roemer. "Right in our faces."

They moved across the park to a rocky ledge which overlooked the broad swale. They rested against a dead stump and listened for elk.

"We'll wait here until daylight," said Roemer. "There oughta be elk somewhere in the saddle."

"I thought we'd have heard a bugle by now," Webster said.

"They may not be in the rut yet," whispered Roemer. "I don't think all those elk up and disappeared."

When the entire saddle eventually became visible, they could see large numbers of elk slowly moving away from them.

"The elk are going the wrong direction," said Webster.

"Don't worry. They won't go far," Roemer said. "They'll probably bed down in that heavy pocket of timber."

"Can we get close without them seeing us?" asked Webster.

"We'll wait until they're all out of the saddle and then sneak down the ridge line. We should have more than enough cover."

When the last two elk disappeared into the timber, Roemer motioned to Webster. They crossed the sagebrush park and wound through the thick timber along the ridge top. About half way down the slope they came to a barbed wire fence.

"Forest Service?" asked Webster.

Roemer nodded and used one of the steel posts for support. He stepped across and then held the top wire down for Webster. Roemer leaned toward Webster and whispered, "We'll pussyfoot along now. We could run into elk anytime."

Roemer now crouched slightly as he advanced toward the elk and the pace slowed to a crawl, each step taken slowly and deliberately. They eventually eased out onto a rocky outcropping sitting above a narrow pass in the ridge line.

"This looks like a great place to set up," said Roemer as he removed his cowboy hat and replaced it with a camou-flaged baseball cap. "Elk could come into that dip from three different directions. I really don't want to bugle unless I hear a bull first. Why don't you go down within bow range of the pass and I'll hunker down here and use the cow call for awhile."

Webster moved down the slope and knelt behind a juniper. As soon as Roemer saw Webster reach this cover, he blew the cow call, imitating the mew of a cow elk and then followed with the answer of a calf. He frowned slightly at the tone of the call and slightly re-adjusted the rubber bands before calling again. He intermittently repeated the calling pattern as he watched and waited.

At first light, the mature tom pressed his long body tightly against the ground and watched the elk feeding across the saddle toward a clump of trees. He had instinctively chosen this location with the hope the elk herd would feed through the narrow opening below him. It was obvious now that the nearest elk would pass no closer than 200 yards from his point of ambush.

He concealed himself in the bottom of a dry stream bed, and moved into the timber. He repositioned himself above a game trail. He could periodically hear the elk in the big herd talking to one another, the mewing of the cows and the beeping of the calves coming from scattered locations throughout the thick timber of the shaded slope.

Away from the main herd and closer to his new position, he heard a cow call and a calf answer. It was the calf's call that piqued his interest. The sound wasn't exactly right.

To the instinctive ear of the predator, this slight defect in pitch suggested weakness. The calf could be sick or injured, easy pickings for the opportunistic carnivore.

The lion backtracked again and focused on the location of the calf. The call continued, emanating from the same part of the timbered slope. The tom bounded to within a couple hundred yards of the calf and began a cautious stiff legged approach. He moved silently within fifty yards of the calf, the long tail curling nervously above him. The lion hoped to see the calf at this distance, but the young elk was bedded just over the lip of the ridge and obscured from his view. This lip allowed the lion to close the gap to 10 yards without any possibility of detection.

The lion stopped in midstride and waited for one final bleat to hone in on the exact location. At the first note of the next call, the lion bounded over the lip and with claws extended, launched his tawny body toward the calf.

It wasn't until the lion was airborne that he recognized the form below him as a human being and not a calf elk.

One moment there was nothing in the opening. The next moment the length of a bull elk filled the small clearing. From his crouched position, Kirk did a quick double take at the suddenness of the elk's appearance. The bull cocked his head from side to side looking intently through the undergrowth. With each turn of his head, the ivory tips of the antlers glinted in the morning sunlight.

Kirk counted five tines on one beam of antler and six tines on the other. The elk was not a trophy but was certainly a fine specimen to take with a bow.

Kirk grinned as he observed the facial expressions of the bull. The animal seemed highly perplexed and extremely cautious.

The bull stood a frustrating ten yards out of bow range. Time seemed in slow motion. Kirk double checked his bow and nocked arrow assuring that all he needed was to rise, draw and shoot if and when the bull moved closer.

At the bleat of a calf, the bull again started moving forward. Kirk tensed, firmly grasping his bow and position-ing his fingers on the nock of the arrow. Kirk heard a loud thud and a crash in the brush down the ridge from his place of hiding. At the sound, the bull elk bolted, disappearing as quickly as he had appeared.

The right front paw slammed between John Sharp's shoulder blades. The lion used the same paw as a leverage point to push himself away from the human form. The lion landed on its left side but immediately righted itself and in an instant scrambled over the bank and out of sight.

The contact pitched Sharp forward and he toppled to the

ground. The cumulative impact of the lion's paw and the ground knocked the wind from him and he gasped to catch his breath.

He rolled over and looked up to see Kirk standing over him.

"You okay?" asked Kirk.

"Hell no, I'm not okay," answered Sharp as he picked himself and his cowboy hat off the ground. "The damn lion bent the brim of my hat and I must have spent two hours shapin' it this way."

Seeing that no harm had been inflicted other than to the hat and his pride, Kirk chided, "I'm not going to take you along anymore if you can't be quiet. I had a bull comin' in and you go and scare him off."

"I saw the bull," Sharp said. "I was concentrating totally on him. I hear something behind me and the next thing I know the sky's raining mountain lions."

"I just caught a glimpse of him before he went over the edge," said Kirk. "Looked like a full sized lion. Didn't seem like he wanted to stick around much after he figured out you weren't an elk burger."

"All I remember seeing were teeth and claws," said Sharp dusting off his hat. "We've had a lot of excitement for one morning. What do you think we ought...."

The full scale bugle of a bull elk filtering down the ridge interrupted Kirk's question.

"Looks like the excitements not over with yet," said Kirk grabbing his bow. "You ready to give this bull a go?"

"You bet. Why don't you get out in front and I'll stay back here and bugle."

"Remember to watch your rear end," whispered Kirk as he moved past Sharp.

Kirk ducked behind the first available patch of cover

and checked the wind once again to assure that their scent wasn't blowing straight to the elk. As he settled into a shooting position, the bugle of a bull elk reverberated from Sharp's position below him.

The bull up the ridge answered with a series of grunts. Sharp responded with a squeal and several grunts of his own. He broke several branches from a dead tree emulating a bull raking the brush with his antlers.

The exchange of bugles and grunts continued for almost an hour, but the bull never moved any closer.

Sharp crawled forward and joined Kirk.

"He must have some cows," Sharp said. "He wants to act macho around his harem so he'll always answer but he ain't gonna risk losing a cow to come to a fight."

"You may be right," said Kirk, "but if he has cows I think he'd have rounded them up and headed 'em out by now. Let's move ahead and press his hand a little. I'll move out in front about a hundred yards. You follow buglin' just like you're going to come in and take his prettiest cow."

They moved forward in tandem, but even though they moved closer, the bull remained entrenched in his position on the ridge line above them. Kirk was about to leave his new cover when he caught a quick flash of movement through a small opening. He readied himself and waited.

Kirk focused on the next opening that would reveal the advancing animal.

Into this opening appeared a man dressed in camouflage stalking cautiously down the ridge toward Sharp's bugle. Kirk's first reaction was disgust followed by disappointment.

Kirk signaled vigorously to Sharp who bugled one more time and then gave Kirk an "ok" sign. The hunter angled about twenty-five yards to the right of Kirk's position and eased closer to the sound of the bugle.

Sharp lay flat on the ground as the hunter edged through the undergrowth.

The hunter kept moving a few steps at a time. Kirk thought the hunter would surely see Sharp lying on the ridge. The man stopped and stood listening for the next bugle to define his course. Kirk smiled as he saw Sharp reach out and grab Ray Webster's leg and softly say, "Boo".

Webster screamed. Sharp looked innocently up at the country western singer and said, "Hi, Ray, how's it goin'?", and then grinned broadly.

Kirk bounced down the ridge and joined them.

"Son of a bitch," said Webster. "You scared ten years off my life."

"I'm sorry," laughed Sharp, "but I couldn't help myself."

"You ought to have seen the look on your face," said Kirk. "I wish I'd had a video camera. The *National Enquirer* would have paid big bucks for that clip."

"You're right about that," Webster said. "I was sure that bull would appear at any time. Didn't expect to see other hunters. I forgot that we'd crossed the fence onto Forest Service land. I guess there wasn't any bull at all, was there?"

"I heard at least two bugles beyond you," said Kirk. "If you were the only one doing the calling then there's still a bull up the ridge." "That's Pete," said Webster. "I've always been out in front of him waiting for something to come by. My heart and blood pressure sure wish I'd stayed waiting instead of trying to stalk the bull we heard down here."

The three men heard a branch crack and turned to see a concerned looking Pete Roemer running down the ridge. Roemer spied the three men together and instantly guessed what had happened.

Roemer removed his ball cap and looked Kirk and Sharp up and down.

"What a pair to draw to," Roemer said. "The things you see when you don't have a gun."

"Good to see you too, Pete," said Sharp.

"I'm betting you're the bull elk I've been conversing with all morning."

"I'm afraid so," said Sharp.

"And I'm also bettin' that Ray here got antsy on his stand and stalked right into your bugle and you jumped out from behind a bush or some other such nonsense."

"You're batting a thousand," said Kirk.

"Getting attacked by us sure beats being attacked by a mountain lion," said Sharp.

Sharp related the details of the earlier encounter with the lion as Kirk and Webster reclined on the thick carpet of pine grass.

"That's an incredible story," said Webster. "I wish I'da had the video camera then the *National Enquirer* would be payin' me the big bucks."

"And then I could sell them the story of you selling them the story," said Kirk, "and we'd all make money."

"You three'd better save all that money to buy beef steak," said Roemer. "At this rate you sure as hell ain't gonna be dining on loin of elk."

"What do you think happened to the big herd?" asked Webster.

"After that scream, I'd guess they're about three counties away by now," said Roemer as he dropped his pack and sprawled out on the ground next to the other men using the pack as a pillow.

Webster turned to Sharp. "I hear you beat me out of buying the Chappel property. You could turn right around and make a nice little profit if you wanted to sell it to me. Would that be of any interest to you?"

"Thanks, but no thanks."

"I thought that'd be your answer," said Webster. "But no harm in asking. Let me know if you change your mind. I am glad you got those sections rather than some developer. The last thing we need is a bunch of houses, kids and dogs in that area."

"I feel the same way," said Sharp.

"We ain't gonna kill anything but time if we sit here chewing the fat," said Roemer as he looked at the position of the sun in the sky. "Let's get movin'."

They walked about a hundred yards down the ridge together, then Webster and Roemer split off to loop back to their horses. After parting company, Sharp and Kirk hadn't taken another twenty steps when an elk jumped up directly in front of them. The brush popped and cracked and tan bodies rose and flashed through the timber. Hooves pounded against the forest floor.

Kirk and Sharp scrambled to the ridge top and watched the fleeing elk cross the broad swale heading for the Webster boundary line fence. Sharp threw an imaginary rifle to his shoulder and aimed at the large six point bull that followed the main mass of elk. Kirk gave a quick bugle with his diaphragm call, but the elk never hesitated in their flight.

"Damn it anyway." Sharp said. "You let your guard down one minute and you'll spook elk every time."

"Those elk weren't bedded down over 150 yards away," said Kirk looking back to their former position. "They sat tight right through all the commotion."

"Now that they're back in Webster's they'll probably be there all season," said Sharp.

"Or they'll trickle right back out into the saddle at dusk this evening," said Kirk.

"That may be, but one thing's for sure, we got skunked this morning."

"It wasn't a total loss. You'll remember the events of this morning for the rest of your life no matter how long you live."

"No doubt about that."

William J. loved to ride. But like many of his contemporaries, he believed a horseback ride had to serve some purpose. The thought of getting on a horse and riding down a road and then riding back merely to be riding was not even open to consideration. A trip to fully view Mort Chappel's sections offered the perfect excuse to straddle a horse.

He parked the horse trailer alongside the weathered set of corrals and the lopsided loading chute. He walked around the corrals examining the condition and noting the needed repairs.

He happily found the corrals to be in better condition than their outward appearance indicated. A dozen new split rails, a couple railroad ties, a handful of long spikes and half a day's labor would make the corrals completely functional.

He rode the western perimeter of the property first and dropped into the deep coulee which divided the lower section. Many rocky breaks and timbered draws branched out of the main canyon and he spent considerable time and effort crossing the drainage.

As he crisscrossed around the several timbered fingers, he closely examined each twist and fold of the topography enjoying the satisfaction of knowing that every rock and tree would belong to the ranch as soon as they signed the closing documents.

He crossed the main fork of the deep canyon and angled his horse up the opposite side of the drainage. Once on top, he let Snowball rest and then rode south along the rim of the canyon until he reached the boundary fence that separated the Chappel sections from the vast holdings of Webster Enterprises.

He noted the sharp contrast between the vegetation on either side of the fence line. The grass on the Webster side of the fence was waist high while the forage on the Chappel side was just starting to regrow from its trimming earlier in the summer.

A well-worn cow path had been chiseled along the Chappel side of the fence by cattle seeking access to the lusher grass of Webster's. It seemed like such a waste to William J. He doubted if any of Webster's handful of Long-horns had ever ventured out of the creek bottoms to graze these lush slopes.

He followed the trail along the perimeter fence for a half mile and then angled across the face of a steep knob to avoid the near vertical fence line. On top of the knob, he beheld a panorama of the Missouri River valley, the extensive sweep of the Webster holdings and a good portion of the Sharp summer range.

He could see many black cattle scattered throughout the parks and the scrub timber as he followed the boundary fence between the Chappel property and the Sharp pastures. He came to a horse gate built in the gap between two trees on the fence line. He rode his horse alongside the gate and opened it without dismounting. He flung the wire gate open intending to come back through once he had checked on his cattle in the vicinity.

The first coulee he came to contained several cows and calves grazing contentedly among scattered stands of jack pines. At his appearance on the horizon, the cattle "turned tail" and thundered across the swale and disappeared into the timber on the far side.

William J. kicked his horse and galloped after the fleeing cattle for no purpose other than the joy of the chase. He caught and raced past the lead cow turning her back into the mass which then turned straight down the drainage. The rancher reined in his horse and admired the good health of the calves that ran below him bucking and shaking their heads.

He followed behind at an easier gait and then cut back through the thick timber to loop back to the horse gate.

As soon as he entered the stillness of the sheltered timber, William J. caught the strong stench of a dead animal. He made a large circle trying to determine the source of the smell. He detected no scent above or below the thick patch of timber, so he dismounted and led his horse up through the thick canopy letting his nose be his guide.

Deep within the thicket, he found traces of black hair which increased in quantity until he came to the decaying carcass of a black calf, teeming with maggots. The white horse balked.

William J. tied the horse to a nearby sapling, and ignoring the putrefying smell, removed his jack knife and cut the yellow ear tag bearing "13" from the skull of the dead steer calf. He stuffed the tag in his pocket and led the horse out of the thicket. He remounted and rode back toward the Chappel property.

As he dismounted to close the horse gate separating the properties, he noticed the flutter of two magpies at the very top of the swale he had just galloped through. He dropped the gate pole and swung back onto the horse.

With considerable trepidation, he urged the horse to climb the bench above the swale. The bench area contained a thick cover of silver sage making the exact location of the birds difficult to find. The distinctive call of the magpies reoriented him and he slightly altered his course in the direction of the sound.

There in the sage lay the body of another calf. Clearly visible on the exposed shoulder were parallel slices in the hide conforming to the raking claws of a mountain lion.

The "2104" yellow tag in the left ear identified the calf as a heifer and the white tag in the right ear told the rancher this calf had been artificially inseminated from the sperm of the registered bull, "Power Point." "It had to be the best calf," said William J. He removed the ear tags and grimly rode back toward the horse trailer.

"Let's see now," said Doc Adams counting on his fingers, "if I got it figured right, so far, you've called in two women, one mountain lion, one country western singer and no elk."

"Hey, I had an elk coming in when the lion attacked," said Sharp. "I think I get credit for that bull."

"He was just coming to see a lion eat an elk hunter," interjected Kirk, "so you can't count him."

As a full moon eased over the horizon, the three men stood on the narrow foot bridge of the Dry Creek cabin talking over the roar of the waterfalls beneath them.

A set of headlights coming up the road interrupted their conversation. A pickup truck pulled into the parking lot and the driver got out and walked briskly toward the cabin.

The three men turned and watched the grain dust covered face of William J. Sharp come into the beam of light.

"I thought you were combining," said John.

"I was but I quit. I thought you'd like to see these," said William J., pulling the pair of ear tags from his pocket. William J. related the details of his morning ride.

"Lion?" asked John.

"No doubt. You could see the claw marks on one calf. I called the livestock inspector. He's going to come take a look at 'em in the morning. I thought you might like to come along."

"Yeah, I'd better do that. Kirk, looks like you're on your own tomorrow."

"Don't know how I'll get along without your elk calling abilities," said Kirk.

"You might as well eat before you go," said Doc Adams. "Garth should just about have those ribs ready."

"Don't mind if I do," said William J. "I was late getting out of the mountains so I missed lunch. That fried egg and two slices of bacon I had for breakfast are pretty much used up."

The men moved across the bridge and entered the log cabin. They quickly filled their plates with pork ribs, fried potatoes laced with bacon and onions and corn on the cob. No one spoke for several minutes as the hunters eagerly devoured the late night meal.

"This lion business is getting plum out of hand," said William J. "I haven't seen anything like it, but then I've only lived here seventy some years."

"I always kind of liked the idea of having lions around," said Garth Hart. "It always seemed so natural, so wild. But now that we've got 'em, I'm not so sure anymore."

"An ecosystem will only tolerate a finite number of predators," said Kirk. "Unfortunately human beings are the most efficient predator going. I'm not sure there's room enough for lions and the number of humans we insist on cramming onto this planet."

"That's only the half of it," said Doc Adams. "At least human predators can be controlled when it comes to big game populations. But if lions are the main predators after a winter kill, the lions are still gonna need to eat. They can't just go down to the local Chinese restaurant and order take out. They'll keep on killin' until the deer are all gone."

"In some ways that's exactly what's happening right now," said John Sharp. "The deer population skyrocketed and so did the lion numbers. Now that the deer populations are dropping, the lions are having to look for other food sources. Unfortunately our cattle and little girls seem to be the easy alternative."

The discussion of the merits and demerits of mountain lions dominated the conversation around the table. After dinner, John and William J. left for the valley and for the first time in Kirk's memory the hunters dispensed with the nightly card game. The hunters immediately went to bed in anticipation of rising early the following morning to renew the pursuit of the illusive wapiti.

Chapter VII

Sunday, September 7th

John and William J. stood with arms folded and watched as livestock inspector Brad Logan knelt next to the carcass of a dead calf. Logan flicked maggots into a mason jar. He then photographed the carcass up close and from a distance.

William J. led the inspector up the swale to the remains of the heifer calf. Logan repeated his examination and maggot collection.

Isn't it a little early to be collecting bait for ice fishing on Canyon Ferry Lake?" asked John.

Logan tapped the side of the jar containing the mass of white larva. "We collect maggots as a timing device. Flies lay their eggs in an animal within very specific periods after death. By looking at the stage of development of the larvae, the boys at the lab, within certain parameters, can make a pretty good estimate as to the time the animal died."

"Probably could make a kitchen timer based on the same principle," William J. said smiling.

"Maybe so, but I wouldn't get Mom one for her birthday if I were you," said John. "But it would be nice to know whether these calves died before or after they killed the lion on Thursday."

"I can't say for sure," said Logan, "but if I had to guess I'd say both died before Thursday."

"There's a chance then that the lion responsible is already dead," William J. said.

"The lab boys ought to have a time frame for the death once they look at these babies," said Logan holding up the jar.

"We can handle three losses." said William J. "But many more will make things pretty tough around here financially."

Some men found solace in the arms of other women. Ben Green had always found solace in the mountains. After flagging traffic for the funeral procession on Friday, he had left for the Elkhorn Mountains. Two days of hiking and grouse hunting had allowed him to finally set aside the bloody image of the remains of Faith Benson.

Ben arrived home well after dark feeling relaxed in both body and spirit. While recounting his adventures to Beth, the phone rang. Ben heard the voice of Carla, the night dispatcher, come on the line.

"Ben, there's a Mr. Clay at the office. He's filing a missing person report on his wife. Do you want to do anything tonight or wait until morning?"

"I'd better meet with him tonight. I'll be right there."

Steven Clay was dressed in a red checkered flannel shirt with suspenders clipped to brand new blue jeans. He also wore heavy soled hiking boots. He had a full beard and long salt and pepper hair pulled back into a small pony tail.

"I don't know if the dispatcher explained our missing persons policy to you," said Ben. "Our policy requires a person to be missing for over twenty-four hours before we issue a missing persons bulletin."

"My wife has been missing since Friday night," said Clay.

"You're just reporting it now?" asked Ben.

"We had a fight," said Clay. "She left in the car. I thought she'd drive around until she cooled off and then come back. When she didn't, I thought she might have gone somewhere for the weekend."

"You live in Headwaters County?" asked Ben.

"We just built a log home in the Dry Creek subdivision."

"Where did you move from?"

"Lakewood, California."

"Does your wife still have family in Lakewood?" asked Ben.

"Kathy grew up there. Her parents and a sister still live in a suburb of Lakewood."

"She's almost had enough time to drive all the way there," said Ben doing some mental calculation of time and mileage.

"I've already called the in-laws," Clay said. "They promised to call if she shows up there."

"Any chance that she might be staying with friends in this area?"

"That's one of the problems," said Clay. "We haven't been here all that long and I've been occupied with building the house. We really haven't made any friends yet."

"What is the make and model of the car?" asked Ben reaching for a pen and a report form.

"It's a blue Honda Civic with California plates. I'll have to look at the registration to give you the exact license number."

"What was she wearing when she left?"

"Jeans, a white sweat shirt and sandals. Here's a picture of her."

Ben took the picture from Clay. It showed a clean shaven, well groomed Steve Clay holding a smiling woman with short black hair and bangs, framing an attractive face.

"We'll enter the car and your wife's identity in the computer network tonight," said Ben. "Since you don't have any idea as to her destination, there doesn't seem to be much to be said for mucking around in the dark tonight. I'll call out the Search and Rescue squad in the morning and we'll search locally. I wouldn't be surprised though if she turns up at her parents' house sometime tonight or tomorrow. Let me know if she reports in. I don't want to have to call out the Search and Rescue volunteers if I don't have to."

Steve Clay assured Ben that he would contact him as soon as he heard from his wife and then asked to accompany the Search and Rescue unit the following morning.

A concerned Beth met him at the door. "What's up?" she asked trying to get some reading from the look on his face.

"Looks like another case of a woman 'seeing the elephant' and going back to civilization after trying to live in the woods," said Ben, who related the details about the missing women and the plans for the following day.

"I have an idea that the where abouts of Mrs. Clay are going to be learned from a divorce attorney rather than from the efforts of the Search and Rescue squad," said Beth.

Chapter VIII

Monday, September 8th

Ben called Kirk and told him about the pending search for Kathy Clay.

"What do you need from me?" asked Kirk.

"We've got those rescheduled traffic cases this morning. Do you think you could get 'em moved again?"

"The judge isn't going to like it," said Kirk. "But I think you've got a good enough reason. It sounds like she could be anywhere."

"You're right but I still gotta look."

"I'll sweet talk the judge into continuing those cases one more time, but the next time they're set you'd better be there no matter what."

"Will do," said Ben. "I'll be there with bells on."

"Anything else I can do for you?

"As long as you're asking, just tell me where to start looking for a blue Honda Civic with California plates."

"Did you say a blue Honda Civic with California license plates?" asked Kirk.

"Yeah, I did. Why?"

"A car matching that description has been parked alongside the Dry Creek Road just above the Sharp cabin since before daylight Saturday morning and was still there when I came out last night."

"Really?"

"Really."

"The couple lives in the Dry Creek subdivision so that makes sense. I guess we'll start looking there."

"Good choice. They'll be calling you 'Sherlock' Green yet," laughed Kirk.

"A firm grasp of the obvious is just one of my many talents," Ben said. "I'll let you know what we find."

Ben leaned out of his office looking into the dispatch center. Deputy Tucker, about to go off shift, was pouring coffee for Deputy Woods who was about to replace him.

Ben called the two deputies into his office and quickly briefed them on Kathy Clay's disappearance and Kirk's sighting of the car.

"I'd like you two to drive up Dry Creek and see if the car Kirk saw is still there and confirm if it's the Clay's vehicle. Tuck, do you feel up to a couple more hours without sleep?"

"You bet. Heaven knows I can use the overtime."

"Alright then, you should be able to get there within thirty-five or forty minutes. I'll wait here with the Search and Rescue. Once we hear from you we'll make our plans."

Ben fidgeted by the radio until Deputy Wood's voice crackled into the dispatch center.

"43-1, this is 43-4, come in."

"43-4, go ahead," said Ben.

"We're at the Clay vehicle. It's right where Kirk described. What did you say the Clay woman was wearing when she left home?"

"Blue jeans, Zena's to be exact, a white sweatshirt and Birkenstock sandals," said Ben checking his memory against his notes.

"Every item you just named is layin' on the front seat," said Woods.

"Are there any rips, tears or blood stains?"

"Negative," said Woods.

"It still doesn't explain why she's naked in the mountains?"

"She's from California," said Woods as if such fact were ample explanation for such conduct. "What do you want us to do next?"

"Just sit tight. We'll be there shortly."

Ben, accompanied by Steve Clay and the Search and Rescue squad, drove up the Dry Creek drainage. Ben pulled in alongside the Honda Civic. Steve Clay jumped out and ran to the vehicle before the Wagoneer came to a complete stop.

"These are Kathy's," said Clay holding up the jeans and sweatshirt. He quickly rummaged in the back seat and pulled out a green canvas bag.

"She keeps her running gear in this bag," Clay said to Ben. "She must have gone jogging."

"Woods, why don't you take the Search and Rescue members and Mr. Clay and walk the county road in both directions. Tucker and I'll drive up this old logging road."

At its junction with the main Dry Creek drainage, the gulch was fifty yards wide. The logging road was flanked on one side by a flat grassy meadow and on the other side by a small stream which flowed through a labyrinth of meanders that crisscrossed the crooked drainage. The steep cut banks and graveled washouts reflected that the stream seasonally carried a volume of water many times in excess of the trickle that currently gurgled through the rocky stream bed.

As Ben followed the winding road up the bottom, the drainage quickly narrowed until there was only sufficient room in the bottom for the road and the stream itself. The road periodically crossed the stream over narrow metal culverts which were beginning to washout on the upstream side leaving just enough road surface for the Wagoneer to pass over. The slopes on either side of the roadway steepened limiting their view from the car.

"Something would have to be right in the road to see it," said Ben.

"I'm getting a crick in my neck," said Tucker as he tried leaning out the passenger window to look up the slopes that towered above them.

"This is a waste of . . . .," Ben started to say when he saw something laying in the roadway directly in front of the patrol car. He slammed on the brakes. The law enforcement vehicle skidded to a stop on the hard packed roadway. Both doors of the patrol car flung open as Ben and Tucker scrambled from the vehicle, neither believing what they thought they saw. There in the right hand wheel track lay a detached human leg, the sinews and tendons of the hip bone protruding garishly from the bloody end.

Ben surveyed the scene trying to look everywhere at once. An ashen faced Tucker moved on past the severed limb. Hidden in the long grass and mature stalks of Mullan, he discovered the scattered portions of what was once a human being.

"43-4, come in," Ben said into the radio. "Woods, we've found a body. Bring the search party back to the Clay vehicle and I'll meet you there. I don't want Mr. Clay to see this. It looks much like the scene on Greyson Creek with the Benson girl, only worse."

"Won't he have to make a positive identification?" radioed back Woods.

"It's a waste of time," said Ben grimly. "No one's going to identify what's left here without dental records and finger-prints."

"Another lion attack?" asked Woods.

"That'd be my guess. I'll meet you in a few minutes."

Ben instructed Tucker to start cordoning off the area. He walked down the logging road to meet the others. Ben gently maneuvered Steve Clay into the passenger seat of the patrol car. He softly but straight forwardly described the discovery of the body. By the time he had finished, Clay sat slumped in the vehicle in a state of shock.

"I need to go see," Clay said finally.

"You'd better stay here," said Ben.

Thirty minutes later Deputy Woods approached the patrol car carrying a manila evidence envelope.

"I know this isn't easy." said Woods. "But we'd like you to examine this."

Woods removed a gold running shoe from the envelope and handed it to Clay.

"It's Kathy's," Clay said. "She replaced the regular white laces with lavender to match her jogging suit. It's really her body, isn't it?"

"I'm afraid so," said Ben "Why don't you let a deputy take you back to town? There's really nothing for you to do here."

"I think I'd just like to sit here," replied Clay numbly.

Ben walked up the gulch counting his paces as he went. By the time he reached the body site, Tucker and the Search and Rescue unit had finished cordoning off the area.

Ben called to Tucker who was busy operating a 35 millimeter camera, "Why don't you knock off and go home and get some rest?"

"That's alright," Tucker said. "If it's all the same to you, I'd just as soon stay and finish up here. After seeing this, I ain't gonna be able to sleep anytime soon."

Ben who was also the county coroner, stepped across the yellow plastic boundary ribbon. He examined the remains which had been gathered and placed on an open black body bag along with the other gold running shoe.

Pronouncing the individual dead seemed a meaningless

act but he dutifully made the finding on his report form. For the cause of death, he entered "preliminary finding of death due to mountain lion attack pending autopsy." Ben thought the autopsy a wasteful exercise.

Ben walked through and scrutinized the entire area. He finally said, "Let's head back to town. There's nothing more that can be done here."

When Ben parked the Wagoneer in front of the sheriff's office, he was confronted by an agitated and insistent William J. Sharp.

"You've got to do something about this lion situation," said William J.

"What lion situation are you talking about?" asked Ben.

"A lion got two more of our calves," said William J. "We just can't afford to lose anymore. Something's got to be done."

"You haven't heard then?" said Ben.

"Haven't heard what?"

"We just found the body of a jogger killed by a mountain lion," said Ben.

"This just underlines my point. We gotta do something about the lions."

"I agree, but I'm currently under order from a Federal District judge, which pretty much puts me out of the lion huntin' business."

"Well, under the circumstances, there must be something that can be done."

"Let's go up and visit Kirk," said Ben. "This legal mumbo jumbo is his bailiwick."

The two men started to cross the alleyway which separated the sheriff's office from the courthouse when the dispatcher leaned out the door of the sheriff's office and called to the sheriff.

"There's a Dr. Hanning on the phone. Do you want to take it or shall I take a message?"

"I'd better take this," Ben said. "Will, go on up to Kirk's office. I'll be there in a minute."

"Sheriff Green," said the well modulated voice of Dr. Hanning, "I have finished my examination of the body of Faith Benson and of the dead lion you sent me. I thought you would want to know my findings."

"Yeah, I know," said Ben. "We got the wrong lion."

"No, not at all," said Hanning. "The lion I examined is definitely the lion that killed the child. Our Forensic Odontologist matched the incisor pattern on the left buttock of the child with one of the incisors of the adolescent lion. Additionally, there were cloth and fiber fragments in the lion's stomach which are identical to the clothing worn by the child. You captured the lion responsible for the death of Faith Benson."

"I don't know if that's good news or bad news," said Ben who explained the finding of Kathy Clay's body to Hanning.

"You have another killer lion?" asked Hanning.

"You tell me," said Ben. "We'll be transporting the remains to you for examination within the hour."

Ben completed the arrangements for the autopsy of Kathy Clay and then hurried to the courthouse.

When Ben arrived, William J. was already seated in one of the hand carved oak chairs in Kirk's inner office.

"How are we gonna get the restraining order released?" asked William J.

"The court has set a hearing date on the 18th of September in Helena," Kirk said. "We have the opportunity to appear at that time and show cause, if any, why the temporary restraining order shouldn't be made permanent pending the outcome of Animals Forever's underlying lawsuit. The restraining order is going to remain in effect at least until that time."

"It's just too damn bad that Slats Smith didn't find the right lion," said William J.

"He did," said Ben, who related Dr. Hanning's findings.

"Then there's another lion killing people," said William J.

"Either that or there's a mistake about the date of Kathy Clay's disappearance." said Ben.

"Whether there's two lions or ten that still doesn't get rid of the restraining order," William J. said.

"Maybe or maybe not," Kirk said as he reached for the file folder and began quickly paging through the file to find the restraining order itself.

Kirk read carefully line by line through the precise language of the order. He placed a pencil in the file to mark the location of the order and looked up and asked, "Is Dr. Hanning certain the lion you shot Thursday is the lion that killed the child?"

"As certain as those forensic guys get."

"And Kathy Clay wasn't attacked until after the lion that killed Faith Benson was shot?"

"According to her husband, she never even left home until late Friday afternoon," Ben said.

"We don't need to worry about the effect of the restraining order at all," Kirk said. "Ben, if you're willing to risk being held in contempt of the Federal district court then I think I have a plan. The order very expressly limits 'Headwaters County Sheriff Ben Green or anyone on his behalf from chasing, capturing, killing, or in any way harming or harassing the mountain lion responsible for the death of Faith Benson.' That lion's already dead. You're going to chase and kill the lions that killed Kathy Clay and the Sharp Ranch cattle. Our position is that the restraining order in no way, either expressly or impliedly, prohibits such conduct."

"A rather legalistic argument, isn't it?" asked Ben.

"Absolutely," said Kirk with a slight grin. "Animals Forever will be fit to be tied, but if you're game, there may be a small window of opportunity to kill the lions responsible before Animals Forever can slam the window shut or before some other person is mauled. What do you think?"

"Let's go for it." said Ben. "I haven't been held in contempt in a long time."

Heidi Singer was bored. From the small table in front of the bookstore, only the large "F" in PIKE'S FARMERS MARKET was visible. The stream of customers and well wishers had remained steady through the noon hour but now in early afternoon the stream had slowed to a trickle. Each time she glanced at the clock, the hands seemed in the same position.

It was a welcome relief when the clerk approached and announced, "Ms. Singer, you have a phone call. You can take it in my office." Curiously, Heidi entered the small office filled with books and stacks of invoices.

"Heidi Singer," she breathed into the receiver.

"Hi ya gorgeous," called the cheery voice of Jefferson Kirk. "You selling lots of books in Seattle?"

"We did really well earlier," said Heidi, "but it's dead right now. What's up?"

"I'm afraid I have another story for you," said Kirk, who related the recent happenings in Headwaters County.

"What's your plan of action?" asked Heidi as she searched on the cluttered desk for a pen and a blank piece of paper.

"Sparks are going to fly over that interpretation," said Heidi as she thought about the reaction of Grover Arlen and Animals Forever.

"Things may get plum interesting around here," said Kirk.

"Well, there's certainly at least two good stories in the mix," said Heidi. "Give me some more of the details of this latest attack."

Finishing the briefing with Kirk, Heidi returned to her autograph table. She impatiently sat for another fifteen minutes mentally drafting the opening to two feature stories. Finally unable to contain herself, and with no customers in sight, she returned to the small office where she made a series of phone calls. Within twenty minutes the book tour was on hold. Heidi had booked a flight to Montana to do an in-depth feature piece on the latest lion killing and the pursuit of the lion by Sheriff Ben Green.

When Ben pulled into the cluttered courtyard, Slats Smith's lion hounds noisily announced his arrival. At the racket, Slats wandered from the old chicken house which now served as a combination shop and junk store. He was dressed in greasy coveralls and carrying a crescent wrench.

"Hello Ben," Slats called. "You sure didn't need to drive all the way out here just to bring me my check."

"I already told you, you don't get paid until after the first of October. But I do need to retain your services again."

"Have lion hounds, will travel," said Slats. "When do we leave and what are we a chasin'?"

Ben explained the details of the search for Kathy Clay and the need to proceed rapidly because of the anticipated actions of Animals Forever.

"I guess I'm in," said Slats. "But I might have to up my rates some since I have to do the work on credit."

"Pay's the same as before," said Ben. "Take it or leave it."

"I'll take it," said Slats extending a grease covered hand. "But what did you do with Warden Berg?"

"The higher ups at Fish and Game are nothing but a bunch of gutless bastards," said Ben. "When Berg tried to get clearance to help me, he was told in no uncertain terms not to assist in any way. They don't want to risk the negative publicity. Their solution to the lion problem pending the hearing on the restraining order is to issue a pamphlet listing tips on how to remain safe in lion country. So it's just you and me."

Slats examined the map spread on the hood of the Wagoneer. "Did the lion leave any tracks along the creek or on the old logging road?"

"I looked both places," said Ben. "But the road is packed as hard as concrete and the creek in that area doesn't have enough water to make a good mud pie."

"We'd better drag my harrow and rug around the roads circling that country and make a tracking bed like we did before."

"When do you want to do that?"

"I'm working on a compressor motor that goes to my chest freezer. As soon as I get that up and running again, I'll head for the hills and make a big loop with the harrow. There's no use in both of us goin'. I'm sure you got other things to do. I'll drag the Ridge Road and cut down through the Shaw Homestead and follow the Dry Creek road out. We'll check for tracks at daylight tomorrow morning."

"Sounds good to me," said Ben. "God knows I have plenty of other things to do this afternoon. Unless you hear different, I'll meet you at my office about 5:30 in the morning."

Ben turned the Wagoneer around in the driveway. As he drove away, he saw Slats in the rear view mirror. Slats was walking toward the old shop with wrench in hand gesturing and yelling all the while at the barking hounds.

"I should have gone with Slats," said Ben as he pulled in front of his office. Awaiting his return were a film crew from Helena, a print reporter from the *Helena Independent Record* and the editor of the community weekly. Ben tersely told them about the discovery of the body of Kathy Clay and the ongoing investigation. He reluctantly let the film crew center him under the sign reading "Headwaters County Jail." The correspondent adjusted the brim of Ben's felt cowboy hat to lift the shadow from his face.

"Sheriff, in light of this finding and Animals Forever's restraining order what are your plans?" asked the reporter.

"I intend to re-review the restraining order with Head-waters District Attorney Jefferson Kirk as soon as I'm finished here," said Ben. "We'll make a firm decision after considering all our options. Now if you'll excuse me I'll be on my way to Mr. Kirk's office."

When he arrived at the reception area of Kirk's office, Marge waved Ben through. Kirk was sitting with his black cowboy boots propped on the oak desk reading one of the many law books piled on every available flat surface within reach of his chair.

"Just how long can you go to jail for contempt of court?" asked Ben.

"No more than life," Kirk said without even looking up from his law book. "But as old as you are, life really isn't that long of a sentence."

"Very funny. Do you still feel comfortable with your interpretation?"

"The press and Animals Forever may give you a lot of heat, but I think our reasoning's sound."

"Then you'll serve half of the sentence if the Federal District judge throws me in jail?"

"No, but I'll come and see you every Sunday."

"Thanks for nothing. That sets my mind right at ease. The Fish and Game won't touch our plan of action with a ten foot pole and the press is already hounding me about my plans. I was reluctant to tell them that we were going to ignore the restraining order and go back to chasing lions. I didn't know what to say, so I just told them I was on my way here to consider all our options in light of the restraining order."

"Relax. Until Animals Forever amends the order, you're home free. Also, I don't think you need to be secretive with the press. If you're up front with them, I think that will demonstrate our rightness of purpose and our clear conscience. If our position is openly assertive that the restraining order no longer applies, we are in a better position with the public and the court. Otherwise, it may seem like we're trying to be devious and underhanded."

"You're probably right. Do you think I ought to make a statement about our plans?"

"I wouldn't volunteer anything but I'd sure be totally forthright if asked. Were you able to contact Slats Smith?"

Ben explained the plan for the following day.

"If you want to be totally up front with the press," said Kirk," why not take a reporter along? Heidi's flyin' in tonight. She just called to bum a ride and pump me for a story. Take her along on the chase. It's pretty hard to say you were being sneaky or underhanded when you've invited the press along."

"Do you think she can keep up?" Ben asked.

"Unless the book tour has softened her up, she won't have any problem. I took her straight up the side of Sulphur Bar last hunting season and she handled it fine."

"Never did mind having a pretty woman around," said Ben. "It's fine by me if she wants to tag along. After watching Slats fawn all over her the other day, I'm sure he won't mind."

"I'm sure she'll want to go. I'll ask her as soon as I pick her up and have her give you a call to arrange a time to meet you in the morning."

"As long as she's going, why don't you come along, too? If we put the dogs on a track, we could use someone to drive the truck. You know those roads about as well as anyone. It doesn't take the hounds long to put a lot of country between them and the truck. It'd be nice not to have to backtrack to get the vehicle."

"I guess I could get away," Kirk said after glancing at a large calendar on the wall and flipping through his appointment book.

Chapter IX

As she walked out of her room at the Mustang Motel, Heidi Singer looked like she had just stepped from the pages of an L.L. Bean catalog.

Heidi crossed the parking lot carrying the morning paper. She opened the door of Kirk's four wheel drive and pulled herself into the passenger seat.

"Good morning," said Kirk smiling.

"What's this nonsense about the woman jogging in the nude?" said Heidi dispensing with any greeting of her own and showing Kirk the headline on the front page of the *Helena Independent Record*. "You didn't mention anything about it."

"The press will certainly run with the most sensational aspect of a story," said Kirk as he read

"LION KILLS NUDE JOGGER."

"No traces of Kathy Clay's jogging clothes have been found," said Kirk. "That prompted the speculation about the jogging in the nude."

"What did happen to her jogging clothes?"

"The sheriff has several theories. The jogging outfit only consisted of some brief type running shorts and a halter top. As grotesque as it may sound, Ben thinks that because the halter top and shorts cover the softest and fleshiest parts of a woman, they may merely have been eaten by the lion. The attack took place on Friday night and the body wasn't discovered until Monday. There was plenty of time for other animals to carry off the fragments of cloth."

"What kind of animals?"

"That country's full of coyotes and pack rats. Also, a bloody scrap of cloth is just the kind of treasure that a raven, camp robber or magpie would swoop down, pick up and fly off with. Or just maybe the lion carried the scraps of clothing far enough away from the site that the Search and Rescue crew and the deputies didn't find them."

"Well, I don't believe she was jogging in the nude," said Heidi.

"How can you be so sure? It sounds exhilarating."

"If you had boobs, you'd know. It would be downright painful for one thing."

"Not everyone is built like you," said Kirk.

"Trust me. She wasn't jogging in the nude."

From the motel, Kirk drove the deserted early morning streets of Townsend to the sheriff's office. Ben Green was waiting by the Wagoneer when they arrived.

"Where's Slats?" asked Kirk.

He heard the roar of an unmuffled engine at the edge of town. The noise grew louder until they could see the head-lights coming up Main Street. The vehicle turned onto the side street and pulled into the alleyway by the sheriff's office. Slats jumped from the vehicle and popped the hood on the flatbed truck.

Seeing Kirk and Heidi, he asked, "Did we pickup some hitchhikers?"

"Two", said Ben.

"An attorney and a pretty woman" said Slats. Looking directly at Kirk, he said, "I guess you gotta take the good with the bad."

"Don't know what you think's so bad about a pretty woman," said Kirk.

Slats lifted the hood of the truck and attempted to examine the engine in the dark. He borrowed Ben's patrol

142

flashlight. After superficially examining the radiator hose, he handed the flashlight to Heidi.

"Heidi, could you get me a screwdriver? It's in the red tool box in the back next to the dog kennel."

Heidi took the flashlight and walked behind the flatbed. A blue plastic tarp covered objects of various sizes and shapes which had been randomly stacked on the truck bed.

Heidi grabbed a corner of the tarp and flung it up and over the bulky objects in the very rear of the bed. She directed the beam of light into the back of the truck and screamed.

Kirk and Ben ran to the rear of the truck. Propped in the large dog kennel stood a full grown mountain lion. Rigor mortise had bared the fangs and frozen the mouth in a perpetual snarl.

Slats laughed and joined the other three at the rear of the truck.

"Here's your lion, sheriff," said Slats. "Signed, sealed and delivered."

"What the hell . . . .?" said Ben.

"I found her track yesterday just before sundown," Slats said pointing to the she lion. "I'd pulled the harrow and rug over a bunch of roads until I'd made a complete circle. I went back up the Ridge Road a piece to see what kind of tracking bed I'd made. I hadn't gone a half mile when I look down and see a lion track in the area I'd swept not two hours before.

"The track was comin' out of one of the forks of the drainage where the Clay woman was found. I was so excited I didn't know whether to shit or go blind. I had a good hour and a half of daylight in front of me, so I put the dogs on the track. She must have had a full belly 'cause the dogs had her treed within thirty minutes.

"I was afraid I'd run out of light so I really busted my butt after 'em. I caught up and shot her out of a big ponderosa.

"There was an old logging road down the ridge from the tree. I backed my truck right into the road bank and slid her down the slope and loaded her up.

"It was really late when I finally got out of the hills. I didn't know quite what to do. I didn't know if the lion had to be examined right away or what. I'd just finished repairing my old chest freezer where I keep all my trapping pelts and hides. It was empty so I went home and stood her up in the freezer just like she's a standin' now. She's hard as a rock, but I was afraid she might spoil."

"Do you think this is the lion that attacked Kathy Clay?" asked Ben.

"No way to know for sure but all the earmarkings look right. She was heading north out of a branch of the same gulch not more than two and a half miles from where they found the body. I'm not as sure about this lion as I was on the other one, but if you want to go double or nothing on my bonus money, I'll take the bet."

"We'll need to get the carcass to the pathologist," Ben said. "Dr Hanning's examining the body of Kathy Clay today. I'm sure he'd like to examine the lion carcass at the same time."

"Providing the lion carcass thaws out in time," Kirk said.

"I wonder if we ought to check the roads you swept for more tracks," Ben said.

"Wouldn't be a bad idea," said Kirk. "You'd better find all the lions you can before Animals Forever modifies the restraining order."

"I need to make some arrangements to get this lion to Great Falls," said Ben.

"If you're busy why don't I check the roads," said Slats.

"I guess we don't need to be driving around the hills holding on to one another's hands," Ben said.

"As far as I'm concerned, Heidi can drive around the hills holding my hand anytime she wants," said Slats.

"Thanks for the offer," said Heidi. "But I think I'd better run with this latest development while I have the chance. Not only is this an amazing story, but as of 6:00 a.m., it's also an exclusive."

"If I'm gonna check roads, I'd better get movin'," said Slats. "It'll be daylight before long and I've still gotta pick up my dogs. Let's throw the lion in the Wagoneer so I can get out of here."

Slats backed the flatbed truck up to the sheriff's vehicle. The three men lifted the lion and placed it in the back of the Wagoneer and closed the door. The lion stood rigidly on all fours staring out the back window.

"Ben, if you'd hook some brake lights to her eyes, you'd never have to worry about being rear ended," said Slats as he backed into the street and roared away.

As soon as the tail lights of Slats' vehicle disappeared around the corner, Ben locked the Wagoneer and then excused himself to try to find someone to transport the dead lion to Great Falls. Kirk, Heidi and the lion were left in the street.

"I don't know how you feel," said Heidi. "But I feel like I'm all dressed up with no where to go."

"I was all geared up for the thrill of the chase," said Kirk. "At least you had the option of driving around in the mountains holding hands with Slats Smith."

"I'm afraid even that would seem anticlimactic after looking this lion directly in the face," Heidi said. "But I was looking forward to getting out in the hills."

"We still can," said Kirk. "You've been wanting some exposure to archery hunting. Let's just up and go."

"I was serious when I told Slats I needed to start writing.

This story is a lock for an AP byline if I can get it done and out."

"How long will that take?"

"Most of the morning, I'm sure."

"Let's head to the mountains as soon as you finish. We can fly fish Greyson Creek this afternoon and bow hunt this evening when it cools off."

"It's a date," said Heidi. "But the sooner you get me back to the motel, the sooner we can leave."

The three dogs acted in concert. The Australian Shepherd/Border Collie crosses were a family and a team. Maggie, the mother, raced to the head of the black Angus cow which had turned back against the flow of the main herd.

When the cow bellowed and lowered its head to chase Maggie, Tucker, one of her many offspring, darted to the rear of the cow. With precise instinctive timing, Tucker bit one back foot as soon as it touched the ground and at the exact moment that the other foot lifted off the ground. In this position, the cow was physically incapable of delivering a kick and Tucker was capable of delivering his punishment for the cow's misdirection with impunity.

The cow turned and sped back toward the main herd. At this point, Daddy Dog, the patriarch of the Sharp Ranch dogs, launched himself into the fray and clamped his jaws firmly on the cow's tail. The cow pulled the dog, half bouncing and half running, across the countryside until he was brushed off by a large clump of silver sage. Sufficiently chastened, the mother cow totally abandoned her efforts to cut back, and ran well into the middle of the mass of black cattle.

John Sharp grinned broadly at the dogs' antics. Doc Adams, who was clearly enjoying his day away from his medical practice, eased his white Arabian alongside Sharp's gelding, Strawberry.

"You'd better give those dogs an extra biscuit tonight," called Adams. "If that cow'd turned back we might have lost the whole bunch."

"You're right about that," said Sharp nodding. "But they're starting to line out now."

A half mile up the ridge Sharp could see William J. pushing the lead bunch of cattle through the north pasture gate. Further down the ridge, hired man, Joe Durham, pushed a second bunch of cows and calves. Sharp and Doc Adams, with the aid of the dogs, brought up the rear. Cows ran back and forth between the three groups of cattle looking for their respective calves.

Cattle trailed better when spaced out along the trail rather than moving them in one big group like a gopher through a snake. The early morning start had been chosen to avoid the steep pitch out of the Dry Creek drainage in the heat of the day.

The cow/calf pairs would be herded to the top of the ridge into upper Greyson Creek. The riders then intended to round up all the cattle in the Greyson Creek pasture. The entire herd would then be moved to fresh grass in the pastures to the west.

The hope was that the new feed would give the cows increased milk production thus giving the calves a double shot of nutrition from sucking the mother cows and from the tender new feed itself.

"The calves look good," said Adams as he rode back and forth behind the line of cattle.

"Another month of easy living ought to really put the bloom on 'em," said Sharp. "I just hope the market's good. Prices have been off some. Calves were a dollar a pound two years ago. Last year they were seventy-five cents. They were

147

holding about seventy cents but I guess they slipped over a nickel last week."

"I don't know how you stand the pressure," said Adams. "I know I wouldn't want to run my business knowing my income might drop over twenty-five percent in one year."

"I sure don't need to go to Vegas to do my gambling," said Sharp. "You have to treat cattle prices just like the weather. It's just one of the things you don't have any control over. You take the good with the bad and hopefully you're still in business the next year."

"I think I'll keep my medical practice and remain a weekend cowboy," said Adams. "There just isn't as much pressure performing surgery."

"It wouldn't be so bad," said Sharp, "if the expenses ever went down but they seem to go up no matter what the cattle market does."

"Do you know the difference between a rancher and a newborn puppy?" asked Adams suddenly with a slight grin.

"No, what?"

"After three months the puppy quits whining."

"I take it you're not shedding any tears for me yet?" said Sharp breaking into a grin.

"Not when you get to go to work with a view like that," said Adams making a sweeping gesture with his arm as the broad green meadow with its beaver ponds and vast quaking aspen grove came into view as they climbed the slope. "Besides, the violin music was starting to give me a headache."

"You're probably right," said Sharp. "I shouldn't complain. But I'll tell ya, ranching would be a whole lot easier if I'd win Lotto."

"What would you do with yourself if you won all that money?"

"I'd just keep on ranching until it was all gone," said Sharp.

With the cattle strung out along the trail and seemingly reconciled to the pasture change, Sharp relaxed for the first time that morning. He leaned back in the saddle and let the horse choose its own course behind the cattle. He breathed deeply, taking in a full measure of the cool mountain air. He basked in the warmth of the morning sun filtering through the thin canopy of trees which bordered the trail.

The movement of a lone black baldie cow running back down the ridge from the lead bunch of cattle interrupted his reverie. The cow veered wide of the second group of cattle avoiding Joe Durham who couldn't leave his position to cut her off.

Flanked by the dogs, Doc Adams turned the Arabian and galloped to meet the determined white face. At the sight of the advancing horse and rider, the cow increased her pace. Adams looped wider, putting the cow between himself and the main herd. Sharp lagged behind the herd, maintaining a position which served the dual purpose of remaining a deterrent to any cattle wishing to turn back and offering a show of resistance to the black baldie.

Adams hazed his horse along the neck of the running cow, forcing her to turn back in the direction of the herd. With the dogs at her heels, the cow initially ran in a straight line toward the other cattle and then she suddenly whirled and doubled back escaping through the narrow gap between Adams' and Sharp's horses. Adams spurred his horse and reined to give chase.

"Let 'er go," shouted John, calling him back.

"I almost had her," said Adams, turning and riding alongside John Sharp.

"We must have left her calf behind," said Sharp. "From the look of her bag, I'd say she hasn't been sucked today. We'll let her find her calf and get 'em both later."

The remainder of the drive to the top of the ridge was uneventful. The riders followed behind the trailing cattle joking and swapping stories of past cattle drives, letting the cow dogs perform the little serious effort required to push the now compliant cows over the ridge.

"Remember the wreck of '93?" asked Adams.

"God, who could forget. We must have had sixty calves go back without a mother among 'em. I wore out two good horses that day."

"I could have," said Adams. "My old plug could hardly break into a trot by sundown. But we survived it and got 'em there."

"We probably should have made some T-shirts saying 'I survived the wreck of '93.'"

"I'd have bought one," said Adams. "Did you ever think why is it that we recall adversity so fondly?"

"I don't rightly know," said Sharp, "but we all tend to do it. I've met a few old timers who firmly declare that World War II was absolutely the best time of their lives."

"It must have something to do with conquering adversity," said Adams.

"Kirk maintains that in the long run it doesn't matter whether an experience is good or bad as long as it's memorable. After twenty years even the most mortifyingly embarrassing moment tends to be funny."

"Under Kirk's theory, in another twenty years your present lion problems will be a stitch," said Adams.

"He might be right. I just hope I'm here laughing about it. But even then I don't think you'll convince Roger and Emma Benson that the death of their daughter was a good thing," said Sharp soberly.

"You're right about that," said Adams. "I guess Kirk's theory has its limitations."

When the cattle crossed the ridge top into the Greyson Creek drainage, the herd collectively, as if by some signal, began running down the slope toward the creek bottom.

Sharp and Adams joined William J. and Joe Durham who had dismounted and stood on the lip of the ridge watching the last of the herd disappear over the final bluff before the bottom. A thick veil of dust hung over where the herd raced across the exposed dirt of the soft slope.

"That went pretty well," said William J. "Did we get 'em all?"

"We had one cow go back for a calf," said Sharp. "While you're eating lunch and rounding up, I'll ride back and see if I can find 'em."

Sharp quickly ate a sandwich and remounted. Following a well-defined game trail, he rode back into the Dry Creek canyon.

Sharp scanned the greens of the grasslands and timber and the bright yellows of the fall quaking aspens looking for two black spots of contrast representing the location of the cow and calf. His visual search produced nothing, but as he turned to leave he heard the distinctive "beller" of a cow reverberating in a coulee at the base of Berberet's knob.

Sharp angled the horse off the ridge and crossed the broken terrain to the coulee. The continual bawling of the animal served as a constant point of reference. Strawberry splashed through the muddy bottom below a galvanized water tank. About two hundred yards above the tank, the cow stood next to a mound of leaves and grass.

The black baldie stood her ground as the rider approached. It wasn't until Sharp was almost on top of the mound that he discovered the mound was actually the partially eaten carcass of a black calf covered by a thin veneer of vegetation.

Sharp swung off the horse and scraped the grass and

leaves from the skull of the dead animal. He grimly hacked the yellow ear tag from the one remaining ear.

The majority of the calf remained intact. The lion had apparently covered his kill in hopes of returning for another meal.

Sharp remounted and headed for Greyson Creek leaving the cow for another day. By the time he reached the creek bottom, the round up had been completed and a mass of black cattle dotted the large meadow. John announced his finding to the others who sat holding the cattle while the cow-calf pairs "mothered up."

"I was just going to leave the cows in the pasture below and open the gate on top and let them work their way over the ridge," said William J. upon hearing the news. "But I think we oughta move 'em across the Flathead Indian trail and down into the Ross Gulch pasture. Maybe we can get 'em out of the lions."

"What's going to keep the lions from following?" asked John. "A barbed wire fence sure ain't going to do it."

"Do you have a better idea?" asked William J.

"No, I don't."

"Let's get 'em going then," said William J. "It's gonna be tough going up the ridge."

By the time the last calf trudged through the gate into the Ross Gulch pasture, riders, horses and cow dogs were all spent. John Sharp dismounted and closed the wire gate.

"How long do you think we'll have to wait until we look back to this afternoon with fond memories?" Sharp asked Doc Adams.

"I'm not sure I'll live that long," said Adams.

"Let's head for the Deep Creek Bar," said William J. "Drinks and dinner are on me."

Holding a copy of the *Los Angeles Times,* Grover Arlen stood at the front of the conference room waiting for the staff of Animals Forever to arrive. Once the staff was seated and settled, Arlen snapped open the paper to reveal the headline, "LIONS INVADE MONTANA SUBDIVISIONS."

"I don't know if this is a problem or an opportunity," said Arlen. "I think we need to put a spin on the recent events in Montana so that it becomes an opportunity and not a problem."

Noting the puzzled looks Arlen related the recent developments in Montana including the attack on Ray Webster's Longhorns.

"We currently have a court date on our restraining order on September 18th. If we don't make some statement or take some action, a groundswell of sympathy may be generated for these victims and landowners negating all public relations value prior to the hearing."

"The celebrity status of Ray Webster is certainly going to heighten the public interest," said Victor Meade, the comptroller. "What kind of action did you have in mind?"

"I'm glad you asked because the one idea I have directly impacts your department. We need to head off any sympathy that may arise because of the economic hardship caused by the cattle losses of the ranchers. I can already hear the wail and whine of some old wrinkled rancher in a beat up cowboy hat that the loss of a couple animals out of a herd of several hundred will put him out of business. I fully expect that we will be accused of bringing about the elimination of the family ranch because of our restraining order. That's why I think, we need to offer full reimbursement to every rancher who has a documented livestock loss caused by a mountain lion attack."

"Have you any idea of the cost of such a program?" asked Meade. "We really don't have anything budgeted to pay those costs."

"The costs will be minimal," Arlen said. "We'll take a hard line on the documentation necessary to entitle reimbursement. The media will pay far more attention to our announcement of the reimbursement program than to any isolated instance of failure to pay because of insufficient documentation."

Victor Meade smiled once again appreciating the ability of Grover Arlen to manipulate public opinion.

"We need to issue a statement which boldly asserts a mountain lion's right to engage in natural conduct," said Arlen. "If the staff concurs, I intend to counter this headline with a press release which forcefully states that lions are not invading Montana subdivisions but rather the subdivisions are invading the territory of the lions. We'll present the subdivision dwellers as the destroyers of habitat and the cattle owners as greedy entrepreneurs who exploit our natural resources for profit. Does anyone see anything objectionable to such an approach?"

The staff members who were universally young and idealistic looked to one another and then almost in one voice said, "Go for it."

When the staff left, Arlen and his Ronald remained behind in the conference room. Arlen dictated a short and pointed press release to be distributed immediately to the media. As he finished talking and stood to leave, Arlen asked, "Any questions?"

"Only one. Why did you seek staff approval before issuing this statement?"

"Just undertaking a little preventative CYA," said Arlen. "If anything goes awry, I don't want the board of directors to be in a position where they can portray me as a 'loose cannon' acting solely on his own. If push comes to shove, I want to be

154

able to claim that no actions were taken without staff approval."

Kirk stopped the Blazer on the north rim of the Greyson Creek canyon. Ahead of the vehicle, a steep two lane track followed a narrow sliver of ridge to the bottom of the drainage.

Greyson Creek appeared as nothing more than a blue ribbon meandering through the wide grassy meadow. The north facing slope on the opposite side of the canyon was thickly timbered with stands of spruce and fir.

Before descending into the canyon, Kirk turned in the hubs on the front wheels and pulled the gear shift into four wheel drive low range.

Heidi Singer placed one hand firmly against the roof of the Blazer as the vehicle tilted sharply forward and Kirk eased the Blazer down the ridge. Kirk laughed.

"Relax," he said. "This is a piece of cake."

"Pretty hard to relax when you're only a few feet away from death," said Heidi as she looked out the passenger window into the bottom of the sharp coulee some hundred feet below.

"You're that close to death every time you pass an oncoming car on the freeway," said Kirk."

Heidi held her breath and remained rigid until the Blazer once again resumed a horizontal position in the relative flat of the creek bottom. As he turned down the drainage, Kirk navigated solely from memory as the two wheel track disappeared into a sea of waist high meadow grass.

Kirk stopped the Blazer a mile downstream in the widest and flattest meadow on the creek. With the efficiency and skill developed from repetition, he retrieved his fly rod from the cylindrical carrying case, threaded the floating fly line through the eyelets and secured a tapered leader to the line.

"Do you remember what I told you about casting?" he asked as they walked through the tall grass to the waters edge.

"Bring the rod tip back to at least the one o'clock position but never past the two o'clock position. Pause. Bring the rod tip forward to the ten o'clock position," she said in a sing-song voice.

When they reached a broad graveled bar, Kirk handed Heidi the rod and moved to her left side to avoid her back cast. Firmly grasping the cork grip, Heidi stripped out several feet of the ivory colored fly line. Deftly making two false casts, she whipped the fly toward a nearby riffle.

The grasshopper imitation shot forward and bounced off a rock in the middle of the stream. The fly looped and landed gently in the calm eddy created as the swift water drafted around the beach ball sized boulder. The dry fly paused momentarily before the current caught the line. As soon as the fly began to move again, a twelve inch rainbow surged from directly behind the rock and in one motion inhaled the fly and turned to reclaim its prime feeding location.

Heidi lifted her wrist setting the hook. The silver fish broke the surface of the water and jumped two more times before making a run downstream. Heidi played the fish, keeping steady pressure on the line without jerking the hook from its lip. She worked the trout easily to the water's edge. She knelt by the creek bank and gently removed the hook from the sharp-toothed mouth of the tired fish. She held the brightly colored trout aloft momentarily to show Kirk her success and then eased the fish back into the sparkling water.

"What do you think now Mr. 'A Way to a Man's Heart is through his Fly?'" she asked.

"I think you've got a great teacher," he said.

Kirk shook his head slightly as she moved upstream. Call it chemistry. Call it magic. Call it infatuation. Call it lust. It didn't matter what one called it. He had to admit to himself how attracted he was to this woman and how absolutely easy it was to be with her.

Bolstered by her success, Heidi eyed a deep clear hole in the sharp corner of one meander. She mentally measured the distance and stripped several lengths of line on the ground at her feet. She pulled the line with her left hand making a single "haul." She methodically whipped the rod back and forth making a series of false casts. All went well until she shot the line forward, targeting the fast water at the top of the meander. The leader caught the rod tip and several loops of line cascaded to the ground around her.

"Nuts, I thought I finally had the hang of it."

"You were doing great until the last cast," said Kirk stepping forward. "You forgot to pause to let the line go fully behind you before you started forward again."

Kirk took the rod from her and skillfully snapped the line forward simultaneously working the lever on the automatic reel, retrieving several feet of slack line. With the line still airborne, he made several false casts and then began stripping more line from the reel spool.

Graceful lengths of the ivory colored fly line arched behind him and he whipped the rod forward one last time. The fly settled gently on the surface of the water at the upstream edge of the corner hole. The current bobbed the imitation on the surface a few inches from the opposite bank.

Kirk tensed as he saw the fish dart from beneath a clump of overhanging willows. He forced himself to wait for the trout to reach the fly and then more by feel than by sight, he set the hook. The small fish came out of the water and dangled helplessly on the end of the leader. Kirk caught the five-inch brookie in his left hand and quickly returned it to the stream.

"You make that look so easy," said Heidi.

"Let me show you," said Kirk as he slipped directly behind her and placed his hand over hers and moved her arm in conjunction with his own.

He stripped forth line letting her feel the timing of the back cast. After false casting several times, they jointly whipped the rod forward sending the fly into a deep pool. At the sight of a fish dimpling the surface, they jerked up on the rod yanking a three-inch rainbow trout from the stream and shooting the miniature fish straight back at them.

Heidi screamed and ducked and then back pedaled into Kirk who, attempting to retreat lost his balance. They toppled onto the sand bar as the tiny fish, too small to be hooked, looped over the top of them and landed in the water where the creek meandered sharply behind them.

Laughing loudly, they lay entangled on the stretch of sand. Kirk bent forward and kissed her. She returned the kiss and ran her hand up across his chest and gently brushed her palm against his cheek. Kirk eased his hand down her back and made a return trip up her inner thigh.

Thoughts of fly fishing quickly faded from their minds. Heidi dropped her hand and snapped open the buttons on his western shirt letting her hand rake through the hair on his chest.

Kirk paused momentarily and removed the canvas fish bag which had been draped over his shoulder. From a side compartment, he removed a small square packet containing a shiny emergency blanket. With one hand, he opened the blanket and spread it across the flat of the sand bar. He gently lifted Heidi onto the blanket and kissed her again.

Items of clothing soon dotted the sand bar. As he moved his hand from her breasts on across her soft dimpled tummy, he said, "So much for your vow of celibacy pending commitment."

She whispered back, "There's no sense in being a fanatic about it. Besides, so far I've caught the biggest and the most fish and I'll do whatever it takes to beat you in a fly fishing contest."

Kirk shifted his weight pulling her against him and kissing her again. He reached beyond her and grasped the handle of the fly rod. With a quick twist of his arm, he made a roll cast flicking the fly and leader into the water of the nearby corner hole. It doesn't get any better than this he thought as he looked at her, felt the warm sunshine on his back and listened to the gurgle of the mountain stream.

Later as they retrieved their clothing, Heidi picked up the lightweight emergency blanket. She shook the sand from the aluminum space age material and began refolding the blanket.

"I suppose you carry this just for conquests of lonely women?"

"Actually," said Kirk. I got that blanket as a high school graduation present. I've carried it in my fish bag ever since. I've envisioned a lot of possible scenarios for its use, but today's wasn't one of them."

As the shadows lengthened, Kirk shaded his eyes against the western sky. "We'd better get movin' if we want to go hunting."

Kirk followed the same narrow ridge out of the canyon they had descended. They traveled west along a narrow trail on the canyon rim. Kirk stopped the Blazer in a saddle which offered a view of the two hogback shaped promontories which the locals appropriately had named "The Hogbacks."

Kirk handed Heidi an extra set of his camouflaged clothing. She pulled the pants on directly over her other clothes. She bent over and rolled up the pant legs, but when she stood up, the pants fell to her knees.

"This'll never do," said Kirk who rustled through his backpack until he found a length of cotton rope. He threaded the rope through the belt loops of the camouflage pants and tied the ends together with a square knot.

He pulled a small compact from the backpack. Kirk smeared the mud brown colored makeup on his index finger. He dabbed streaks of color across her face and completed the camouflage pattern with streaks of the leaf green and black makeup.

"An admirable job even if I do say so myself," said Kirk as he sighted over his thumb. "Archery hunting ought to be a woman's dream sport."

"How's that?"

"You get to buy a complete new wardrobe and wear lots of makeup."

"I'm just sorry the grunge look isn't still in vogue in Seattle," said Heidi as she examined herself in the side mirror of the Blazer.

They eased into one of the many timbered gulches which stood before them. The temperature dropped markedly as they moved out of the fading sunlight into the shadows.

Many timbered fingers and hidden folds greeted them as they moved to the west. Kirk frequently pointed to the ground, revealing the hoof prints of elk or the oval shaped elk droppings.

As they scrambled out of one steep bottom using branches above them as handholds, the high pitched bugle of a bull elk shattered the stillness. The bugle had been de-scribed to Heidi as "flute like", but that description fell far short in its depiction. Thrilled, Heidi smiled broadly up at Kirk who had frozen in his position on the ridge and was listening intently.

Another bull answered the challenge of the first bull

with his own high pitched squeal followed by a series of low throaty grunts.

They crawled the last fifty yards to the ridge top and stopped behind a wide juniper bush. They stood up and eased to the edge of the bush. Kirk parted some branches so they could see the landscape beyond.

A dozen cow and calf elk were grazing in a long grassy park just east of the saddle which divided two promontories. At the edge of the timber, a mature six point bull elk stood like a statue peering into the thick timber.

This cream colored bull remained motionless until another bugle reverberated from deep within the timber. At this sound, the old bull pirouetted and thrashed his antlers against a clump of sage brush. Pieces of sage and dirt flew into the air landing on the back of the angry elk.

Another bull elk burst from the timber approximately 300 yards above the light colored herd bull. The challenger had five points on each side of a tall narrow rack. The five point trotted into the clearing and skirted around the cow and calf herd.

Kirk motioned for Heidi to follow him. They ducked back into the small drainage and hiked down to a narrow finger of trees which offered cover to a point a hundred yards below where the cows and calves were feeding seemingly oblivious to the antics of the males.

Kirk and Heidi slowly moved up the ridge until they could see the elk again. The younger bull was cautiously approaching a cow elk that had strayed a considerable distance from the others.

The older bull galloped across the park. In one motion, he hazed the errant cow back toward the main elk herd and whirled to greet the challenger. The five point turned and made an inglorious retreat to the cover of the timber. The older bull raked his antlers up and down the trunk of a small fir tree stripping off the branches and revealing the bright yellow wood and sap beneath the bark.

Kirk gently pulled Heidi back into the cover and they moved along the edge of the timber until they were behind a small fir tree. He drew an arrow from the bow mounted quiver and nocked it on the bow string.

Kirk made a mewing sound with his cow call. The six point bull immediately grunted an answer, but stayed fixed in his location.

Kirk waited a few minutes and then placed the diaphragm elk call in his mouth. He brought the corrugated grunt tube to his mouth and served up a challenging bugle of his own. The old bull answered but refused to budge.

This frustrating process repeated itself for the next forty-five minutes. The bull would always answer but stayed about seventy yards from where they were concealed. An enthralled Heidi watched and listened to the concert not caring if the bull came in or not.

Kirk was about to back up and try looping back to the bull from a different angle when he caught a flash of movement out of the corner of his eye. He turned to see the smaller five point silently slipping through the timber not twenty yards away.

The five point disappeared behind some thick brush but soon reappeared in the five-foot gap between the trunks of two large fir trees about ten yards below them.

Kirk tensed and waited. One ivory tipped antler entered the opening. Kirk drew the compound bow and held the nocked end of the arrow against the anchor point on his cheek. The full head and antlers of the elk emerged in the clearing and then the bull stopped.

Kirk felt the muscles in his arm ripple as he held the bow at full draw. The bull remained still and peered at their place of hiding. Just when Kirk felt he could not hold the drawn bow any longer, the bull snorted and whirled back into the timber loudly snapping branches as he ran headlong through the undergrowth.

Kirk relaxed and lowered the bow. They turned their attention back to the mature bull just in time to see the bull and the last of his cows slipping into a finger of timber. "I think we're done for the day," whispered Kirk.

"That was really something," said Heidi. "He was so close and what a sound."

By the time they hiked out to the Blazer, it was dark. A multitude of stars covered the sky.

As they climbed into the vehicle, Kirk asked, "Well, what did you think?"

"That has to be the most exciting thing I've ever experienced in the outdoors," said Heidi.

"I was good, wasn't I?" said Kirk with a slight grin.

"I'm talking about the elk, you idiot."

"I thought you meant something else," said Kirk, feigning surprise.

"I bet."

"I don't know about you" said Kirk. "but I'm famished. What do you say to dinner and drinks at the Deep Creek Bar?"

"Sounds like a perfect ending to a perfect day."

They followed a two track road reaching the highway just below the large log framed building, the only bar and restaurant on Deep Creek. They knelt by the creek before crossing the covered foot bridge to the bar and washed off as much makeup as possible with the cold mountain water.

William J. handed the unopened menus back to the waitress and ordered for the entire group.

"Rib steaks around."

"How would you like those cooked?"

"Rare," said William J. sounding astonished that the waitress even needed to ask. "Just run 'em twice around the corral and bring 'em out."

Kirk and Heidi found this boisterous group upon entering the high open beamed dining room of the log structure.

"Come join us," called William. J.

"What's the occasion?" asked Kirk slipping into the chair next to John Sharp.

"We're celebrating the end of a gawd awful afternoon of trailin' cattle," said Doc Adams.

"Worse than the wreck of '93?" asked Kirk who had been one of the participants on the infamous drive by which all others were compared.

"Almost," said Sharp, "we caught a little breeze coming up the north side of Greyson Creek or we'd have lost 'em all for sure."

"Sounds like a good time," said Kirk. "I wish I could've been there."

"I bet you do," said Sharp. "What weighty matters kept you away?"

"We fished Greyson Creek and then bow hunted the Hogbacks."

"Bow hunting, Hell. You two've probably just been up foolin' around in the woods," said Adams with a grin.

The reddening of Heidi's face told him that he must have hit close to home. "Anything you want to admit to, Heidi?"

164

"I wouldn't have taken my camouflage makeup off if I'd have known you were going to embarrass me so," said Heidi. "Now if you'll excuse me, I think I'll retire to the ladies room and remove the rest of this makeup. What I've got left obviously isn't enough to do any good."

William J. called for two more rib steaks and ordered another round of drinks. John Sharp related the discovery of the lion killed calf and the need to move the cattle.

"Once a mountain lion gets a taste of beef, he'll probably just follow the herd," said Kirk.

"That's what I'm afraid will happen, but we had to try something."

"How many calves have you lost now?"

"Today's makes four," said Sharp.

"Look on the bright side," said Kirk, "with the price of cattle down, at least you haven't lost as much money."

"I'm not sure that's the way you look at it." Sharp shook his head. "Only an attorney could see the positive side of losing calves the same time the market's down."

"Any chance the lion Slats killed is the lion that killed this last calf?" asked Adams.

"It's possible that it's the same lion," said Sharp. "As the crow flies, the calf I found this morning is not that far from that area. But I'm not holding my breath. I thought the same thing about the last lion killed. The calf I found this morning hadn't been dead long."

"The cattle losses have certainly been overshadowed by the human deaths," said Heidi slipping into the chair next to Kirk. "I think it's about time though that I write an in-depth story about this aspect. Would you be willing to give me an interview about how the lion attacks are impacting the ranch?"

"I guess it couldn't do any harm," said William. J. as the

steaks arrived. "It might be nice if our side of the story got told for a change."

Heidi tentatively poked her fork into the still red steak. She thought about sending it back to the kitchen, but then shrugged. "When in Rome . . . ."

Chapter X

"I wonder sometimes why I ever take a day off," said Kirk as Marge Johns handed him a thick stack of message memos all with calls which needed to be returned. Kirk retired to his office to sort through the various crises and quasi-crises that had developed in his absence. Despite his instructions not to be disturbed, Marge buzzed him.

"What's up?"

"Tanner Trent's on the line. I thought you'd want to take it."

Kirk picked up the phone and said hello to the famous California attorney.

"Good morning, Mr. Kirk," Tanner Trent said warmly. "I just called to see what you intend to do with all your free time."

"What free time is that?"

"Why I heard Sheriff Green ordered the chase and killing of another lion. Or did I hear wrong? I just deduced that if the sheriff were in jail for contempt of court he wouldn't be bringing you any cases to prosecute so you'd have lots of time on your hands."

"Another lion was killed," Kirk said.

"It's good to know my sources are correct. I hope you realize that I'll be instituting contempt proceedings against Sheriff Green on behalf of Animals Forever. Will you accept service of process on behalf of the sheriff or will I have to retain a process server?"

"Read the order," said Kirk.

"Whatever possessed the sheriff to defy a Federal Court order?" asked Trent.

"Read the order."

"I'm assuming he undertook his actions without seeking your advice."

"Read the restraining order."

"What do you mean?"

"Your restraining order is moot."

"That can't be," said Trent.

"Read the exact language of the order," said Kirk who cited the pertinent language from memory.

"Even if that is the language, the sheriff still defied the spirit of the order," said Trent.

"Tell Steve Clay or Emma Benson about the spirit of the order," said Kirk. "If it weren't for you and your restraining order, Ben Green and Slats Smith would have been free to pursue other lions and maybe Kathy Clay would still be alive today."

"Mr. Kirk, I have misplaced my file and rather than waste your time, let me locate the order and the specific language to which you refer. I'll get back with you shortly."

As soon as Trent hung up, Kirk rummaged through his file and again re-read the exact language of the judge's order.

Pete Roemer tied the big appaloosa to the railroad tie which served as the gate post for the heavy wooden corral gate. The ranch foreman then dashed across the courtyard to the A-framed chalet. He opened the ornate wooden door, ducked his head inside, and called, "Ray, you'd better come take a look at this."

Webster saw Roemer kneeling alongside his gelding. As he approached the horse from behind, nothing appeared out of place, but when he moved next to Roemer, several long even gashes were clearly visible on the neck and front shoulder of the tall horse.

Bright red parallel strips of flesh protruded through the horse hide and two long streams of blood trickled down the front leg to form a small red pool next to the hoof. The shoulder muscle quivered violently as the horse stood nervously eying the two humans.

"Lion." said Webster using the word both as a question and an epitaph.

"I found the gelding standing all wide eyed at the end of the horse pasture," said Roemer. "He was wilder than a March hare. I had to rope him to catch him."

Webster felt a sick feeling in the pit of his stomach as he looked at the gaping wounds. "Is he going to be all right?"

"We need to get him to the vet," said Roemer. "Those wounds need to be cleaned and stitched backed up. I'll get the horse trailer and take him to town if you want to stay and go hunting."

"No, I'll go with you," Webster said.

Roemer backed the goose necked trailer along the corral fence as close as he could get to the injured animal. After considerable coaxing, the gelding lunged forward into the trailer. Webster swung the trailer door closed and latched it shut.

"He's still bleeding pretty good," said Webster as they backed the trailer around the courtyard and started for town.

"The wounds aren't as bad as they look," said Roemer. "A few stitches will close 'em right back up. A horse's got a lot more blood than you think. It looks to me like he's a pretty lucky horse. A few inches either way and the lion would've hit a major blood vessel and he'd have been history."

"Do you think we oughta report this attack?" asked Webster.

"It couldn't hurt anything. We'll swing by the sheriff's office on our way through town. I'd like Ben Green to see these cuts before they're sewed up."

When they reached Townsend, Roemer double parked the pickup truck and horse trailer on the street in front of the sheriff's office. He left Webster in the vehicle while he crossed the street to the office door. He entered and re-emerged a couple minutes later followed by Ben Green.

"Pretty nasty lookin' cuts," said Ben. "I'll have a deputy follow you out to the clinic and take some pictures to document the damage."

"We gotta do something about the lions," said Webster. "At the price I paid for this appaloosa, lion food's pretty pricey."

"The lions are gettin' bolder," said Roemer. "The appie here was in a two acre horse pasture not a hundred yards away from the chalet."

"We're doin' what we can," said Ben. "Slats Smith's checking for lion tracks as we speak. If it's alright with you, we may try picking up the lion scent in your horse pasture."

"Fine by me," said Webster. "It makes me sick to see that beautiful horse flesh sliced to ribbons."

"If I can get Slats rounded up, we'll be up with his dogs late this afternoon," said Ben.

Ben watched the horse trailer roll down the street and disappear around the corner. As he turned to go back to the office, the dispatcher called to him from the doorway, "I've got the pathologist from Great Falls on the phone for you."

"I've completed part of my analysis of the lion carcass and the body of Kathy Clay," said Dr. Hanning.

"What'd you find?"

"Our Forensic Odontologist identified two incisor patterns on the woman's abdomen which exactly match the

170

incisors of the lion. I was also able to extract some fleshy material embedded under the front claws which I sent for laboratory analysis."

"Did you find any fibers or clothing fragments?"

"Not under the claws. The digestive tract of the lion is still a frozen mass. I won't be able to examine the contents until it thaws."

"So does it look like we got the lion that killed Kathy Clay?"

"My preliminary findings are consistent with that conclusion," said Hanning. "I do need to complete a more detailed analysis of several items. I identified an unusual wound to a rib bone which I want to examine microscopically. Also, do you know what activities the victim may have been engaged in immediately prior to the attack?"

"Based on the best available information, we think she was jogging," said Ben. "Why do you ask?"

"I discovered a foreign substance in the fold of skin of the inner elbow."

"What type of substance?"

"A grayish semi-liquid greasy substance possibly petroleum based."

"I don't have a clue what it could be," said Ben.

"It may be a sports cream or even suntan lotion," said Dr. Hanning. "In any event I sent it over to the lab along with the matter extracted from beneath the lion's claws for testing."

"Any idea when you'll complete the examination?"

"I put a rush order on the lab work," said Hanning. "I have the lion's body in an examination room with an external heater turned on high. It shouldn't take too much longer. I shall report my findings to you as soon as I finish the exami-nation."

"Thanks for the update," said Ben. "Let me know if you need anything more from me."

Ben thought about calling Steve Clay to ask about the foreign substance discovered during the autopsy, and then decided against it. The explanation was probably simple enough. No use in disturbing the still grieving husband at this point. If Dr. Hanning's testing didn't reveal the source, then he'd make an inquiry of Steve Clay.

Tucker entered and flipped a folded copy of the morning paper onto the desk.

"What's this?" asked Ben.

"Thought you'd be interested in Animals Forever's latest propaganda."

Ben scanned the news story which extensively quoted Animals Forever's president Grover Arlen. He folded the paper and headed for Kirk's office.

"Have you seen this?" asked Ben.

"I have," Kirk said. "It's also being carried on the radio."

"This makes the cattle ranchers out to be nothing more than greedy robber barons. According to this, the only form of mankind lower than a rancher is some misguided human being who chooses to live in a subdivision in the mountains."

"The problem with this type of article," Kirk said, "is that there's just enough truth interwoven with all the BS that it appears credible. I agree that people shouldn't be living up in those mountains. They destroy the very lifestyle they're looking for, but they don't deserve to be kibble for mountain lions either."

"At least maybe the Sharps can get some money for their calves under this reimbursement program," said Ben. "Animals Forever claims they'll pay for any cattle killed by mountain lions."

"This reimbursement program sounds really swell on

172

the surface," said Kirk, "but there's lots of key details omitted from this story. It fails to mention who's going to determine if a calf was killed by a lion. How is the price going to be fixed? Is it market price at the time of the kill or at the time the calf would have been shipped? How much paperwork will be required? What about the calf which just shows up missing and is never found? I think I'll reserve judgment on this so called 'reimbursement program' until we know more details and see how it's actually implemented."

"It still gravels me that people over two thousand miles away are trying to dictate policy to us," said Ben. "They treat us like dummies who are too unenlightened to ever possibly understand what's best for ourselves or our land."

"They tend to be condescending," said Kirk. "I get really tired of those types wanting mutually exclusive things. They want to live a modern lifestyle with lavish homes made of wood and equipped with all the latest appliances, but they never want a tree cut or mineral mined. We need a certain amount of wilderness, but we need some land uses which are somewhere between wilderness and rape, pillage and plunder. I wonder how many of 'em even consider that the shoes they're wearing are just pieces of an old dead cow."

"I think the most of 'em think Big Macs are manufactured in Detroit," said Ben.

"Some celebrities are the worst," said Kirk. "They'll wail about dozens of environmental issues, but they haven't the slightest compunction about crisscrossing the country in their private jets. They personally deplete more natural resources in one year than a thousand members of some African tribe will consume in a lifetime."

Ben nodded. "But if a couple of 'em decide a mountain retreat in Montana would be fashionable, they're among the first ones to buy into the subdivisions that are 'invading' the mountain lions."

"That's what's happened in the Flathead and the Paradise Valley," said Kirk. "I'm afraid the celebrity rush to Headwaters County may not be far behind."

"We've already got Ray Webster," Ben said. "We may just be seeing the tip of the iceberg, but you'd never think of any of this by reading this article."

"If you don't like this article from Animals Forever, I'm sure you're not going to like their next one," said Kirk who related the call from Tanner Trent.

"That's just wonderful," said Ben. "Do I need to go home and pack my toothbrush?"

"I'll be surprised if they actually seek a contempt citation, but you can almost count on being personally blasted by Animals Forever for your actions."

"That's why I get paid the big bucks," said Ben as he tugged on the brim of his black cowboy hat and retreated through the doorway. Heidi Singer flagged him down in the hallway. Ben told her about Dr. Hanning's preliminary findings and the attack on Ray Wester's horse. "You can't believe the interest this case is taking on," said Heidi.

"I can believe it," said Ben. "You can't believe the number of requests for information that the dispatchers are fielding—reporters, news services, radio stations and everything in between."

John Sharp rummaged intently through a chest of drawers.

"What are you doing?" asked Misty.

"I'm trying to find some ammunition," said John. "I very deliberately packed it away in a safe place at the end of last hunting season. I just can't seem to locate that 'safe place.'"

174

A high powered rifle with a hardwood stock leaned against the counter.

"Why do you need your rifle and ammunition?"

"The dead calf I found yesterday was only partially eaten. The lion had covered the carcass with grass, leaves and sticks. It obviously intended to come back for another meal. If it does, I intend to be waiting."

"You can't just shoot a mountain lion," said Misty. "It's against the law."

"I know that," said John. "But I'm not going to sit idly by and let a mountain lion destroy our future. Between the lions and the cattle prices we're close to a serious financial crisis."

"There's got to be another way," said Misty. "What kind of example are we setting for the boys if we pick and choose the laws we intend to obey?"

"The right to defend one's property is a well established principle of law," said John. "If by some slim chance, I'm caught, I fully intend to rely on that right."

"But you're not planning on getting caught?"

"Not on your life and if I do kill a lion, I'm sure not going to broadcast the fact to the world. This case is getting too much attention as it is. I don't want to make a federal case out of it. I just want the lions to leave the cattle alone."

"A federal case is very well what you might make out of it," said Misty.

"Do you have any better suggestions?" said John as he finally located the hard plastic cartridge case containing the 7mm ammunition.

"Animals Forever announced today that they'll reimburse ranchers for all livestock losses caused by mountain lions. Why don't we file a claim for the loss of our calves? What have we got to lose?"

175

"Nothing I guess," said John. "I just don't like thinking I'm in the business of raising mountain lion food."

"I'd much prefer to seek reimbursement," said Misty. "Besides you wouldn't like jail."

"Be alright if I had conjugal visits," said John reaching an arm around her narrow waist.

"Not on your life," said Misty as she pulled away from him and started up the stairs. "If you go to jail for shooting a mountain lion, don't expect any conjugal visits from me."

"Who said I was talking about conjugal visits from you?" John said with a grin. "But for now you win. I'll hold off hunting lions for the present and I'll check on filing a claim for reimbursement. However, my patience won't last if the lions get another calf. If that happens all bets are off and I'll declare war on the mountain lions. Agreed?"

"Agreed," echoed Misty as she stopped and allowed him to catch and embrace her.

The hounds sat silently in the homemade kennels oblivious to the traffic and congestion around them. Their disinterest and placidity disappeared when they saw an orange tiger striped cat in the alley across from the sheriff's office. At the sight of the domestic tabby, the hounds began baying and clamoring against the sides of the kennels.

Slats Smith rushed out of the sheriff's office and yelled, "Shadup you mangy mutts!"

His admonition for silence sent the cat scurrying down the alley and the dogs howled even louder at the departing blur of orange. Ben emerged to investigate the commotion.

"Once a lion hound, always a lion hound," said Slats. "If you want to have some fun, we can let the hounds loose."

"Fat chance," said Ben. "We'd be a week rounding up dogs and we'd probably have to call the fire department to get the cat off a telephone pole or out of a tree."

"Where I come from in Missouri, the local sheriff had a special tool for gettin' cats out of trees and off poles," said Slats. "You oughta think about getting one yourself."

"What special tool is that?" asked Ben.

"Twelve gauge shotgun," said Slats. "Works like a charm."

"I swear you could personally set back community relations thirty years," said Ben as he spread an aerial map across the hood of Slat's flatbed pickup truck.

Ben located Webster's chalet.

"It's big country," said Slats whistling softly as he outlined the area which constituted the vast Webster holdings with his index finger. "If the lion doesn't tree right away, we can figure on a tough hike."

"No one said it'd be easy," said Ben as he placed his weathered 30.06 in the cab of Slats' truck. "What do you think's the best plan of attack?"

"It's not rocket science. I'd say we go to Webster's and dump the hounds into the horse pasture and see if they pick up a scent. If they don't, we come home and if they do, we go to chasin' lion."

"Simple but effective," said Ben. "Let's finish packing up and give it a go."

Ben walked back into his office and retrieved a portable radio and large battery case which he placed on the front seat between himself and Slats.

"I suppose you do have to be able to be reached in case of an emergency," said Slats as he eyed the electronic equipment.

"I'm a hell of a lot more concerned about callin' in for a ride home when this hunk of junk you call a truck breaks down," Ben said.

Slats drove down Main Street with the dogs yapping all the way. A mile out of town the portable radio squawked and the dispatcher requested that they return immediately to the sheriff's office.

Slats made a wide U turn in the middle of the highway and drove back through the small town. Deputy Woods stood in front of the sheriff's office when they arrived. The deputy ran to the passenger side of the flatbed and handed Ben a fax.

Ben Green scanned the document.

"What's up? asked Slats impatiently.

"Looks like we're out of the lion chasin' business," said Ben. "The Federal District Court has modified Animal Forever's restraining order. This in no uncertain terms makes it clear that until the hearing on the 18th, I can't even look at a cat let alone chase one and that includes the one that just ran down the alley."

In 1855, General L.L. Stevens established a pathway to be followed by the Flathead Indians in their annual journey from their villages west of the Continental Divide to their traditional buffalo hunting grounds on the eastern plains of Montana. Most of this trail had, with time, been lost to cultivated fields and paved highways.

On the Sharp Ranch, a faint two wheel track clinging to a long ridge from the headwaters of Greyson Creek west to Ross Gulch is the only visible remainder of this historic route.

The mature tom stepped from the thick undergrowth onto this fragment of history and instinctively pondered his options. The carcass of the dead calf above the water tank at the base of Berberet's knob offered a sure meal. But the carcass was a long distance from his present location and even though the sharp pain of the horse kick to his ribs had subsided to a dull ache, the lion preferred a closer meal.

The trail to his west was dimpled with the tracks of the Sharp cattle. The lion turned to the west and trotted briskly along the ridge line. At the barbed wire fence which crossed the trail, he gathered himself and bounded gracefully over the gate clearing the top strand of barbed wire by a good two feet.

The lion continued his brisk pace until he heard the distinct bawl of a calf calling for its mother. He immediately slowed to a stalking speed and eased off the Flathead Trail itself into the upper reaches of Black Butte Gulch.

This area which had been clear cut some thirty years before consisted of large grassy meadows interspersed with thick clumps of fir and quaking aspens. A grown over logging road graded around the many swales and cuts of the broken terrain.

The lion entered the old clear cuts and spied a calf. The calf grazed along the old logging road a half mile away from the black mass of cattle which lay around several blocks of salt scattered by the Sharps on one of the finger ridges.

The lion's attention focused exclusively on the black calf. He picked a point halfway between the calf and the salting ground. He stalked deliberately to this point using every piece of available cover. He pressed his long body tightly against the lip of the cutbank above the logging road and waited.

The calf came forward with none of the wariness of a deer or elk—a point not lost on the instinctive memory of the lion. The calf walked unsuspectingly to the point of ambush. The lion bounded from the cut bank not even noticing the pain in his side.

Pete Roemer and Ray Webster sat outside the A-framed chalet waiting for the sheriff to arrive. Webster idly picked on his guitar as he leaned against the wall and basked in the late afternoon sunshine.

A chipmunk peeked over the edge of the redwood deck at the strange sound. Roemer rolled a beer nut across the planks toward the curious animal. The chipmunk darted over the edge, fielded the nut and scampered back beneath the deck with his prize.

The phone rang inside. Roemer motioned for Webster to remain seated on the floor of the deck and ran into the living room with the cathedral ceiling and large stone fireplace.

"Who was that?" asked Webster when Roemer returned.

"A local couple wantin' to know if they could use the Paradise meadow for their wedding."

"That's the fourth call of that type this week," said Webster. "Don't people realize that one of the main reasons I come to Montana is to get away from telephones?"

"A certain amount of that comes with the territory," said Roemer. "If you own property, you have neighbors, and neighbors in Montana expect you to behave neighborly."

"I suppose so," said Webster, "but I still want some peace and quiet when I come to Montana. I suppose if a big subdivision goes in next to us that all of those 'Montanans' would consider me to be their next door neighbor."

"Certainly."

"That's why I wanted the Chappel sections so badly," said Webster. "I wanted to avoid that possibility."

"I doubt if the Sharps will ever subdivide so I think you're pretty safe along that boundary. But even if you had more property, you would still have people to contend with on the other side of any property you bought. You can't own it all."

"That's the built in Catch-22," said Webster. "The more property you own the more neighbors you have and the more burdens that come with land ownership. If you deny access in any way, then you're the son-of-a-bitch celebrity owner."

"And if you give me that job, I'm the son-of-a-bitch ranch foreman for the son-of-a-bitch celebrity owner," said Roemer.

"There ought to be a way to have a buffer zone between your property and the rest of the world," said Webster.

"Buy an island," said Roemer as the phone rang again and he dashed back inside.

"Who was it this time?" asked Webster when Roemer returned.

"Ben Green," said Roemer who told Webster about the new restraining order.

"You know I even played at a benefit concert for Animals Forever," said Webster.

"You're kidding?" said Roemer.

"Nope. It just seemed like the thing to do at the time. Ya know when I was in Nashville, mountain lions in the wild seemed natural and right. Now that I'm here and they're slicing my favorite horse to ribbons, I'm not as thrilled with the idea."

"Depends on whose ox is being gored or horse being clawed, I suppose," said Roemer.

"I just liked lions better in the abstract than in the concrete," said Webster. "But I guess there's no use sitting around here. The elk are a buglin' and we'd better get after 'em before the phone rings again."

Chapter XI

Thursday, September 11th

Ben called Dr. Hanning's office. The receptionist put him on hold. The weather forecast and three country western songs from the FM radio station in Great Falls played on the line while he waited. At least, he thought, it wasn't elevator music.

Dr. Hanning came on the line.

"Sorry to keep you waiting," said Hanning. "I was waiting for the last lab report to arrive in hopes it could explain the conundrum with which I've been presented. The toxicologic examination of the contents of the stomach of the lion revealed human tissue and hair consistent with the blood and hair of Kathy Clay. We also found flesh embedded in the lion's claws with the same blood type of the woman."

"So the human blood in the flesh found in the lion came from Kathy Clay?"

"I can't positively make that assertion," said Hanning. "While we can totally exclude people by the use of blood typing, we cannot say with certainty that a specific person was the source of that blood. We can only assert that the blood is consistent with a specific person's blood type and look to the percentage frequency of that particular type occurring in the human population. We can also look to determine whether a person is what we call a 'secretor' or a 'nonsecretor.' In this case, Kathy Clay's blood type occurs randomly in about twelve percent of the human population. She is also a nonsecretor. The percentage of people who are nonsecretors and of that blood type is about six percent. We can of course do more specific testing with DNA analysis but that would take another month and be relatively expensive."

"No great mystery in those findings," said Ben. "The chances of the lion eating someone other than Kathy Clay, who is also only six percent of the population, seems statistically improbable. I'd say for all practical purposes, the evidence says the lion ate flesh from Kathy Clay."

"I agree," said Hanning, "but the blood and hair samples are only one part of the source of my puzzlement. My dilemma developed when I examined a suspicious looking injury to a rib bone. The microscope clearly reveals a cutting type wound which suggests infliction by a knife."

"You're saying we have a homicide?" asked Ben.

"No, I'm saying I found a cutting type wound which suggests that it was inflicted by a knife. Forensic science can't offer any explanation for who or how it was inflicted. That's your job."

"You're sure that the rib wasn't just bitten by a sharp tooth?"

"Absolutely. The microscope doesn't lie. The edges of the wound are even and distinct. A wound inflicted by a knife and one by an animal bite may appear similar to the naked eye but the difference is like night and day under magnification."

"Was the knife wound the cause of death?"

"That's my dilemma," said Hanning. "Both the knife wound and the injuries inflicted by the lion could be fatal. I'm waiting for the analysis of the foreign substance I found in the fold of skin in the elbow. I'm hoping the identity of that substance will shed some light on the cause of death."

"Other than the knife wound to the rib, did you find any other wounds or marks not made by the lion?" asked Ben.

"Nothing that can't be attributed to a lion or other animal."

"What do you mean, other animal?"

"Whenever a body is exposed in the open, there are usually some superficial wounds attributable to rodents or scavenger birds," Hanning said. "I found a few such wounds corresponding to those sources, but not as many as one might have anticipated. But other than the knife wound, I found no other mark or wound inconsistent with a death by lion attack."

"Did you find any trace of clothing?" asked Ben.

"No fiber fragments were discovered—not in the digestive tract of the lion or under the claws," said Hanning.

"You're not giving me much," said Ben.

"I can only report what I find."

"Or don't find," Ben said. "I've got about fifteen different news services waiting for your conclusive opinion as to the cause of death and what you're telling me is that as of now you don't know."

"That's it in a nutshell," said Hanning. "And we may never know based on my findings. The lab analysis of the foreign substance may reveal nothing. Your investigation may have to supplement my findings in order to determine the cause and manner of death. For the moment, I'm declaring the cause of death as inconclusive pending further investigation. I'll fax you my findings as soon as we hang up."

"Call me with your analysis of the foreign substance," Ben said. "Hopefully that'll tell us something."

Ben went to the fax machine located in the dispatcher's office and waited for the incoming transmission. He took the fax to Kirk's office and casually tossed the report from Dr. Hanning onto his desk.

Kirk idly scanned through the first page of the document sorting out the meanings concealed within the medicalese. Yawning, he turned the page. When he reached the second paragraph of the second page, Kirk tensed and jerked upright in his chair.

"A knife wound?"

"That's what it says."

"Not exactly what we expected."

"That's the understatement of the year", said Ben.

"What do you think it means?" asked Kirk.

"I hoped you might have some answers."

"It's either a homicide or a suicide," said Kirk.

"How could it be a suicide?" asked Ben.

"Consider a scenario in which Kathy Clay is badly mauled by a mountain lion. She's unable to walk and in excruciating pain. Things look completely hopeless so she stabs herself. I remember reading about a hunter who fell and broke his leg. He crawled along for a few hours and then shot himself. Or how about a scenario where Kathy Clay, despondent over a fight with her husband, retreats to a remote area in the mountains and stabs herself. Her body is then scavenged by a mountain lion?"

"Where's the knife and her clothing?" asked Ben.

"Pack rats and scavenger birds," Kirk said. "The report indicates that there was some physical evidence of both."

"I'd say those possibilities are about as likely as someone coming along and stabbing the body after the lion made its kill. You don't really think either of those things really happened, do you?"

"No, I don't," said Kirk. "I don't know the why or the how of it, but I think we've got ourselves a homicide."

"That's what I think, too," said Ben. "The question is what do we do about it."

"I'd say we'd better take a close look at Mr. Steven Clay," said Kirk. "He readily admits to having a fight with her before her disappearance. Is there anything in retrospect which you see as suspicious about his actions?"

"They say hindsight is 20/20," said Ben. "But looking back I find it rather odd that the woman disappears on Friday afternoon and her husband doesn't file a missing person report until Sunday night."

"That struck me, too," said Kirk. "Although his explanation at the time seemed legitimate."

"What do you make of the evidence of the lion attack itself?" asked Ben.

"Perhaps the lion's just a convenient scavenger no different from the pack rats or camp robbers," said Kirk.

"Now there's a scenario Animals Forever would love," said Ben. "I can hear it all now: 'Sheriff kills lion doing what lion's do naturally.'"

"You can count on that type of argument if that's the case," said Kirk.

"The $64,000 question," said Ben, "is where do we go from here? We still don't have a murder weapon, an eyewitness or any other evidence for that matter. And the press will soon be descending on yours truly wanting to know the conclusion of the autopsy. What do I tell them?"

Kirk pondered the situation for several minutes.

"We definitely have some investigative work ahead of us and it would be considerably more productive if that work could be performed without public scrutiny.

"For now I'd suggest that we tell the press that the cause of death is inconclusive pending further investigation and not make any public disclosure about the discovery of the knife wound."

"Where do you think we ought to focus our investigation?" asked Ben.

"First, I think you ought to make a few subtle inquiries into Steve Clay's background. Second, I think we need to address the mystery of the missing clothing and now also the missing knife. I think knowing their whereabouts would be highly illuminating."

"We didn't make an extensive search of that area," said Ben. "The cause of death seemed so apparent, we didn't spend a lot of time scouring the terrain."

"That might be the place to begin," said Kirk. "You could always call out the Search and Rescue squad again and have them comb both sides of the gulch where the body was found."

"That's an option, but Gallatin County has a fancy dog trained in Germany," said Ben. "He's supposed to be able to do some amazing things in locating people and objects. I'll check with the Gallatin County Sheriff and see if we can borrow the dog and his handler for a morning. In the meantime, I'll have a record check made on Clay."

"We can't keep the information about a possible homicide under wraps for long," said Kirk. "We'll need to get cracking."

"I'm out of here," said Ben jumping to his feet. "I'd appreciate it if you'd issue a short press release regarding the forensic report."

"I've got you covered," said Kirk.

John Sharp stopped his flatbed pickup truck on the old logging road next to the salting ground. He and Joe Durham walked through the group of black cattle congregated around the scattered salt blocks.

The cattle reluctantly stood up at the approach of the two men. John critically eyed each calf mentally guessing its weight. Seeing cattle in this remote corner of the pasture pleased the rancher.

"The cattle'd never got this far back if we hadn't put the salt here," said Sharp.

"It does get 'em out of the creek bottoms," said Durham.

One Angus cow failed to move out of their path quickly enough for the liking of the hired hand. Durham ran a few steps toward the animal waving his arms and shouting. The cow ran a few steps and then turned and looked blankly at them.

"Cows are stupid," said Durham as is if he'd just discovered that fact.

"It's a good thing too," said Sharp. "Cows are hard enough to deal with as it is. There'd be hell to pay if those mama cows were smart enough to understand that we're just raising their babies so that they can be killed and eaten."

"Wouldn't make a bit of difference," said Durham. "Every morning before I throw the rolled oats into the trough, I tell the steers in the feed lot that if they eat the oats, they'll get fat and we'll eat 'em. But do they listen? Noooo... They belly right up and suck up all the grain they can."

"I guess they can't say they weren't warned," said Sharp as he mentally pictured Durham delivering the daily lecture to a corral full of black steers. "But if cows are so stupid, how come we're the ones constantly busting our butts to make sure they have food and water while they just lie around and eat."

"You may have a point," said Durham pointing to a heavily muscled Angus bull standing at the edge of the group of cattle. "Look at that bull. What a life. All he has to do every year is eat, drink and get twenty-five to thirty cows pregnant. I wish I could make a living the same way."

"You've got my permission," said Sharp. "But you may want to check with Kirk. I think it may be against the law. Although in this age of tolerance for sexual orientation, who knows anymore. In any event, I ain't payin' your wages until I see what kind of calves you throw."

"That's not quite what I had in mind," said Durham.

"But that may be the only way you get some intelligence bred into the herd. I swear the cattle get dumber every year."

"You're getting older and crabbier every year," said Sharp. "You just need to be a little more laid back and develop a little patience."

"Hell's bells, I've got patience I ain't even used yet," said Durham.

After checking the cattle, the two men climbed back up the ridge to the truck. Sharp mounted his spotting scope on the window of his truck.

Sharp focused across the deep chasm of Black Butte Gulch onto the many parks of the ridge plateau called Mundin Flats. Beyond the flats, the 10,000 foot snow capped "Old Baldy" peak provided a majestic backdrop. Cumulus clouds lolled like continents in the deep blue Montana sky.

"I never get tired of that view," said Sharp.

"Looks the same as when I was a boy," said Durham. "It's kind of nice to know that some things don't change."

"It may change," said Sharp. "I've heard the property to the north may be subdivided. I'd sure hate to see roads and houses on that skyline."

"I guess it's there's to do with as they want," said Durham. "But somehow it still don't seem right. Some country ought to be there just to look at and maybe feed a few cows and a couple elk."

Sharp started the truck and drove around the bend in the old logging road. He hadn't gone three hundred yards when a black mound appeared before them in the center of the roadway.

"What the hell." said Sharp at the sight of the dead calf.

Sharp threw the gear shift into neutral, set the emergency brake, and jumped out of the vehicle leaving the door wide open. Grim faced, Sharp stood over the remains of the dead calf. A mountain lion had struck again. Possible courses of action whirled through Sharp's mind. He was too upset to settle on a specific plan of action, but one thing was clear to him, action would be taken.

Kirk entered Ben's office. He handed a stack of neatly typed press releases to the dispatcher who was on the phone talking to some branch of the media.

"If you look on your map," said the dispatcher, "Townsend is halfway between Glacier and Yellowstone Park."

"How's the public relations business?" asked Kirk as he handed Ben the press release.

"It's crazy," said Ben. We've had calls from all over the world—Britain, Japan. You name it, we've heard from 'em."

"I didn't see the morning paper. I suppose Animals Forever took you to task. I'm surprised though that Animal Forever's wail and the preliminary autopsy report would generate that kind of interest."

"Animals Forever did deliver a pretty good broadside against me," said Ben. "In their book, I'm the bastard of the year for killing the lion even though the tooth marks are all over her body. But today the media hardly cares about either of those stories.

"Do you know what earth shaking story is overshadowing those concerns? Ray Webster's horse. Heidi Singer's sidebar article about the attack on the horse is all anyone wants to talk about. A little girl is slaughtered by a mountain lion and the press is mildly interested, but let a mountain lion claw a country western superstar's horse and the press is in a feeding frenzy."

"You're kidding." said Kirk.

"Unbelievable isn't it? In some ways it's great. Here I thought I'd be on the media hot seat about defying the 'spirit of the restraining order.' The press has hardly asked about that issue. Do you know the number one question asked of me and the dispatchers?"

"What?" Kirk asked.

"The name of Ray Webster's horse."

"What is the name of Ray Webster's horse?" asked Kirk.

"Damned if I know." said Ben. "All I know is that it's a big appaloosa gelding that Webster paid way, way, way too much money for."

"Looks to me like Webster's appaloosa has kept your feet from the fire."

"Only good thing an appaloosa ever did for me."

"You just never did like appaloosas," said Kirk.

"My pappy told me that there were two reasons the Indians rode appaloosas," said Ben. "They were the only horses slow enough to catch on foot, and after an Indian brave got on and put up with an appaloosa's nonsense for awhile, he was fightin' mad by the time he got into battle."

"Where's Webster? He can at least answer the name question."

"He and Pete Roemer are out hunting and are conveniently unavailable for comment," said Ben. "So every reporter calls here. With all this attention, I'm afraid when the news of the knife wound hits, all hell's gonna break loose."

"You're right about that," said Kirk. "How are you coming with your background check?"

"I visited briefly with Kathy Clay's parents," said Ben. "They just needed to talk to someone about their daughter so I really didn't have to ask a whole lot of questions. They told me that Kathy married Clay right after she graduated from college. He was several years older and a successful investment counselor at a well-known brokerage house. They were concerned about the age difference but the marriage seemed to take.

"Clay always had a dream of moving into the mountains and away from the city. After he put his twenty years in with the brokerage firm, he retired, sold their home, bought a lot in the Dry Creek subdivision and moved to Montana."

"Sounds like a common dream," said Kirk. "Did Mrs. Clay share in it?"

"Her parents said she gave lip service to the move, but they both noticed some disillusionment in recent weeks. Kathy kept telling them that Steve seemed a different person since the move. She complained about missing her friends and family and many of the social amenities of the city."

"How have the Clays been supporting themselves?"

"They had a pretty good nest egg left after they sold their California property and built here. Also, Clay draws a monthly pension check. Kathy's father did say that Clay had hoped to start an investment counseling business from his home to supplement their income. Apparently, he was having difficulty getting it off the ground. But that just seemed to be a minor setback. They really had a lot going for them. There didn't seem to be any motive for murder."

"Unless Kathy Clay intended to leave," said Kirk. "A divorce would have totally derailed Steve Clay's dream. He may have envisioned years of hoping and planning going right down the drain. So he killed her."

"Not much of a motive, but people have killed for less," said Ben, "and I do know from talking to the contractor who did the work on their new home that they did have some major cost overruns. Those extra expenses combined with the failure of his consulting business and the strained marriage may have put him right over the edge."

"I wonder if Mr. Clay happens to be the beneficiary of any life insurance policies issued on his wife's life?" asked Kirk. "It'd be worth the effort to seek an investigative subpoena to see if such an animal exists and if any recent changes may have been made in the policy.

"I'll approach the court for the subpoena first thing in the morning. We don't have much of a window of opportunity to gather information. We definitely want to interview Mr. Clay before he knows he's a suspect."

"While you're getting the investigative subpoena for the life insurance policies, I'll be looking for her clothes," said Ben.

"You got the dog?"

"Yeah. The Gallatin County sheriff owes me a couple favors. The dog handler is meeting me first thing in the morning and we're going up Dry Creek to the site where the body was found."

"Are you taking the Search and Rescue unit and the deputies?"

"No. According to Sergeant Frank, the dog handler, the fewer human smells in the area, the better. Having to sort through multiple smells only confuses the dog and slows the process."

"Makes sense to me."

"It's just going to be Sergeant Frank, the dog and me."

"By the end of the day, we may have enough information to corner Steve Clay," said Kirk.

"The lab report on the foreign substance ought to be back by then, too," said Ben. "It may just all come together. God, how I love when that happens. Did you see anything else of significance in Hanning's findings?"

"After I talked with you this morning, I went through the pathology reports of Faith Benson and Kathy Clay from soup to nuts. Neither lion had a single cattle hair or beef tissue in the digestive tract or under the claws."

"What do you think that means?" asked Ben.

"I have a hunch that one lion is killing all the cattle and it's not one of the lions involved with the human encounters. When you mark the cattle kill sites on a map, they really aren't all that far apart. One lion flip flopping over the ridge between the Sharp Ranch and Webster's could be doing all the damage."

"Probably a young lion," said Ben, "or an old one that's developed a taste for cows and discovered that they're a whole lot easier to catch than deer or elk."

"That's all academic at the moment," said Kirk. "With the modified restraining order in effect, no one's going to be killing any more lions."

The dispatcher called to Ben. "There's a reporter on the phone wanting to talk with you about Ray Webster's horse."

Kirk smiled at Ben's grimace and hurriedly left the office. Kirk returned to his office and dictated an application for an investigative subpoena citing the discovery of the knife wound and the other limited details known to law enforcement.

Kirk proofed the subpoena over Marge's shoulder as she typed. As soon as the subpoena and related documents were finished, he placed them in his briefcase. He would make the half hour drive to Helena first thing in the morning and present the request for the subpoena to the District Judge. If the request were granted, he could have the life insurance policy in hand by noon.

"There ain't no way on God's green earth," said William J. Sharp. He disgustedly threw the two inch stub of a pencil

194

onto the round oak table. William J. had never learned to trust a calculator. Neat columns of figures filled the many pieces of crumpled paper which covered the table top.

Mary Sharp scurried from the kitchen to see what was disturbing her husband.

"I've figured and re-figured our budget a dozen different ways," said William J. "I can't make it pencil out so that we can swing the purchase of the Chappel property. I'm not even sure we can make our other land payments."

"The lion kills have made that much difference?"

"The lion kills are just part of the problem," William J. said. "Calf prices went down another four cents today. If the calves would bring what they brought two years ago, the lion kills would only be a minor inconvenience. This year the lion kills may just be the straw that breaks the camel's back."

"What are we going to do?" asked Mary.

"Frankly, I don't like any of our options. We could just forfeit the earnest money and let the Chappel property go, or we could try to sell it to Ray Webster at a profit, or we could just up and subdivide it ourselves. Maybe we could get some of the easy money that the out-of-staters are throwing at Montana."

"What's wrong with either of those last two options?" asked Mary.

"I really don't want to have a subdivision on both sides of us. One is enough and to tell you the truth I wouldn't feel right about making a profit off of Mort Chappel's offer to sell. He gave it to us at the price he did because he thought we intended to use it to run cows the same as he and his father before him. If Mort had an heir, that property would've never been for sale."

"There aren't any easy choices," said Mary, "but we can't afford to lose the $5,000 in earnest money either."

"Damn the luck." said William J. "Why couldn't the Chappel property come up for sale in a year when the cattle market was up? And why is this the year that the lions develop a taste for beef steak."

"I suppose we ought to get together with Misty and John and make a decision," said Mary.

"You're right. We'd better have a ranch meeting and decide what to do."

"Maybe Animals Forever will come through with the reimbursement for the lost calves. John contacted them and a field representative is supposed to be here in a couple days to investigate."

"That money wouldn't hurt anything," said William J.

Kirk felt a debt of gratitude to Ray Webster's horse. The widespread coverage of Heidi's story on the mauling initially diverted her attention from her suspicions concerning the autopsy report on Kathy Clay.

Flushed by her success, Heidi gleefully related the many inquiries from the mainstream media and the tabloids.

"I tried my damndest to track down the name of Webster's horse before my deadline the other day. I couldn't reach Webster or his foreman so I regretfully had to omit that one detail. In retrospect, that was the hook which made for a lot of the interest and the follow up inquiries."

"What is the name of Webster's horse?" said Kirk.

"Spot."

"You're kidding."

"No, but you've got to admit, it's an appropriate name for an appaloosa."

"It may be an appropriate name for an appaloosa but

I'm not sure it's an appropriate subject for this much media attention."

"This business still amazes me," said Heidi. "In my career, I've written articles about a thousand different subjects—some with far reaching consequences— but the story which generates some of the most interest is some fluff piece about a country singer's horse."

"What earth shattering story are you bringing us tomorrow, the names of Slats Smith's lion hounds?"

"That's a thought," said Heidi. "But actually I filed a story this afternoon about the citizen's group that formed today in response to Animals Forever's statements."

"What kind of citizen's group?" asked Kirk.

"Steve Clay and Roger and Emma Benson announced the founding of a group to be known as "People First". They assert their right to be safe on their own property and to defend themselves from mountain lion attacks. They vented their outrage that the press seems so concerned about the welfare of Ray Webster's horse when they themselves have lost loved ones."

"You can't really blame them," said Kirk. "If it'd been one of my kids, I'd probably feel the same way."

"This conflict with people and lions isn't going to end with the hearing on the restraining order, is it?" asked Heidi.

"No. Most people believe in private property rights and in the right to defend one's property. These same people would also express the belief that mountain lions should have the right to exist in the wild. It's the conflict of these two rights that creates the problem."

This discussion was interrupted by the waitress bringing the Horseshoe Cafe's daily special of homemade soup and cornbread. The discussion drifted from topic to topic, from the serious to the ridiculous. Kirk again had to admit to himself how much he enjoyed her company.

"Did you get the final autopsy report this afternoon?" asked Heidi.

"Nope," replied Kirk tersely.

"When do you expect it?"

"Tomorrow."

"You know something you aren't telling me, don't you?"

"Yup."

"You aren't going to tell me, are you?"

"Nope."

After dinner, Kirk escorted Heidi across the street to her room at the Mustang Motel. They kissed. "I really do need to finish a piece and make some phone calls," she said before kissing him again and slipping through the door.

Kirk drove a circuitous route along several back roads to get home. He mulled over and over his feelings and the status of their relationship. Maybe it was time to take the big plunge again.

He entered his log home by way of the patio door in back. The phone rang as he started up the stairs to the loft. His spirits lifted as he heard his daughters' voices, each on an extension phone.

"Hi, Dad," they called.

"We heard about Townsend on the news," said Jenny. "A mountain lion clawed Ray Webster's horse."

"You watch out for Nugget," Lisa said. Forty-five minutes later, Kirk had received an update of every happening at their grade school. He knew who was cool and who was not. He knew that Lisa had a secret admirer and that Jenny knew the identity but wasn't telling. He knew all these facts which, on one hand seemed so trivial, but yet somehow seemed vital. Finally he looked at his watch.

"You two need to get to bed," he said as he remembered the time zone difference. "It's a school night."

"Ah, Dad," they said. "Don't hang up yet. Mom wants to talk with you."

"Jeff, how are you?" asked Sarah Kirk.

"I'm doing pretty good considering. Although I have a feeling things are really going to bust loose around here in a day or two."

"I don't know how to say this other than right out," said Sarah. "And I don't want you to say anything at all right now. I just want you to think about it. The girls miss you and Montana terribly. I think maybe we ought to give it another try. We really did have something once and I think it's worth trying to get it back. Tell me you'll think about it."

"I'll think about it," echoed Kirk numbly.

Long after the line had gone dead, Kirk sat in a state of shock still holding the receiver. A gamut of emotions and memories raced through his mind. Feeling emotionally and physically exhausted, he slowly climbed the stairs to the loft and fell back on the bed without bothering to remove his clothes.

Chapter XII

Friday, September 12th

The sleek black dog bounded gracefully from the metal dog carrier onto the ground next to Ben Green's Wagoneer.

"Platz." said Sergeant Monte Frank.

At the command, the dog stretched flat on the ground revealing the brown markings on his face and neck. The German Shepherd eagerly looked up at the handler in anticipation of the next command.

"Platz?" asked Ben Green.

Frank explained, "Dogs like Hans here are trained in Germany for the first eighteen months of their lives. They learn all their commands in German."

"We are introduced to our dog in an intensive three week training program. We can change the commands to English but it just slows down the training process. It's much easier for us to learn the German. Sometimes we modify or change a command.

"It's an ongoing learning process both for the dog and his handler. The tracking command is 'Suche.' Hans learned that command for tracking both humans and objects with human scent such as clothing. Early in our training process, I discovered that using the one command for both types of searches confused Hans. With time he's come to understand 'Suche' for human tracking and 'Little Suche' for tracking clothing or related human objects. So he now understands one command that's part English and part German."

"It's a sad commentary," said Ben. "There's one bilingual officer attached to the entire sheriff's department and it's a dog. What type of bark does he make when he's on a track?"

"Because Hans is trained for human apprehension, he trails without barking."

"How in the hell do you keep track of him?" asked Ben.

"You trail with him on a leash," said Sergeant Frank. "If he gets off the leash, you have no way of knowing where he's gone unless you hear a perpetrator in the distance begging for mercy."

Sergeant Frank and Hans followed Ben to the location in the narrow ravine where Kathy Clay's remains had been discovered. Ben opened the brown paper bag containing the jeans and sweatshirt recovered from her Honda Civic.

Sergeant Frank pulled the items of clothing from the bag and extended them toward the dog. Hans probed the items of clothing thoroughly with his long pointed nose.

"Hans, little suche."

The soil under the body recovery site remained stained from the blood and other body fluids. At this location, Hans' quivering body indicated a positive reaction for human scent consistent with that of the clothing. Outside of this immediate area, the dog failed to detect any more of the targeted human scent.

The two law officers and the dog worked up the old logging road until it dead ended at a gigantic slash pile near the top of the drainage. Here they crossed the small mountain stream and worked their way back down the drainage through the thick undergrowth of willow and dogwood.

By the time they recrossed the stream and climbed the steep bank to the Wagoneer, the residue of moisture from the early morning frost had soaked through their pants and boots.

"I never detected a positive reading once we left the body site," said Frank as he flopped down next to the vehicle.

"I think we've done all we can here," said Ben. "Let's go

back down the coulee to where the car was discovered. We'll see if Hans has any better luck there."

Kirk bounded up the sandstone stairs outside the Lewis and Clark County Courthouse two stairs at a time. He tried to decipher the Roman numeral MDCCCLXXXV carved in stone above the arched doorway.

He hurried to the second floor and wound his way along the dark narrow corridor which led to the chambers of Nelson P. Ross, State District Judge in and for the First Judicial District of the State of Montana.

At Kirk's appearance in the doorway, the graying judge waved Kirk into the court's private sanctuary. Kirk dispensed with any greeting and slid the application for an investigative subpoena across the desk to the magistrate.

Judge Ross carefully scrutinized the application and the proposed subpoena through the narrow lenses of his bifocals. He then neatly set the legal documents back on the desk.

The judge paused and retrieved one of the many pipes from the pipe rack on the corner of his desk. He loaded the pipe with a generous supply of tobacco from the leather pouch which hung from the back of his chair.

The judge struck a farmers match with his thumbnail and drew the flame to the bowl of the pipe. He sucked on the pipe, exhaled a large cloud of sweet smelling smoke and then leaned back in the oversized swivel chair.

"When I read the article, I suspected the husband as the perpetrator," Ross said. "I guessed you'd be in asking for some kind of order for production."

Kirk gave the judge a puzzled look.

"You don't have a clue what I'm talking about, do you?"

"I'm afraid not, Your Honor," said Kirk.

Judge Ross dug in his leather satchel and tossed the morning copy of the *Helena Independent Record* across the desk to the prosecutor. The bold faced headline on the front page proclaimed: "ANIMAL RIGHTS GROUP CLAIMS NUDE JOGGER VICTIM OF HOMICIDE".

The article under the headline cited the discovery of the knife wound to the rib and Dr. Hanning's inconclusive finding as to the cause of death. The article quoted from the preliminary autopsy report itself and then went on to quote Animals Forever's president Grover Arlen.

Arlen suggested that the Headwaters County authorities assigned the blame for the death to the mountain lion because they were unable to solve the murder. Arlen particularly denounced Sheriff Ben Green for killing the second mountain lion when in actuality, Kathy Clay died at the hands of another human being.

Stunned, Kirk set the paper back on the judge's desk.

"Your application pretty much confirms the facts set forth in the paper," said Judge Ross. "Their sources must have been accurate."

"Apparently so," Kirk said.

"Your application seems in order and in accordance with the statute," said Judge Ross. He reached for a quill pen next to an old fashioned ink well and signed the subpoena with his characteristic flare.

Kirk drove across Helena to the copper-domed state capitol building. He went to the insurance division of the state auditor's office and delivered the investigative subpoena and his fax number to an acquaintance in the legal department.

Kirk began the return trip to Townsend. As he drove, he pondered the article in the morning's paper and his thoughts kept returning to the one overriding question. How did

Animals Forever get access to Dr. Hanning's preliminary findings?

"This is the last cottonwood as you come up the creek," said Ben as he reached down and picked up one of the broad yellow leaves which lay next to the corrugated trunk of the massive tree. "The elevation must rise just enough at this point that they won't grow any further up the creek."

"I hadn't noticed, but I see what you mean now that you mention it," said Sergeant Frank.

Ben had parked on the Dry Creek road across from the pull out where the officers had discovered Kathy Clay's car. For the second time that morning, they crossed the road to the mouth of the tributary drainage which intersected Dry Creek.

"Let's work our way up the logging road to the body site and then come back on the other side of the creek like we did before," said Ben.

The Sergeant nodded and again proffered the dead woman's jeans and sweatshirt to the dog's discriminating nose.

"Little suche," commanded Frank as he began to lead the dog up the old logging road away from the former location of Kathy Clay's car.

Hans began pulling toward the sharp cut bank of the stream and Frank jerked once on the choker chain collar sternly. "No, this way. Little suche, little suche."

Hans returned and they began moving from side to side up the roadway. Ben followed several feet behind so he wouldn't interfere with the tracking process.

They returned to the body recovery site where Hans' body language once again indicated his detection of the scent

204

of Kathy Clay. They crossed the narrow stream and began working down the opposite side of the canyon.

In this lower wider portion of the drainage, the creek bottom was not as brushy. Large juniper trees shaded a ground covering of rust colored spongy moss. Hans wound through the maze created by the many junipers until they reached the point where the small stream flowed into a culvert crossing under the Dry Creek road.

The officers climbed up this steep portion of the road closing the complete circle of both sides of the drainage. The two men stretched out in the shade of the cottonwood tree and rested from the exertion of the climb.

Hans jerked against the leash in the direction of the cut bank.

"Platz." said Frank.

"Well, at least it was worth a try," began the sheriff. "I think . . . ."

"Wait a minute," interrupted Frank as he sat upright and slapped his palm against the side of his head. "Maybe I'm not as dumb as I look. Hans here's been trying to pull me toward the creek ever since we got here. I've been pulling him away and insisting he look elsewhere. Maybe he knows something we don't."

"We were just on the other side of the creek," said Ben. "If there's anything in that direction, he should have picked up the scent when we came back down the coulee."

"Unless whatever he's looking for is between here and there," Frank said.

Once again Sergeant Frank let the dog smell the jeans and sweatshirt. He unsnapped the leash from Hans' collar.

"Hans, little suche," said Frank.

The dog bolted across the road and disappeared over the bank. Ben and Sergeant Frank raced in pursuit.

Beneath the cut bank was a wide meander in the creek bed. Sometime over the ages, the small mountain stream had bypassed this loop of creek bed leaving a small flat space between the cut bank and the stream itself.

Hans stood in the middle of this space. Every muscle quivered from one end of his body to the other.

A long root protruded from the less steep portion of the bank and Ben used it as a rope easing his way into the bottom.

Ben crossed the flat gravel bar to the German Shepherd.

"Bingo." Ben said.

There loosely piled on the washed gravel surface lay two items of clothing.

Ben left Frank with the dog and returned to the Wagoneer for some evidence bags and his 35mm camera, then hurried back to the site.

After photographing the clothing in place, he carefully lifted the lavender halter top and examined it for any tears, rips or stains. He saw none and placed it into a brown paper bag. He followed the same procedure with the matching pair of running shorts.

A few feet closer to the cut bank, Hans stood in place, the muscles rippling under his sleek coat.

"What's he on to now?" asked Ben.

Frank walked over to Hans and examined the ground. He knelt, retrieved one of several small slips of paper and then quickly dropped it.

"What've you got?" asked Ben.

"To phrase it as nicely as I can," said Frank, "Hans has found where someone took a dump in the woods."

Ben joined Frank. On the ground scattered around a mound of human feces lay several small slips of paper.

206

"Lottery tickets," said Frank. "Apparently whoever crapped here did so without the benefit of toilet paper. They had to make do with losing lottery tickets."

"Looks like pretty shitty evidence to me," said Ben with a grin.

"At least it's evidence," said Frank. "It's way more than we had ten minutes ago."

Ben placed the lottery tickets and the feces into separate evidence bags.

Ben pulled himself back up the bank using the convenient root for support. Frank handed the evidence bags up to Ben and then pulled himself up the bank.

"If any of those tickets are winners, you gotta share with Hans and me," said Frank as they carried the evidence bags across the road to the Wagoneer.

"Deal," said Ben.

"How is it," Heidi asked. "that you can't tell me about a possible homicide, but you can give the complete forensic report to Animals Forever?"

"I never gave anything to anybody," said Kirk.

"It had to come from you or Ben Green," said Heidi. "I already checked with Dr. Hanning's office and they didn't release anything."

"I haven't a clue who gave them the report, but I intend to find out," said Kirk as he motioned Heidi into his private office.

Marge Johns handed Kirk a stack of message notes as he walked past the reception desk.

"Most of these are requests for call backs from the press," said Marge as the phone rang again.

"So what can you tell me about Animals Forever's allegations?" asked Heidi.

"Not much," said Kirk. "Apparently Animals Forever, you and everyone who had fifty cents for a morning's paper knows as much about this case as I do."

"So you can confirm the presence of the knife wound on Kathy Clay's body?"

"I can confirm that Headwaters County law enforcement officials are treating this case as a potential homicide and are conducting their investigation accordingly."

"Who is the focus of the investigation?" she asked.

"At the moment, we are suspicious of everyone," said Kirk. "Are you sure you were in Seattle on the night of the disappearance of Kathy Clay, Ms. Singer?"

"Isn't it true that Steve Clay is the primary suspect?"

"Like I said, no one is above suspicion at this point," Kirk said with a slight edge to his voice. "I'm afraid you have way more questions than I have answers."

"It's not just me," said Heidi pointing at the stack of call back messages on his desk. "Animals Forever's allegations hit like a bomb shell in a munitions factory. The general mystique of mountain lions combined with the celebrity element provided by Webster's horse created plenty of media interest on their own. The murder possibility took the story to critical mass."

"I sure didn't want to conduct this investigation under this type of public scrutiny," Kirk said. "I still can't believe Ben released the forensic report."

"But if he didn't, who did?"

"That's a whole 'nuther investigation," said Kirk as the interoffice intercom buzzed.

"Sorry to interrupt," said Marge, "but John Sharp is in the office and needs to visit with you for just a second."

"Send him in. We're just about finished anyway. I've already told Heidi all that I know about this case."

John Sharp strode through the doorway holding his gray felt cowboy hat in his hand.

"What brings you to town in the middle of the day?" asked Kirk.

"I'm lookin' for someone to help move some cows in the morning and wanted to know if you'd like to come along."

"I thought you just got done moving cows."

"We did," said Sharp, "but a lion got another calf at the top of Black Butte Gulch. We're gonna wean the calves and truck 'em back to the home ranch. I've got a lot of the neighbors lined up with their cattle trucks, but I need a few warm bodies to sit a horse to round up in the morning and then move the mother cows after the calves are weaned."

"Unless things go totally out of control, I'd be up for that," said Kirk. "Nugget could use the exercise."

"How 'bout you?" asked John turning to Heidi.

"I haven't ridden since I was eleven," said Heidi.

"Doc Adam's Arabian gelding is at the ranch and Doc can't go. You might as well come along."

Heidi turned and looked questioningly at Kirk.

"You'd do fine," said Kirk. "Doc's horse ain't got a mean bone in his body."

"I've got the nagging feeling that I'll regret this," said Heidi. "But I'm in."

"Great," said John. "I know you're busy with all the hoopla about murder and such. I'll get out of your hair. See you both bright and early in the morning."

As soon as John left, Heidi quickly refocused on Grover Arlen's suggestion that Headwaters County authorities blamed the death of Kathy Clay on a mountain lion to cover up the homicide.

"What a crock," Kirk said. "How could we do a cover up when we didn't even know it was murder until we received Dr. Hanning's report?"

"Good point," said Heidi as she reviewed the notes of her interviews.

"In fact, if you look closely at Dr. Hanning's report, there isn't one finding that's inconsistent with a death caused by mountain lion attack."

"Are you saying the death is not a homicide and is really due to a lion attack?" asked Heidi.

"All I'm saying is that based on the evidence available at the time, the sheriff's office was justified in their conclusions and the course of action they followed."

Heidi folded her notes and stood to leave.

"Where are you off to?" asked Kirk.

"I need to finish putting a story together and if I'm going to ride a horse in the morning, I need to pick up some cowboy boots and blue jeans. I'll see you later."

"Don't forget a cowboy hat," Kirk called after her.

Kirk spent the next two hours fielding calls from the media. Late in the afternoon, Ben came in.

"How'd Animals Forever get access to Hanning's report?" Ben asked.

"We've been blaming you," said Kirk.

"It's a good thing I'm back to defend myself. They sure as hell didn't get it from me."

"Did your dog come up with anything?" asked Kirk.

Ben informed the district attorney about their search and ultimate discoveries.

"Do you think there's a connection between the lottery tickets and the clothing?"

"In that location, there'd almost have to be," said Ben. "The tickets themselves were all issued prior to the date of Kathy Clay's disappearance. The oldest ticket was sold last April and the last one was sold in the middle of August. Each ticket plays the same numbers, 6,8,12,23,24 and powerball 3."

"That's not uncommon," said Kirk. "A lot of people always play the exact same numbers."

"I'm always afraid of doing that myself," said Ben. "The time I didn't buy a ticket would be the time my numbers would come up."

"Maybe the lottery tickets belonged to Kathy Clay," said Kirk. "How about a scenario in which she changes to go jogging but then nature calls. She doesn't have any toilet paper so she grabs some losing lotto tickets and climbs out of sight over the bank.

"She takes off her jogging clothes and does her business. On a whim, she decides to jog up the remote road in the nude."

"Great. We're back to a nude jogger theory," said Ben rolling his eyes. "Why'd she leave her jogging clothes in the bottom and more importantly how'd she get a knife in her ribs?"

"How 'bout while jogging naked, she comes across a bow hunter scouting elk the day before the opening of the season? He thinks he's come across the wild nymph of the woods who fate has provided to fulfill his every sexual fantasy. He grabs her and she fights him. He panics and the next thing you know she's dead and left to the whims of a marauding mountain lion."

"The sad part is that you've had even more outlandish theories," Ben said.

"I don't suppose you can learn anything from the lottery tickets themselves?" Kirk said.

"That's what I've been working on," said Ben. "I visited with Lottery Headquarters in Helena. About all they could tell me was that the tickets were all losers and that they had been purchased at Bob's Grocery here in Townsend. I plan on checking with the clerks to see if Kathy Clay ever purchased Lotto tickets."

"You may be able to do better than that," said Kirk.

"How so?"

"Bob's maintains an alphabetical file of Lotto entry forms for customers who play the same numbers week in and week out," Kirk said. "It saves time in the checkout lines if customers don't have to mark their numbers each and every time they play. If Kathy Clay was a regular player, there may be an entry form on file."

"I'll check that out first thing."

"If that doesn't pan out you can always ask Steve Clay about it when you interview him."

"Steve Clay has already contacted the office," said Ben.

"What's on his mind?"

"The dispatcher said he was irate that he first learned his wife may have been murdered by reading it in the morning paper."

"I can't blame him for being upset if he's innocent," Kirk said. "Seems like that's the type of reaction one would expect if he truly didn't know."

"Or the type of reaction one would expect if he wanted to appear innocent," said Ben. "I suppose I'd better call him and assure him that we didn't give out that information."

"Such an approach may be a better lead in than calling him up and asking him to come in and tell you about killing his wife," said Kirk. "It's really too bad you couldn't have interviewed him before the murder allegation went public. He may be very defensive."

"I'll just have to use my witty and charming nature," said Ben.

"God help us. I assume the dog didn't come up with a knife?"

"That's affirmative."

"How about the test on the foreign substance found on the body of Kathy Clay?" asked Kirk.

"I called Hanning's office. They said they'd get the results faxed to me tonight or first thing in the morning. I'll report back to you as soon as I know something more," Ben said as he rose and walked toward the door.

Marge Johns entered Kirk's office and handed him several pages of a fax.

"This just came in from the auditor's office," she said.

The first page under the cover sheet was a memo from Kirk's friend in the legal department of the auditor's office. The handwritten note read, "Kirk, this is the only life insurance policy I could locate on the life of Kathleen Murphy Clay. Hope it helps. You owe me for the quick service. Matt."

The next page was a copy of a document with a highly detailed graphic design of a bald eagle standing on the globe of the world. Under the eagle logo, fancy scrolled writing proclaimed, "AMERICAN FIDELITY LIFE INSURANCE & TRUST COMPANY".

Kirk leaned back in his chair and put his feet up on the oak desk and began to read the lengthy document and its amendments.

Later that evening, Kirk stroked the stiff bristled brush across Nugget's flank one last time. He stood back and admired his work. Nugget's coat had been the beneficiary of Kirk's nervous energy. He had brushed and re-brushed the horse while trying to call Ben. The sleek golden hide shone in the moonlight.

As he labored, he had replayed all the events leading up to the discovery of the knife wound to Kathy Clay. He had considered a dozen different scenarios but he had to admit to himself that at the moment all were nothing more than mere speculation.

His legal training told him that at the moment, he couldn't even prove the murder itself beyond a reasonable doubt let alone who did it.

Also nagging his consciousness was Sarah's bombshell. He had finally come to accept the divorce and the separation from his children. The possibility of reopening a chapter of his life that he thought closed seemed overwhelming.

He allowed himself to think about the possibility only briefly. The thought of having the children with him once again brought a smile to his lips. But the image of a smiling Heidi Singer also loomed strongly in his consciousness. He promised himself that once the current work-related crises were resolved, he would force himself to deal with his personal life.

Kirk pulled the halter rope free and led the overly groomed horse to the small corral where he could easily be caught in the morning. Kirk grabbed the cordless phone and dialed Ben's number.

Ben picked up the phone on the fourth ring.

"Where you been?" asked Kirk.

"Workin'."

"Did you do any good?"

214

"You were right about the lottery ticket file at Bob's grocery, but unfortunately there's no card on file for Kathy Clay. I asked the clerks and no one had any memory of her ever even buying a ticket."

"Damn. So much for that theory," said Kirk.

"Don't you get tired of being right all the time?" asked Ben. "I did take Bob's lotto card file with me. I'll sit down over the weekend and go through each card and see if I can come up with a match."

"That oughta keep you off the streets and out of trouble," Kirk said.

"It's probably not worth the effort," said Ben. "But it's not like we got a whole lot of leads to go on. How'd you make out with your investigative subpoena?"

"I got a copy of the life insurance policy," said Kirk. "And very interesting reading I might add."

"How so?"

"The policy was issued shortly after the Clays were married. It's a standard term policy in a face amount of $10,000."

"Nothing surprising or particularly incriminating about that old of a policy," said Ben. "And the amount hardly seems enough to prompt a murder."

"That's where it gets interesting," said Kirk. "This policy sat unchanged until the Clays moved to Montana. In June of this year, the base policy was amended to raise the face amount to $250,000 with a double indemnity provision in the event of an accident."

"Need I ask who the policy names as the beneficiary?"

"Mr. Steven Clay," said Kirk. "If Kathy Clay died as the result of a lion attack, he stands to receive $500,000."

"Now that is a sum worth killing for," said Ben whistling softly.

"It's sure something to ask him about," Kirk said.

"I tried talking with Steve Clay," said Ben. "He told me in no uncertain terms that he didn't want to be interviewed in any manner without his attorney being present. He told me to contact his attorney and arrange a time convenient for us both. Hardly seems like the actions of an innocent man."

"I agree, but you're not going to get much out of him with an attorney present. You'd probably better go through the motions though. You can at least get him pinned down to a story so that he can't conveniently change it every time we come across an incriminating piece of evidence."

"I'll call the defense attorney first thing Monday morning and set up a time," said Ben. "We sure don't have anything to lose."

"Anything else I should know?"

"I think you'll be real interested in knowing the results of the analysis of the foreign substance by the lab. All Dr. Hanning can say scientifically is that the substance was fat or grease of animal origin."

"Can he say anything unscientifically?"

"He said that he also applied the Dr. Hanning smell test and if he doesn't miss his guess, it's bacon grease."

Chapter XIII

Saturday, September 13th

A red ball of sun crept over the horizon as John Sharp left the county road and continued up the two track trail which clung to the bottom of the Ross Gulch canyon. He stopped the pickup and horse trailer before a green metal gate.

Bounding from the passenger side of the truck, Kirk ran to the gate, unlatched the gate chain and swung the gate open. John drove through onto the Sharp Ranch property.

Spears of frost covered grass glistened in the headlights. Heidi shivered even though she was plenty warm, sandwiched along with Misty, between the two men. The deep streaks of crimson lighting the morning sky enhanced her feeling of anticipation for the new experience.

The winding road stopped at a set of corrals situated next to a quaking aspen grove. A weathered, hand-hewed log cabin with a sod roof and an old outhouse were the only remnants left of the historic homestead.

"This was the Ross place," Misty said to Heidi. "It was one of many homesteads which covered every tillable 160 acre parcel in this area after the turn of the century. The old school house sat just over the hill."

"What happened to them all?" asked Heidi.

"In this part of the west, 160 acres wasn't and still isn't enough land to make a living," lectured Misty. "Congress based the Homestead Act on the eastern arrogance that because 160 acres was enough acreage in the east and Midwest, it would also be enough in the arid west."

"Just another example of people outside of Montana dictating policy to the poor dumb residents who don't know what's in their best interest," said Kirk. "You'd think sooner or later someone would pay some attention to those who actually live and work on the land."

"Those who don't learn from history are destined to repeat it," said Misty. "The homesteads were eventually all swallowed up by the larger ranches."

"My hearing on Friday with Animals Forever is history repeating itself," said Kirk. "The vast majority of the members of Animals Forever live out-of-state but they sure don't hesitate to tell us how we ought to live."

"A little grumpy this morning, aren't we," said John. "Did someone not get their morning coffee?"

"Don't' get him started," Heidi said. "If he gets on his soap box, we'll be here all day."

"Let's get to movin' cattle," said John. "He can tell it to the cows."

"Probably be a more receptive audience anyway," grumbled Kirk as he climbed out of the pickup.

While William J. and Joe Durham pulled in by the corrals, the two couples unloaded the horses from the trailer. Kirk tightened the cinch on the white Arabian and held onto the halter rope while Heidi positioned herself to mount. She placed her left boot in the stirrup and lifted her right leg to swing into the saddle. Kirk planted the palm of his hand firmly on the seat of the tight blue jeans which clearly displayed the shapely curves of the woman's figure and gave her a boost.

"When I retire, I'm gonna get a job at a dude ranch doin' nothin' but helpin' good lookin' women get on their horses," Kirk said and grinned.

Heidi was too nervous to even attempt a response to his remark. She slipped her right foot in the opposite stirrup and sat stiffly in the saddle.

"Relax a little," said Kirk. "Try to put more weight on

your legs and not balance so much with your arms and shoulders."

After some further instruction, Kirk swung aboard Nugget.

In single file, Kirk, Heidi, John and Misty, flanked by the three cow dogs, rode up a long sloping ridge toward the southeast corner of the pasture. As they topped the ridge, they stopped and gave the horses a short breather.

Across from them, they could see William J. and Joe Durham riding up the opposite slope. The Arabian whinnied at the sight of William J.'s white horse on the north ridge.

"Doc's horse and ol' Snowball are buddies," said Kirk. "That Arab will be the lonesomest horse in the world once William J. gets out of sight."

In spite of her nervousness, Heidi found herself thoroughly enjoying the experience. She talked softly to Doc's horse who, in accordance with local custom, was also named "Doc." She became enthralled at the motion of the animal's ears as they responded to the inflections of her voice. She slowly began to relax and feel comfortable in the saddle.

At the boundary fence, they turned and John called to Heidi, "Head 'em up and move 'em out."

"What do I do?" asked Heidi looking back at Kirk.

"Just ride behind 'em and yell," he said. "I'll show you."

Giving Nugget some rein, he urged the horse in the direction of a cow and calf which stood looking defiantly at the horse and rider. "Hey cow, Hey cow," he shouted as he slapped the palm of his hand against his thigh. The cow and calf turned and raced up the ridge.

Heidi followed his example and turned Doc toward several animals laying in the sagebrush. "Hey cow, hey cow," she called in a tentative voice. The cows remained stationary ignoring her admonitions.

"You call that a yell?" said Kirk. "Let 'em know you mean business."

Drawing a deep breath, Heidi let out a shrill shriek that Kirk thought sounded like a cross between an elk bugle and a train whistle. At this noise, the cattle scrambled to their feet and ran bucking and jumping up the slope following the pair hazed by Kirk.

"You're a natural," shouted Kirk smiling broadly.

The sharp yip of the dogs drew Heidi's attention. She turned to her left and saw the dogs dart into a clump of willows along the spring that welled into a bog at the bottom of the slope.

As quickly as the dogs entered the willows, a mass of black cows and calves exploded out the other side. The cows bawled loudly as the dogs continued their pursuit and nipped at the heels of the stragglers.

Across the rolling pasture, cattle came out of every crevice and swale to investigate the commotion. The cows took note of the advancing dogs and riders and either ran toward the growing herd of cattle, or headed over the ridge in the direction of the corrals.

The riders rode back and forth behind the wide line of cattle. Heidi yelled until she was hoarse.

When the herd of cattle topped the ridge, the cows began running down the long gentle sagebrush slope toward the quaking aspen grove adjacent to the corrals. North of the old homestead, William J. and Joe Durham pushed another herd of cattle down the coulee above the corrals.

Heidi reined in her horse at the top of the slope and watched the scene unfold before her. Cattle streamed down the ridges ahead of the dogs and riders. The sun was now up in the sky offering a measure of warmth. The layer of morning frost had melted and the fall grass and quaking aspen leaves shimmered in the sunlight.

Her overriding impression was of motion. Everywhere she looked dogs, horses and black cattle descended on the wooden corrals.

The white Arabian stood at attention also surveying the scene. At the sight of William J.'s horse across the far coulee, Doc whinnied and started moving forward at a brisk pace.

Heidi grabbed onto the saddle horn and held her breath. The horse broke into a gallop and quickly made up the distance between the ridgetop and the tail end of the cattle entering the quaking aspen grove.

To her relief, Doc slowed to a walk behind the milling mass of cattle. Fortunately, the pasture fence narrowed in the grove of trees, funneling the cattle into the corral and larger fenced holding pen. The crescendo of bawling cows and calves reverberated throughout the aspen patch.

Kirk rode alongside the white Arabian and shouted to Heidi above the din, "Whadya think?"

"Amazing." shouted back Heidi.

She followed Kirk to the corral fence where they dismounted and secured the horses to one of the pole rails.

"What now?" asked Heidi.

"We separate the mother cows from the calves," said Kirk.

"How do you do that?"

"Just sit back and watch."

Kirk let the gate leading into the corral swing open a few feet and then stood in the narrow opening. William J. and John entered the enclosure and began hazing the mother cows toward the gate opening.

Kirk stepped aside letting the mother cows through but filled the opening whenever a calf tried a dash for freedom. Within a short period of time, all the mother cows milled outside the corral fence bawling for the calves still trapped inside.

During the separation process, several stock trucks had arrived at the homestead. Once the cows were "cut out", the neighboring ranchers began herding the calves up the slanted ramp of the loading chute into one of the stock trucks.

As soon as one truck was loaded and pulled away, another truck would back into the loading chute and the loading process would begin again. The corral full of calves emptied in increments of twenty to thirty calves a load. Shortly before noon, William J. and Joe Durham pulled away in the Sharp Ranch stock trucks with the last two loads of calves.

Kirk carried a wicker basket full of lunch from the cab of the flatbed. He joined Misty and Heidi who were sitting on the ground with their backs against the wall of the homestead cabin. They leisurely basked in the fall sunshine.

A concerned looking John strode purposefully from the corral to the truck. From above the sun visor, he retrieved a dog-eared note book and began thumbing through the pages filled with columns of numbers.

"What's wrong?" asked Misty.

"When we were sortin', I jotted down the numbers of a couple dry cows. I want to see if they're the mothers of the lion killed calves or if we're missing some calves we don't know about."

John ran his index finger down the column that corresponded to the ear tag numbers of the dry cows and then across the page to the column which corresponded to the number on the bright yellow ear tag of their calves.

"Damn." he said. "The black bawlie is the mother of one of the calves Dad found next to the Chappel sections, but I can't account for the calf of the other cow. I think we're missing another one."

"There's nothing you can do about it now," said Misty as she tossed him a clear plastic sandwich baggie. "You may as well eat."

John removed the sandwich and took three quick bites. He tossed the remainder to Daddy Dog who sat in the shade of the truck watching his every movement. The dog quickly gulped down the morsel while growling ferociously at the other two dogs who came to share in the treat.

"I've kind of lost my appetite," he said as he flopped down on the ground next to his wife.

Trying to change his mood, he turned to Heidi and asked, "Did you enjoy your first calf weaning?"

"It was glorious," said Heidi. "I'm really glad you talked me into coming. It feels grand being here . . . so romantic . . . such a sense of adventure. I feel like I'm a kindred spirit with all the cowboys who ever rode this range. I feel like all my senses have been heightened by the countless sights, smells and sounds. Things even taste better out here. I swear this is the best sandwich I've ever eaten. I enjoyed the experience far more than I ever imagined."

"A simple 'yes' would have sufficed," Kirk said. "But no doubt about it, you made a memory today."

"Oh God, don't get him started on his 'memories define your life' theory," said John. "We'll be here all day."

"I've heard it before," said Heidi. "You're right. We would be here all day, but I will never forget this morning."

"I sense support for my theory," said Kirk.

"What's on tap for this afternoon?" asked Heidi changing the subject.

"We're going to move these cows west to the Hogback pasture," advised Sharp pointing to the two spiny knobs in the distance. "Hopefully out of lion country."

"Lion country may be just wherever you put the cows," said Kirk.

"You may be right," said John. "But the lions haven't tackled a full grown cow yet. Maybe with the calves at home we'll be spared any further losses."

After lunch, the riders gathered the cows and trailed them across what initially appeared to Heidi as a rolling grassy bench. In reality, the terrain concealed a number of gulches which weren't revealed until they rode up on them. The cows moved slowly but steadily. Heidi caught herself occasionally dozing in the bright afternoon sun.

When the last coulee was negotiated and the cows were finally herded into the desired pasture, the riders retraced their route back to the corrals. The speed of their return was enhanced by several galloping spurts across the flat portions of the grassy bench.

Heidi dismounted by the old homestead cabin. She bent over slightly as she started to lead the horse to the trailer.

"I feel eighty years old," she said. She felt the stiffness in her knees and thighs. "I hurt in places I never even knew I had places."

Smiling, John took the reins from her and jumped the Arabian into the trailer.

"You think you're sore now, just wait until morning," said John.

"I can wait," said Heidi as Kirk offered his hand and boosted her up into the cab of the four wheel drive pickup.

"Let's say we go out tonight for dinner, drinks, and dancing," said John as he turned the truck and trailer around and headed back down the Ross Gulch canyon.

"You've got to be kidding." said Heidi. "All I want to do is fill a tub full of hot water and lay in it until I turn into a prune."

"I have a meeting tonight," said Misty, "so count me out."

"Looks like we've been stood up," said John to Kirk. "Doc Adams, Professor Jackson and a couple more of the boys are supposed to be staying at the Dry Creek cabin. How 'bout you and I head up the creek and see if we can bum supper."

"You sure you don't feel up to going out?" asked Kirk.

"I'm real sure," said Heidi.

"It's a plan then," said Kirk. "Let's drop Heidi off at the motel and we can pick up our gear on the way back through."

Riding cramped in the cab of the pickup did nothing for Heidi's tight, sore legs. At the motel, she would have fallen out onto the pavement had not Kirk caught her.

Kirk laughed and told her, "We're not laughing at you. We're laughing with you."

"Right," she said trying to sound angry, but she couldn't help laughing at her own predicament as she slowly hobbled across the motel parking lot to her door.

Heidi limped into the bathroom and began filling the bathtub. She sat back on the bed and with great difficulty lifted her left leg. With much effort and groaning, she worked off one of the new cowboy boots. She rested briefly and then repeated the process with the other foot. A similar Herculean effort was needed to remove the tight blue jeans.

"You're a wimp, Heidi Singer," she told herself.

She tested the water with her hand and then turned off the faucets. She placed one foot in the tub and then the phone rang.

She thought about ignoring it but reluctantly admitted to herself that old habits are hard to break. She knew that she'd never been able to ignore a ringing phone. Resignedly, she stepped back out of the tub and reached the phone on the seventh ring.

She listened briefly to the caller and then demanded, "Who is this?"

She thought the call a prank but still reached for the pen and note pad on the Gideon Bible.

"Repeat that again, please?" she implored.

The caller repeated the information in the same flat monotone voice. She wrote frantically.

"Where? What time?"

She jotted the information on the pad and then stated, "I'll need to meet you and confirm....", but the line went dead.

She tossed the pad back onto the dresser. She sighed deeply and eyed the inviting bath. Hoax or no hoax, she knew her journalistic curiosity wouldn't allow her to relax and enjoy the luxury of the warm water anymore than she'd been able to ignore the ringing of the phone.

She quickly rebuttoned her blouse and struggled back into the jeans. Completely avoiding the cowboy boots, she slipped on her running shoes and limped out the door to the rental car.

Kirk and Sharp crossed the bridge of the Dry Creek cabin and stepped into the dim ring of light cast from the propane lantern mounted on the corner of the one room cabin.

"I don't suppose a poor starvin' cowboy could bum some table scraps?" Sharp asked of Doc Adams and Professor Jackson who were standing next to a large barbecue grill. Coals of charcoal glowed a bright orange under a mesh grill covered with split halves of chicken.

"It'd be easier to sneak the sun past a rooster than to sneak a meal past you two," said Jackson.

"I suppose we can sacrifice and divide up our meager provisions," said Adams. "My boy'll probably have to go to bed hungry, but we'll honor our Christian duty and share."

"From the amount of chicken on that grill, I'd expect a National Guard convoy to be bivouacked here," said Kirk. "We worked up a pretty healthy appetite chasing cows, I just hope it's enough."

"Did you get the calves weaned?" asked Adams as he used a plastic squirt bottle to quell the flare of the coals.

"It went like clockwork," said Sharp. "The calves are home and the cows are moved."

"I couldn't make it this morning," said Adams. "But I was with you in spirit."

"In your absence, you were represented by your horse," said Sharp. "Heidi Singer rode Doc."

"She got along okay?"

"She did fine," said Sharp.

"And she looks a damn sight better on top of the Arabian than you do," said Kirk.

"She is pretty easy on the eyes," said Adams. "Kirk, you'd better up and marry that girl before she comes to her senses."

"I've considered that option," said Kirk. "But I also talked with Sarah the other night and she's pushing to get back together and see if we can make it work again."

"You're not actually considering getting back with that woman." said Adams. "If you want more pain in your life, why don't you just let me beat you with a broom handle. It'd be a whole lot cheaper."

"You're probably right," said Kirk. "But I really miss Lisa and Jenny and I'd like for them to grow up in a small town away from city influences. It's more than just the kids though. My relationship with Sarah's the only thing in my life

I could never make work. I've always accomplished everything I ever undertook. I'm not bragging because a lot of those things didn't come easy or naturally. It just seemed I could always struggle, sweat and persevere until I found a way to reach a goal.

"I still feel like such a failure because of the divorce. We seemed so right in so many ways. She never acclimated to life in Montana. I just feel like it might be worth the effort to try it again."

"Some people just aren't right for each other," Adams said. "You can't put a square peg in a round hole."

"I've thought a lot about that too," said Kirk. "Look at today. Heidi was thrilled. She felt a sense of romance and adventure in the great outdoors. Even though she could barely walk by the end of the day, she came away from weaning calves thinking she'd had a wonderful day.

"All Sarah would've seen is sweat, bugs and cow shit. She'd have hated every minute and complained all day long."

"So what are you going to do?" asked Sharp.

"I think I'll go hunting," said Kirk evasively as he realized the extensiveness of his out of character confession. "But first I think I'll have a beer."

He walked to the front porch of the cabin and fished a Coors Light from the icy slush of the old washtub.

"So you'll be giving Sharpie another bow hunting lesson tomorrow?" asked Jackson.

"We'll go out for the morning hunt," said Kirk. "I promised Heidi I'd take her fishing in the afternoon."

"It doesn't look like I'm gonna have much need for those bow hunting skills," said Sharp making a confession of his own. "We were going to expand the guiding business into the bow season to help pay for the Chappel sections. With the lion kills and the drop in cattle prices, I don't think we'll be able to swing the deal."

228

"That's too bad," said Kirk. "What ya going to do?"

"We haven't decided. May try selling the property to Webster. We may forfeit the earnest money. We may just sit back and pray that the cattle market takes an upturn before the closing date. If you come up with any good ideas let me know."

"I'll give the matter some thought," Kirk said.

"What about the reimbursement money from Animals Forever?" asked Adams. "Didn't you file a claim?"

"A representative from Animals Forever is supposed to come out with the livestock inspector on Monday to visit the kill sites," said Sharp. "It would sure help if we could get that money."

By the light of Professor Jackson's flashlight, Doc Adams turned the chicken halves and then brushed the pieces with barbecue sauce.

"Jackson, get a plate," said Adams. We're almost ready to eat."

After the hearty meal, Doc Adams pushed his chair back and looking at the huge pile of chicken bones on Kirk's plate asked, "How was your chicken?"

"Burnt," said Kirk. "But just the way I like it."

"From the papers, it looks like you've got another murder to solve." said Adams.

"It appears that way," Kirk said. "Although in some ways this case reminds me more of an arson investigation. With arson you first have to prove the fire was deliberately set and then worry about proving who did it. We're facing the same two step process with the death of Kathy Clay. We've got to first prove she was murdered and then try to identify the party responsible."

"My money's on the husband," Jackson said.

"I'll take that bet, too," said Adams.

229

"I'd lean that direction myself," said Sharp. "I read somewhere that over half of all murders are committed by family members."

"I guess you three have this case pretty well wrapped up," said Kirk. "Based on your gut feelings and betting predilections, I'll file a murder complaint and issue an arrest warrant for Steve Clay first thing Monday morning."

"Glad to be of assistance," said Adams. "Let us know if there's anything else we can help you with."

Heidi Singer felt foolish. Driving from the motel, she turned onto the main street of the small town and drove slowly past the three-block business district. She circled twice around the city park located directly across the street from the Headwaters County Courthouse.

A huge silver water tower with "TOWNSEND" painted on the side stood in the center of the park. Rising above every other structure in the community, the water tower dominated the skyline of the town.

Her surveillance revealed the park to be deserted except for three picnic tables scattered throughout the well-kept grounds. For safety reasons, she parked on the main street under a street light. Trying to appear casual and unassuming, she wandered into the park.

Beneath the water tower, the local V.F.W. organization had erected a four foot tall marble stone as a monument to all war veterans killed in combat. She approached the stone in a roundabout manner.

The closer she got to the stone, the more likely it seemed that the call was nothing more than a childish prank. She wondered to herself if the Candid Camera television series were still running. A practical joke by Kirk seemed even more likely. She closed the distance between herself and the polished piece of marble.

The manila envelope lay so flat on the top of the marble stone that she couldn't see it until she stood directly over the stone itself. Spying the envelope, she self consciously glanced around the park. Seeing no one, Heidi picked up the envelope, pivoted and marched back to her car. She quickly drove back to the motel.

After bolting the door, she sliced open the envelope with a nail file and removed the contents. The graphic design of an eagle perched on a globe first caught her eye. Beneath this logo written in scroll were the words "AMERICAN FIDELITY LIFE INSURANCE & TRUST COMPANY". She quickly scanned down the page to "Insured: Kathleen Murphy Clay." and further down to "Beneficiary: Steven Clay."

Chapter XIV

Sunday, September 14th

"I can't believe you shot a bull with a blunt," said Doc Adams.

"Seemed like the thing to do at the time," said Kirk. "I'm not ready to give up the anticipation that comes with the hunt. I've killed enough elk in my time. Anymore I don't have to kill one to enjoy the experience. I enjoyed thunking that 'ol boy in the ribs just as much as if I'd arrowed him dead right in his tracks."

Adams, Sharp and Kirk walked down the narrow jeep trail. Across the coulee, they could see Professor Jackson and the two boys paralleling their movements down the opposite ridge toward the vehicles parked below on Deep Creek.

The sun had risen high in the sky. The temperature hovered in the mid-sixties. With the morning hunt over, the three men laughed and joked as they lazily stumbled along the trail allowing the other hunters to catch up to them.

"The thanks I get for trying to herd a bull elk your direction," said Kirk trying to sound exasperated. "I guess next time I'll just shoot it myself."

"That's got to be the luckiest bull alive," said Adams. "He blunders into the range of a bow hunter and gets shot with a blunt. Go figure."

"You up for another hunt today?" Adams asked Sharp when they got to the vehicles.

"No, I'd better make sure Kirk gets home safe."

"Didn't know it was your day to watch him," said Adams.

"Can't be too careful," said Sharp. "The last time we let him go on his own we lost him."

Kirk and Sharp loaded their gear in Sharp's diesel and headed down the Deep Creek Highway.

"I've been thinking about your land problem," said Kirk as he looked out over the creek meandering through the hay meadows in the bottom below the highway. "I've got an idea."

"Beginner's luck," Sharp said.

"No really, what do you think about selling a conservation easement to Ray Webster?"

"A conservation easement?"

"It's an easement whereby a landowner sells certain rights to his property such as the right to subdivide, the right to log or graze cattle. It can be any one of the bundle of rights that we attorneys call 'property.' The way it works is that the development rights are transferred to a nonprofit entity like the Land Alliance or the Nature Conservancy. The conservation group then monitors and assures that the land is never developed and is managed in accordance with the terms of the easement. The value of the rights transferred away is tax deductible, of course."

"Why would Webster want to pay for a conservation easement and donate it when he could buy the whole piece when we default on the buy/sell agreement."

"He might find that preferable to having your big new subdivision along his north boundary," Kirk said.

"We aren't planning any subdivision."

"Webster doesn't know that," said Kirk with a sly grin. "As I see it, you don't give a damn whether you have the right to subdivide that property. All you want to do is run a bunch of cows for a few months during the summer. It wouldn't change your use of the property one iota if you conveyed away every right to use the property except hunting and cattle grazing."

233

"You really think Webster might be interested in such a proposal?" asked Sharp.

"What could it hurt to ask? He can't do anymore than say 'no.' Conservation easements have some attractive tax advantages to someone who generates as much income as Webster. I think if some silver tongued individual were to approach him right, Webster could be made to see the wisdom of such an approach."

"You wouldn't be that silver-tongued individual?" Sharp asked.

"With the murder investigation heating up, this may be the week from Hell, but once things calm down, I'd sure be willing to approach Webster with a proposal. Why don't you bounce the idea off William J.?"

"I'll do that this evening," said Sharp. "I know Webster's no fan of subdivisions."

"Your scaring the crap out of him that morning probably didn't help the cause any, but I still think it's worth a shot," Kirk said.

Sharp pulled off of the highway onto the graveled road and stopped at the Kirk homestead. Kirk grabbed his gear and bounded up the stairs into the house.

He noticed the red light on the answering machine and pushed the play button.

"I'm on to a big story and can't go fishing," said Heidi's voice. "I'll call you later."

"I'm sure glad I hurried off the hill," Kirk said. He went back outdoors and quickly assembled his fly rod. He walked across the hay meadow to the water's edge of Deep Creek.

Heidi scrolled back through the rough draft on the screen of her laptop. The article was good. Unfortunately, it was based solely on a purported copy of a life insurance policy.

The source of the policy remained a mystery. She needed confirmation and on a Sunday afternoon it seemed impossible to obtain.

She considered just running the article. She felt certain that for whatever reason, she had been handed an exclusive and timely story. Either or both of those elements could vanish with a day's delay.

She agonized over a dozen different avenues but none offered a solution. She was about to admit defeat and scrap the project for the day.

"Why not get the confirmation straight from the horse's mouth?" she whispered.

She reached for the phone book and found Steve Clay's number. She pondered her approach and then dialed the number. He answered immediately.

"May I speak with Steven C. Clay?" she asked in a business like tone of voice.

"Speaking."

"Mr. Clay I need to verify some information about a life insurance policy with American Fidelity Life & Trust. My records show that policy #A4567892 was issued in 1984 naming you as the beneficiary. The policy was then amended in June of this year. This amendment increased the face amount of the policy to $250,000 with a double indemnity coverage in case of accident."

"Yes, that's correct," said Clay. "I sent you the claim form and a certified copy of the death certificate last week. Is there a problem?"

"No, everything's fine," Heidi said. "I have all the information I need at this time. Have a nice day Mr. Clay."

Heidi hung up. She had a twinge of guilt but then

acknowledged to herself that she hadn't lied or made any false representations about her identity. Heidi proofed the article an additional time and then plugged the modem on the computer into the telephone jack. She pushed the transmission button and fell back on the bed.

"Wire," called Pete Roemer pointing back to the long strand of barbed wire laying in the sagebrush. Ray Webster instantly reined his horse, making a wide detour around the rusty tentacles of steel.

Roemer looked back and did a double take. He reined in the bay stopping crossways in the trail. Roemer gazed intently along the top of the bluff above them.

"What'd ya see?" asked Webster easing his horse alongside the ranch hand.

"I must have mountain lions on the brain," said Roemer. "I thought I caught a glimpse of a lion moving along the bluff. I guess I'm turning into an old woman and starting to see things."

"Must have been a mirage," said Webster as he too scanned the rugged bluff that loomed above them.

Failing to see anything on the ridgeline but rock and scrub timber, the two riders resumed their trek down the narrow trail.

"Damn the wire anyway." said Webster. "That's all we need is to have another horse cut to ribbons."

"I'm trying to get it cleaned up a little at a time," said Roemer, "but there's just so much of it laying around the hills. When the homesteaders pulled out of this country, they pulled up stakes and walked away."

"Think of the work that went into that fence," said Webster as he pointed to the intermittent line of rotting and broken posts still visible on the steep slope. "I'd hate to have to walk that route let alone build a fence along it."

"And to think it was built without the benefit of a chain saw," said Roemer. "I built a lot of fence the same way when I was a youngster."

"There's a lot of history in these hills," Webster said. "I don't suppose you know who homesteaded this place?"

"I haven't a clue," said Roemer. "It'd been abandoned long before I ever came to this country."

"A lot of hopes and dreams went into these home-steads."

"Not to mention blood, sweat and tears," added Roemer.

"And not a thing left to show for all that effort," said Webster.

"Nothing but some old cedar posts and scattered pieces of wire."

"Makes you wonder if a hundred years from now anyone will even know we've been here," said Webster.

"We can always hope that'll be the case," said Roemer.

The mature tom mountain lion raised slightly off his belly and watched the riders fade in the twilight. He clung to the dark shadows and trotted briskly down the side of the bluff on the trail of the horses.

While Roemer and Webster negotiated the switch backs of the trail angling into the narrow valley, the lion paused on a large limestone formation which jutted out of the timber on the knob overlooking the chalet. As the full moon rose and illuminated the meadow beyond the chalet, the lion bounded off the rocky ledge. He raced down the slope until he reached the steep bank overlooking the small stream which fed Webster's fish pond.

Below this bank, a yearling Longhorn steer stood drinking from the creek. The lion sprang from the bank.

In one motion, he clamped the strong jaws on the neck of the steer and pulled the animal to the ground. He ate and then piled the gravel, sand and driftwood of the creek bank on top of the carcass. With his belly noticeably distended, the lion climbed back up the ridge and settled into a bed of pine grass in a thick pocket of timber. After meticulously cleaning his face and paws, the lion stretched out and slept in the long shadows created by the full moon.

The figures were beginning to blur in the light of Ben's desk lamp. He sat comparing the numbers of the lotto tickets found near Kathy Clay's clothes with the lotto entry forms kept on file at Bob's Grocery.

He had started early in the morning and completed comparing all of the file cards from "A" through "M," before allowing himself an excursion on Canyon Ferry Reservoir.

The sun and fresh air had been a welcome respite but now those same elements had left him drowsy. He had forced himself to examine the entry forms indexed in "N" through "V." All that remained were the entry forms behind the single "W,X,Y,Z" index card.

Ben laid out several of the "W" entry forms, "Wade", "Walker", "Watterson". He continued the grueling process and jerked upright in his chair. He placed one of the lotto tickets next to one of the entry forms. There side by side were matching numbers including the "power ball." Ben gazed in disbelief at the name at the top of the lotto entry form.

He called Kirk.

"I finished going through Bob's index cards," said Ben. "In a million years, you'll never guess whose card matches the lotto tickets we found up Dry Creek."

"Don't keep me in suspense. Whose name is on the entry form?"

"Scott Edward Woods."

"Deputy Woods? Our Deputy Woods?"

"One and the same."

"Why are his losing lotto tickets next to Kathy Clay's clothes?" Kirk asked.

"That's an excellent question. I intend to ask him the first chance I get."

"You don't think this explains how Animals Forever got the forensic report?"

"I don't know what to think," said Ben. "I've never had any occasion to doubt Woods in any way."

"He does have a reputation as a lady's man," said Kirk. "You don't think he and Kathy Clay may have had something going on the side?"

"Not to my knowledge," Ben said. "As far as I know, he's been chasin' around with your secretary for the last few months."

"Deputy Woods and Marge Johns have been seeing each other?"

"Didn't you know?"

"She never said a word," Kirk said and laughed. "Wait until I see her."

"How do you think we should approach Woods?" asked Ben.

"Why don't you have him report to my office first thing in the morning," said Kirk. "You can advise him of his

Miranda rights and show him what we got. I think his reaction will tell us a lot. Maybe there's a logical explanation for all of this."

"I'd like to hear it," said Ben. "But I sure do wish it'd been Deputy Anderson instead of Woods."

"Why so?"

"Because I'd have found the entry form at 9:00 this morning instead of having waded through a zillion other cards in the file index."

"You should have started with Z'" said Kirk.

"Now you tell me. See ya bright and early."

Kirk set the phone on the counter and tried to imagine how Deputy Woods could be connected to Kathy Clay, her clothes or to the discovery of bacon grease on her body.

Chapter XV

Monday, September 15th

"Looks to me like we've got somebody else to ask about a possible leak," said Ben tossing the morning paper onto Kirk's desk. Kirk unfolded the paper to view the front page.

A bold headline proclaimed, "HUSBAND TO BENEFIT FROM WIFE'S DEATH". Kirk quickly read the first line of the article under Heidi's byline. The article set forth the exact terms of the life insurance policy and recounted the discovery of the knife wound by the pathologist.

"How'd she find out about the life insurance policy?" asked Kirk.

"Beats the hell out of me," said Ben, "but she must have a pretty good source. She's got the dates, the policy amounts and even the policy number itself pegged. I'd suggest you ask her about where she got her information."

"I intend to," said Kirk. "One thing's for sure, someone is leaking information. I also want to ask Woods some pointed questions about that."

"You'll have your chance. He called me on his patrol car radio just as I was leaving the office. He's on his way."

A relaxed Deputy Woods sauntered into the district attorney's office.

"Good morning, gentlemen," he called as he plopped down in the hardwood chair across from Kirk's desk. "What's up?"

"We need to ask you a few questions," Kirk said. "But first the sheriff needs to advise you of your rights."

Ben pulled the small business size card from his wallet and read the familiar Miranda Warning which advised the deputy of his right to remain silent. The warning further informed the deputy of his right to an attorney and if he couldn't afford an attorney that one would be appointed for him.

"Being fully advised of these rights, do you wish to continue to speak to us?" asked Ben.

"This is a joke, right?" Woods smiled.

Kirk removed an 8x10 photo from a file and slid it across the desk to the deputy.

"The lotto tickets next to the pile of human dung shown in this photo all contain the same numbers as the the entry form you have on file at Bob's Grocery. What do you have to say about that?"

"I knew the Forest Service was adopting tougher rules and regulation, but I didn't know it'd become a federal offense to take a shit in the woods."

Kirk smiled.

"Such conduct is probably against their regulations," said Kirk. "But that's out of my jurisdiction."

"This is what concerns us," said Ben removing another photo which depicted the running clothes.

Ben handed the deputy a third photo showing the position of the clothes and lotto tickets in relationship to each other.

Woods examined the three photos.

"I did take a dump at this site," he said. "After Tucker and I first examined Clay's car, nature called. I knew you and the search and rescue unit were coming up the creek so I climbed down the steep bank to get out of sight. When I got down there with my pants around my ankles, I realized I hadn't brought any toilet paper. I looked through my wallet and pulled out all my losing lotto tickets."

"What about the jogging clothes?" asked Ben.

242

"They weren't there," Woods said. "I'd have noticed that lavender color for sure. There's no way I could've missed 'em."

Kirk asked some pointed questions about the forensic reports and the life insurance policy but the deputy denied any knowledge.

As Woods walked through the reception area after being excused, Kirk noticed the wink Woods gave Marge.

"What ya think?" asked Ben.

"My every instinct tells me he's tellin' the truth. I don't think he's our leak and I think Kathy Clay's jogging clothes were placed there after her death and after the discovery of her body."

"What does that mean?"

"It rules out the jogging in the nude theory. But beyond that I'm not sure. I'm speculating that the presence of bacon grease may be the key clue. If Kathy Clay were killed and the killer wanted to encourage scavengers such as lions and coyotes, bacon grease would be a likely scent lure. I'm betting the killer removed the victim's clothes to encourage predation and to avoid the grease stains."

"So who did it?"

"That's your job," Kirk said. "I'll prosecute someone when you find 'em. In the meantime, I think I'll see if I can have lunch with a certain journalist."

"Where's the brand?" asked Frank Boesk, the representative from Animals Forever. He was a slight man with a goatee and coke bottle lensed glasses.

"It's on the right hip," said John Sharp. "Same place as the other three."

"Let's look at it," said Boesk.

Livestock Inspector Brad Logan and John Sharp turned over the decaying carcass exposing the Sharp brand on the black hide. Boesk made several notations on the pad he carried. He sheltered his remarks on the clipboard like a school child protecting his test paper from the prying eyes of other students.

As with the examination of the other carcasses, Boesk asked only a few pointed questions and kept his conclusions to himself.

"These are the claw marks I noted in my report," said Logan pointing with the sharp end of a stick.

"I've seen enough," said Boesk. "Let's move on."

John joined William J. in the ranch truck. They drove toward the most recent lion kill site at the top of Black Butte Gulch. Logan and Boesk followed in Logan's vehicle.

"What ya think?" asked William J.

"Who knows," said John. "The guy's impossible to read. He hasn't said three words and seems irritated when anyone tries to explain or point out anything."

"You'd think he'd pay a little attention to the livestock inspector," William J. said. "After all, cattle are his area of expertise."

"He projects the attitude that he's the only one who knows anything worth knowing," said John.

"Little man syndrome," said William J. "I've seen it a million times. A lot of short men go through life with a chip on their shoulder."

"He does make it hard to be cordial," said John. "But he can be cantankerous as all get out as long as he gives us the money."

William J. drove across a long sagebrush flat and then

244

climbed through stands of fir trees until he crossed into the grassy clear cuts on the other side of the ridge. He wound the pickup along the old logging road until they reached the most recent lion kill.

"A blind man could find this calf," said William J. acknowledging the putrefying odor in the area of the decaying carcass.

Boesk donned a face mask and walked around the carcass making several notes on his clipboard. When he completed his examination, he returned to the vehicle without saying a word. They returned to the parking lot of the Deep Creek Bar where Boesk had left his vehicle that morning.

William J. and John approached him expectantly.

"Can we buy you lunch?" asked William J.

"No thank you, I really need to be going. I'll file my report with Animals Forever and someone at the home office will review and approve it. You should have a check by the end of the week. Good day, gentlemen."

Boesk ducked into his small foreign car and left.

"What do you think?" asked John.

"I think we oughta have lunch," said William J. "And I think he said 'check.'"

Kirk slipped into a booth at the Horseshoe Cafe across from Heidi Singer.

"Sorry I had to cancel our fishing trip," said Heidi. "Did you see my story?"

"I did."

"Quite a story if I do say so myself. Half a million

dollars seems a sufficient motive for murder. Wouldn't you agree?"

"Where'd you get the policy?" asked Kirk.

"You're not asking me to reveal a source, are you?"

"I most certainly am," Kirk said.

"Well, I'm not going to tell you," said Heidi.

"Look, I obtained that life insurance policy by means of an investigative subpoena. Now all of a sudden you show up with the same information. We suspect a leak in the sheriff's office. We need to find it. So, tell me how you came by the policy."

"I can't help you," said Heidi. "A journalist never reveals sources. You should know that."

"I can obtain an investigative subpoena, have you sworn and placed under oath. Then, I can ask you the same question."

"I still won't tell you."

"I could have you held in contempt of court."

"A contempt charge will be all you'll be holding against me."

"Don't force my hand," said Kirk. "Just tell me how you got the policy. I don't want to have to play hardball."

"You do what you've got to do," said Heidi sliding out of the booth. "I've suddenly lost my appetite. I'll see you later."

"See you in court."

Heidi walked quickly from the restaurant and crossed the street to her room at the Mustang Motel. There were certain compromises a journalist wouldn't make. It was so unfair of him to even ask. She seethed as she replayed the conversation in her mind.

The phone rang and she answered half expecting Kirk to be calling to apologize. Instead the distinctive flat monotone voice intoned, "More information . . . same location," and then the line went dead.

Stunned, she hung up the phone and wondered what she should do. She started for the door, hesitated a long moment and then continued out the door to her car. She drove the now familiar route up Main Street to the water tower park.

Except for a group of kids playing frisbee in the open grassy section, the park was deserted. She hurried up the walkway to the marble memorial.

There as promised lay another manila envelope. She removed the envelope from the top of the stone and discreetly slipped it in her purse.

She returned to the vehicle and immediately drove back to the motel. Once back in her room, she sliced open the end of the envelope and anxiously removed the contents.

She recognized the letterhead of the Montana State crime lab. She read quickly through the document to the analysis conclusion.

"Bacon grease," she whispered.

If Kirk didn't like today's story, she thought with a grim smile, he certainly isn't going to like tomorrow's.

Grover Arlen thumbed back through the report of private investigator Steve Smith, as he waited for Tanner Trent's arrival.

"Mr. Trent is here," said Ronald.

"Show him in and see if you can reach Steve Smith in Montana. If he's there, put him on the speaker phone."

The silver-haired Tanner Trent, immaculately dressed as usual, entered the office and sat on the plush black leather couch. Arlen handed him Smith's report. Trent quickly scanned the document.

"Mr. Smith's on the phone," said Ronald.

"Put him on."

"This is Steve Smith," said the flat monotone voice of the private investigator.

"Good morning, Mr. Smith," said Arlen warmly. "Thanks for the quick background checks on Kirk and Green. How'd you get so much detail in such a short time?"

"In a small town it's easy," said Smith. "I made a few inquiries at the local convenience store to find out the local gossip and then I went to the county courthouse. They have bound books containing every issue of the local paper for the last hundred years. A small town paper tells you who's been to whose house for dinner, every birth, death and other noteworthy happening. I not only know the names of the guests who went to Kirk's fourth birthday party but I can also tell you who won the game of 'Pin-the-Tail-on-the-Donkey.'"

"I also want to congratulate you for getting us the forensic report revealing the knife wound," said Arlen. "And kudos for obtaining the life insurance policy and putting it in the hands of the lady journalist. That was a good stroke."

"I'm not sure I ought to know, but how did you come into possession of those documents?" asked Trent.

"You'd be surprised where you can get and what you can learn with a US WEST hat, a shirt with your name over the pocket and a belt full of strange looking tools," said Smith.

"Don't tell me anymore," said Trent.

"I'm a little disappointed in the amount of dirt you reported on Kirk and Green," said Arlen. "They're both home grown products who made good and by all appearances look squeaky clean. You call that scandal?"

"I can only report what I find," said Smith. "If you want creative reporting, call the *National Enquirer*."

"Mr. Smith may have hit the nail on the head," said Trent. "This report just needs to have a defense attorney's twist on some of the elements to find scandal."

"What elements?" asked Arlen.

"Mr. Smith's report has documented a long term relationship between the district attorney and the Sharp family. John Sharp and Jefferson Kirk grew up on adjoining ranches. They played basketball together. Johnny Sharp even attended Jeffie Kirk's fourth birthday party."

"So they're good friends. So what?" asked Arlen.

"Why would a district attorney refuse to prosecute a husband for killing his wife despite evidence of marital discord, motive and opportunity?" asked Trent.

"Why?" asked an intrigued Arlen.

"So he could place the blame on the mountain lions that are killing the cattle of his long time friends and neighbors. By focusing the blame on the lions, Kirk and Sharp, with the assistance of Ben Green, could dispose of the cattle killing lions with the blessing of public opinion."

"At least that's what the press release of the benevolent animal right's organization will allege," said Arlen. "Tanner, you're a genius. What else?"

"The 'not so secret' relationship of the district attorney and the beautiful journalist," said Trent. "Nothing more than an attempt on the part of Kirk to manipulate the press. Singer was initially taken in but later learned about the cover up and exposed it."

"By now Heidi Singer ought to be in possession of an additional lab report also pointing to murder," said Smith.

"This is beautiful," Arlen said. "I think this thing will all come together. I'll issue a press release today suggesting all those things. Mr. Smith, you keep your ear to the ground. We'll be in Montana on Thursday night for the restraining order hearing on Friday morning. We'll touch base with you again at that time."

Kirk drafted an investigative subpoena ordering Heidi Singer to appear and offer testimony. To expedite matters, he funneled each draft page of the application and subpoena to his secretary for typing before beginning the next page.

He proofed the draft of the documents over Marge's shoulder. He placed the finished product in a file and immediately drove to the courthouse in Helena.

He caught Judge Ross during a recess and presented him with the formal request and the proposed subpoena.

"Trying to endear yourself to the press, eh Mr. Kirk?" asked Ross with a slight grin as he signed the subpoena with his customary flourish.

"Hardly," said Kirk. "I have an idea that I may be back asking for a contempt order."

Kirk drove back to Townsend reminding himself that he'd better brush up on his journalism law and the state of the law regarding testimonial privilege and immunity. Kirk arrived at the sheriff's office late in the afternoon. He delivered the documents to Ben for service on Heidi.

"You'd better be good to Jake tonight and give him an extra biscuit," Ben said after he reviewed the documents.

"Why's that?"

"Because I have an idea that after I serve these papers the only lovin' you're gonna get will come from that dog."

"That's the risk you take," said Kirk. "But it's good to know you've taken a personal interest in my love life."

"I did eliminate one possible source from whom Heidi Singer might have received the life insurance policy," said Ben.

"Who'd you rule out?"

"Steve Clay. I interviewed Clay this afternoon and he denied giving the policy to anyone."

"How'd the interview go otherwise?"

"A waste. Clay's retained Dan Todd to represent him. Todd was present throughout the interview. You know how it goes when the defense attorney does more talking than the suspect."

"Did you learn anything?"

"Not much. Clay adamantly denies any involvement in the murder and portrays himself as a double victim, bereaved husband and now falsely accused murder suspect. He admits to the increase in the policy limits of the insurance policy but claims it was just an adjustment prompted by a review of all their affairs when they moved to Montana. He claims to have been at home working on the landscaping at the time of the murder."

"He's not going to say anything incriminating now that he's got counsel. I sure wish we could've gotten to him before the news of the murder broke."

"If wishes were horses..." said Ben. "We didn't so where does that leave us?"

Kirk paused. "We can prove the murder of a woman in a remote mountain area. We know she and her husband had a fight just before she disappeared. We know the wife was becoming disenchanted with life in Montana and that her leaving would be financially devastating to the husband. We also know that her death would be a financial bonanza to the husband. We know the husband had appeared to be a different man shortly before the murder. We know the husband has no alibi for his whereabouts at the time of the murder. In short, we have a suspect with substantial motive and opportunity.

"Unfortunately we have no other evidence, no murder weapon, no eyewitnesses, no fingerprints, no blood stains. In short, we have no case."

"What else can we do?" asked Ben.

"Pray."

Chapter XVI

Kirk threw the morning paper back onto the oak desk. He paced back and forth between his office and the reception area.

"Next thing you know Animals Forever will be accusing John Sharp and me of committing the murder in order to frame the mountain lions," Kirk said.

"You have several messages," said Marge, handing him a stack of papers.

Kirk flipped through the messages as he paced. The notes were mostly requests for return calls from news agencies.

"These allegations are libelous," said Kirk to Marge even though his early morning review of journalism law told him otherwise. His status as a public figure made him fair game.

"How could we cover up the murder by putting the blame on a mountain lion before we even knew it was a murder?"

He thought the answer appeared obvious. A few calls to the media proved otherwise. The press wanted to find scandal and intrigue.

It became apparent that at least in the mind's eye of the media more than ample evidence existed to arrest Steve Clay for the murder of his wife.

The presence of the bacon grease continued to haunt Kirk. The inner voice he had come to trust over the years nagged at his conscience and told him he had heard or seen something in his recent past related to bacon grease. He couldn't dredge up the recollection.

Kirk retreated to the law library and re-reviewed the investigative files and forensic reports from the deaths of

Kathy Clay and Faith Benson. The review left him feeling even more discouraged.

Reluctantly he closed the file and forced the subject from his mind. With only two days left before the hearing on the restraining order, he couldn't dwell on the murder investigation. He had to prepare the position of Headwaters County in response to Animals Forever's suit.

In an attempt to coordinate a defense, Kirk called Jeremy Haskins, the staff attorney for the Montana Department of Fish and Game, the other named defendant.

"Jeremy, Kirk here. I thought I'd touch base to see what you're planning. It'd be nice if we could present a united front."

"Our position's going to be quite simple," Haskins said. "It's our stance that the Department of Fish and Game is specifically charged by law with protecting, preserving and perpetuating mountain lion populations. We believe it is within our province by law to decide what is in the best interest of the species and not some outside organization such as Animals Forever. The department spent a great deal of money and energy adopting a comprehensive environmental impact statement for the management of mountain lions.

"The Mountain Lion Environmental Impact Statement allows the killing of lions in situations similar to what has transpired in Headwaters County. I intend to put our chief wildlife biologist on the stand and introduce the EIS through his testimony. After that, I intend to point and re-point to the Montana law which gives us the jurisdiction to call the shots. Hopefully the judge will rule from the bench and dismiss the restraining order. What'd you have in mind?"

"I intend to make an evidentiary record of the discovery of the bodies and the actions of the sheriff in chasing and killing the lions. I was also intending to put William J. Sharp on the stand. He grew up in that country and can give a first hand historical perspective relative to the re-establishment of mountain lions in Headwaters County. In light of Animal Forever's allegations of conspiracy between myself and the Sharp family, I may have to rethink that approach. I would, however, be interested in seeing your Environmental Impact Statement prior to the hearing."

"I'll fax you one when we hang up," said Haskins. "Frankly, I'm a little bit nervous about going to court against Tanner Trent."

"Don't worry about it," said Kirk. "He still puts his pants on one leg at a time. It's just that each leg is carefully tailored and costs more than our two wardrobes put together. See you in court."

Kirk heard the whir of the office fax machine which spit out paper for ten minutes. Kirk gathered the lengthy document and retired to the sanctity of the law library.

He read the Mountain Lion Environmental Impact Statement from start to finish.

Kirk learned that mountain lions, *felis concolor*, were once the most widely distributed mammal in the Western Hemisphere. They had roamed from northern British Columbia to the southern tip of South America. In recent years Montana's lion population had reclaimed much of its former habitat, being found in forty-six of the fifty-six counties.

The EIS stated that more attacks on humans had occurred in the past twenty years than during the previous eighty.

The report also recounted that ninety percent of all human fatalities by lion attack involved victims less than sixteen years old. Yearling and two-year-old mountain lions were responsible for over sixty percent of those fatalities. The report attributed the increase in lion/human confrontations to the influx of people searching for a rural lifestyle in lion habitat.

The EIS noted that where mountain lion and livestock

ranges overlap, livestock could be "expected to become part of the prey base." The EIS said, "In areas of higher mountain lion densities, cow/calf pair operations may not be economically feasible." The Sharps would be thrilled to read that conclusion, he thought.

He also learned that mountain lions are one of the few wild animals that breed year-round and that males breed with numerous females whose areas overlap with his own.

"Only man's stupid enough to try to live with one female," he said as he made notes of the salient portions of the document.

The EIS seemed well researched although many of the studies relied upon were twenty to thirty years old—a fact which would not go unnoticed by Tanner Trent and Animals Forever.

The findings of the EIS also seemed consistent with Headwaters County's first hand experiences with the death of Faith Benson. A young child killed by an adolescent lion seemed to fit the pattern.

The legal position advocated by Jeremy Haskins seemed sound to Kirk. Despite some inherent flaws, the EIS at least attempted to approach the subject objectively and scientifically. It went far beyond any research or analysis conducted by Animals Forever.

Kirk's thoughts were interrupted when Marge Johns leaned her head into the library, "I'll see you in the morning."

"Where are you going?" Kirk asked.

"It's five o'clock," said Marge "I'm going home unless you're paying overtime."

"Wow, the day kind of got away from me," said Kirk. "I've still got a lot of work to do yet tonight. I'll see you tomorrow."

Kirk returned to his labor and without the normal office

interruptions, completed most of his research and hearing preparation.

As Kirk sat back in the quiet of the law library in the vacant courthouse, he reflected on the consequences of the pending hearing. Were lions, people and cattle just incompatible? In his tired state, the answers seemed difficult and overwhelming. As difficult as the problems created by having your girlfriend thrown in jail for contempt he thought as he flipped off the lights of the law library and trudged down the courthouse stairs.

"We've only got five more days," Webster said as he swung off the sorrel horse. "After that I'm back on the road for three months solid."

"We were close tonight," said Roemer. "The wind shifted at absolutely the wrong time. A whole lotta things gotta go right for a successful bow hunt and unfortunately one wrong thing can wipe out all the right things."

"It seems like everything that could happen has happened," said Webster.

"I'll unsaddle if you'll get the cook going on dinner," said Roemer.

"You've got a deal," said Webster handing the halter rope to Pete. "I'll have the cook salt down two big T-bones and I'll break out some of that aged Missouri sour mash whiskey."

As Webster crossed the courtyard to the chalet, Roemer pulled the saddles and bridles from the sweat covered horses and hung them in the tack shed. He filled his pockets with handfuls of the alfalfa pellets and fed them to the eager animals as he quickly brushed their sleek hides.

Roemer led the two horses beyond the courtyard to the

gate entering the small horse pasture. He put the horses through the gate and smiled to himself as the horses ran into the pasture and immediately rolled on the ground with all four feet in the air.

Roemer leaned on the gate post and surveyed the meadow. The screech of a magpie at the far end of the meadow where the creek meandered against a high cut bank interrupted his reverie. The flutter of wings of the black and white birds focused his attention. He watched a pair of magpies rise out of the creek bottom, alight on the single branch of a dead cottonwood tree and then drop back into the bottom.

"What the hell," said Roemer as he did a quick inventory of the ranch horses. Satisfied that all horses were present, he reopened the gate and marched across the horse pasture to the boundary fence. He pushed down on the top strand of barbed wire and stepped out of the horse pasture into the grazing land beyond.

He followed a narrow trail down the cut bank and used a fallen quaking aspen tree as a bridge across the small mountain stream. At his approach, the flock of magpies scattered and flew into the tops of the nearby willows where they sat chastising his presence. He kept his eyes fixed on the spot from which the birds had flushed. He entered the broad gravel bar below the steep bluff.

Such a small portion of the Longhorn steer was visible beneath the mass of dirt and sticks that Roemer initially thought the carcass was a beaver. A closer examination revealed the freshly killed steer.

The paw prints of a mountain lion were clearly recorded in the soft sandy soil. Roemer stood up and walked around the carcass. He stopped and slowly gazed across the expanse of mountains above him.

He retraced his path across the meadow to the tack shed. Roemer started toward the chalet to report the discovery to his employer. He stopped halfway across the courtyard and he diverted his course to his own pickup truck. He reached under the seat and pulled out a dusty leather scabbard. From the scabbard, he removed a lever action Winchester .30-30.

Roemer rummaged through the cluttered glove compartment of the old pickup and retrieved a half empty cartridge box. He loaded the rifle and laid it across the seat of the pickup. He would keep the discovery of the steer to himself. He turned his attention to the thought of Missouri sour mash whiskey and headed toward the chalet.

Chapter XVII

Wednesday, September 17th

Kirk had not slept well. He had been disturbed all night by images of bacon grease, mountain lions, hound dogs, Sarah and Heidi. He slipped on his running clothes and sleepily walked out the front door.

As he ran, his head cleared and then, as had happened in the past, his mind served up the recollection that he had struggled so hard to dredge up from his memory. He now remembered where he had recently heard the term "bacon grease" apart from the forensic report.

Unfortunately the incident seemed so trivial that he felt a let down. The incident seemed totally unrelated to the murder of Kathy Clay. He at least felt the relief of not having to keep racking his brain for the answer.

There could be no connection between the recollection unless . . . . And then as he frequently did as he ran, he considered a ludicrous hypothesis and tried to prove it.

He mulled over possible situations which could some-how connect the two events. His mind wandered through each possible scenario as through a maze. He finally imag-ined a scenario which could pull the incident into the context of Kathy Clay's murder and the presence of bacon grease on her body.

He had all but dismissed his theory, but something kept nagging at him as he drove to work. He argued with himself and then quelled his alter ego by promising to check the forensic report as soon as he arrived at the office. A quick scan of the findings ought to quickly dispel his theory.

When he arrived at his office, he read through the report on the autopsy of the lion originally believed responsible for the death of Kathy Clay, but he could not locate the results he sought.

He called the pathologist in Great Falls.

"I have gone through the report of your examination of the mountain lions," said Kirk to Dr. Hanning. "I haven't been able to find the existence of any drug screen on the blood of the lions. Was such a test run or am I missing something?"

"Unless there's a special reason, we wouldn't perform a drug screen on the lion," said Hanning. "We routinely perform such a test on the human victims. Lions aren't usually big drug users."

"Touche," Kirk said. "Could you still run such a test?"

"I still have the blood vials. So sure, it'd be easy to do. What do you suspect?"

"I hesitate to say. It's so outlandish you'd probably just laugh. Also, because of all the information leaks we've been having, I don't want to risk that one of my far out theories might receive some media attention. Why don't you just humor me and run the screen. If it turns up something significant then I'll tell you."

"I'll do it," said Hanning.

At 9:05 a.m. Kirk and a court reporter sat in the courtroom of the Headwaters County Courthouse. As they waited, the court reporter added a new bundle of the narrow columned paper to her recording machine.

"I can't believe anyone would just up and ignore a court order to appear," said Kirk looking at his wrist watch. "Judge Ross will have a cow when he finds out...."

The double doors of the courtroom burst open and Heidi Singer entered with Don Todd at her side. Dressed in a navy blue pinstriped business suit she followed Todd to the front of the room.

"My client and I are here pursuant to your investigative subpoena," said Todd handing the subpoena to the court reporter.

"Are we ready to get started?" Kirk asked.

"No time like the present," said Heidi.

The court reporter asked Heidi to stand and raise her right hand and then administered the oath.

She moved forward and took the witness stand.

"Would you state your name for the record?" Kirk asked.

"Heidi Elizabeth Singer."

Kirk handed a copy of the *Helena Independent Record* to the court reporter who affixed a bright red sticker and handed the paper back to the prosecutor.

"Ms. Singer I'm handing you a copy of a newspaper marked 'State's Exhibit A,'" Kirk said. "On page one there is an article under the byline of Heidi Singer. Did you write that article?"

"I did."

"In that article you repeatedly refer to a life insurance policy issued by American Fidelity Life Insurance and Trust Company on the life of a Kathleen Murphy Clay. In preparing that article did you have a copy of that life insurance policy in your possession?"

"I did."

"Ms. Singer, how did you come into possession of that policy?"

Heidi Singer looked to Don Todd and carefully answered, "After consulting with my legal counsel, I refuse to answer that question. I believe I have a privilege not to testify. I will not reveal my source."

"Do you refuse to divulge the name of the group or individual that provided that policy of insurance?"

"I do refuse."

"Ms. Singer, the day after this article appeared you published another article in which you referred to a forensic lab report from the Montana Crime Lab. In preparing that article did you have a copy of that lab report?"

"I did."

"How did you come to be in possession of a copy of that lab report?"

"I also refuse to answer that question for the same reasons."

"You understand that your refusal to answer these questions could result in you being cited for contempt of court?"

"I do."

"Has your counsel advised you of the possible consequences should the court find you in contempt?"

"He has."

"And you still refuse to answer?" Kirk asked.

"I will not reveal a source."

"I guess we're done then," said Kirk snapping his file folder shut. "I guess we'll see you back in court."

Kirk walked from the courtroom to his office where he dictated a formal request for a contempt citation.

"Are you sure you want to do this?" Marge asked.

"No one is above the law," said Kirk.

Chapter XVIII

Thursday, September 18th

"All rise," the bailiff said. The single television camera allowed by Judge Russell panned the jammed to overflowing courtroom as the Federal District judge walked from his chambers and assumed the bench.

"Be seated," directed Judge Russell and the courtroom came to order.

Kirk and Ben Green sat at one end of the long counsel table. Tanner Trent, Grover Arlen and the local counsel retained by Animals Forever occupied the opposite end. Fish and Game Director Donald Parker and staff attorney Jeremy Haskins sat in the middle of the table directly in front of the judge.

Kirk glanced over his shoulder to the audience portion of the courtroom. He spotted Heidi sitting in the third row with her notepad ready. She wouldn't be hard to serve, he thought.

On his way to the Federal Courthouse, he stopped by the State District Court and presented Judge Ross with a petition for a contempt citation. Judge Ross had issued an order directing Heidi Singer to appear before him and show cause why she should not be held in contempt. Kirk delivered the signed order to Ben for service upon the taciturn journalist.

Federal District Court Judge Myron Russell had a reputation as a no nonsense judge who was not at all hesitant about taking matters into his own hands to expedite a case.

Judge Russell cleared his throat and made eye contact with all the attorneys seated below him.

"Counsel, I should advise you that I have read all of the briefs filed in this matter so I think we can dispense with any lengthy legal arguments. Before we begin, however, I do have one question of Mr. Trent."

"Yes, Your Honor," said Trent rising to his feet.

"I note that your action is limited to the conduct of the Headwaters County Sheriff and the Fish and Game officials within the confines of Headwaters County. If I understand the legal argument as set forth in your brief, isn't your argument just as applicable to the general hunting of mountain lions and in particular to the hunting of mountain lions by the use of dogs?"

"Your Honor raises a very good point," said Trent. "This action began as a reaction to the conduct of Headwaters County Sheriff Ben Green. However, this incident has subjected the entire issue of hunting mountain lions to scrutiny. It is our opinion that the Department of Fish and Game failed to properly census the lion population within Montana before allowing a hunting season. We also believe the hunting of lions with dogs to be inherently cruel and inhumane to both the lions and the dogs.

"Because of these factors, we believe that the hunting of mountain lions ought to be prohibited in all of Montana. In that regard, I should advise the court that in the near future we shall be amending the underlying complaint in this action to affect such an outcome."

"Our inquiry this morning is limited to the events in Headwaters County," said Judge Russell.

"That's correct, Your Honor, but I merely wanted to point out that we believe the court to be correct in its assessment that the arguments presented today can easily be extrapolated to the State of Montana as a whole. There are some important distinctions however.

"Your Honor, in Montana, the general mountain lion hunting season is set to coincide with the presence of snow cover and periods of low birth rates. The snow cover during the hunting season allows hunters to determine if the lion they are hunting is a female with dependent young. Snow cover also allows the opportunity to back track for kittens if a female is found to be lactating after being killed.

"In the instant case the actions of Sheriff Benjamin Green and the Department of Fish and Game were taken without the benefit of snow cover. Their actions are more grievous because young lions are jeopardized by chasing and killing at this time of year.

"It is the position of Animals Forever that no one knows how many mountain lions are inhabiting Headwaters County. When the wildlife biologists don't know how many lions are present in any ecosystem, there is no way they can determine that the death of one lion is not the death of one lion too many.

"Secondly the pathology reports reveal that the lion responsible for the death of Faith Benson has been killed. Also, it has now been determined that the death of Kathy Clay was in fact a homicide and not a lion attack. Despite that determination, the lion which scavenged the body was needlessly slaughtered.

"So the only lions that are now being restrained from being killed are those responsible for the cattle predation. Because Animals Forever has announced and put into motion a program to reimburse ranchers for documented cattle losses suffered as the result of lion attacks, we believe no irreparable harm will be inflicted if the restraining order remains in effect until the resolution of the underlying action."

"Thank you, Mr. Trent," said Judge Russell. "I believe I understand your position. Mr. Haskins, does the department wish to come forth and show cause why the restraining order should not be continued?"

"We welcome the opportunity, Your Honor," said Jeremy Haskins rising quickly. "We would like to call biologist Alfred Plano."

The biologist wearing the Fish and Game uniform with

the distinctive arm patches came forward. He was sworn in and took the witness stand.

Jeremy Haskins asked Plano to recite his extensive educational training in wildlife biology and his many years of practical experience in the field.

Haskins then asked the clerk of court to mark a thick document as an exhibit. Alfred Plano identified the document as the Environmental Impact Statement for mountain lion management in Montana. In answering questions about the management plan, the biologist displayed an encyclopedic knowledge of the charts, graphs, and other data contained within the voluminous document.

Once the management plan was received into evidence, Haskins asked, "Mr. Plano, is the killing of predatory lions allowed under the management plan?"

"Most definitely."

"In your opinion will the actions taken by the Headwaters County and the Fish and Game officials in this case significantly impact the lion population in Headwaters County?"

"It would certainly impact those killed," said Plano drawing a ripple of laughter from the audience. "But in the overall scheme of things, the impact would be minimal. In the long run, the habitat and the prey base are the controlling population factors. If you have both of those factors present, another lion would soon move into and take over the range of any lion killed."

"Thank you, Mr. Plano," said Jeremy Haskins. "Your witness, Mr. Trent."

Trent lifted the management plan off the clerk's table and held it dramatically over his head for all to see.

"This is a very impressive document," Trent said. "I'm sure you're quite proud of it."

"Thank you. I am."

"I'm sure much time, effort and money went into its preparation."

"I can assure you it did."

Trent handed the document to Plano.

"Can you show me in this document where I can find how many mountain lions there are in the State of Montana?"

"You can't count lions like other game animals . . . ." began Plano.

"That's a 'yes' or 'no' question," interrupted Trent.

"No, I can't."

"Can you tell me by examining this document how many mountain lions there are in Headwaters County?"

"No."

"Apart from this document, can you tell me how many mountain lions reside in Headwaters County?"

"Not exactly. I can make some estimates. We do know the numbers have increased significantly."

"On what do you base that statement?" Trent asked.

"Well, for one thing the number of sightings is up three fold from ten years ago and the number of lions killed during the hunting seasons has increased. Even though we have raised the quotas each year, the quotas are being filled more quickly each year."

"Isn't it true that over the last ten years subdivisions have been developed in isolated areas that are prime mountain lion habitat?"

"Yes."

"Could an increase in the number of people in those areas result in an increase in the number of lion sightings?"

"I'm sure it could," said Plano.

"So maybe the sightings are a reflection of the increase in human populations rather than increases in lion populations."

"Sightings are just one of the factors."

"You also testified that the increase in the number of lions killed during the hunting season was also a factor in your determination that the lion population has increased."

"Yes, it is."

"Maybe I'm just a poor dumb attorney from the city but aren't you saying that the more lions that are killed the more lions you have."

"We have quotas," said Plano.

"Mr. Plano, hypothetically, if we went out in one year and killed every mountain lion in Montana, then wouldn't your logic dictate that the lion populations would in fact be larger the following year."

"No of course not. You're taking it to an extreme...."

"Am I? Mr. Plano, who wrote most of the actual language of the management document?" Trent asked.

"I did."

Trent flipped through the document to some specific language he had previously noted.

"Do you recognize this quote?" asked Trent reading from the document. "'The management of mountain lion has been chronically hindered by a paucity of information on population dynamics.' Did you write that, Mr. Plano?"

"I did."

"Isn't that just fancy biologist language for we haven't a clue how many lions we've got and we haven't ever really known?"

"The specific habits of mountain lions make determining

lion numbers very difficult," said Plano. "The species doesn't lend itself to the employment of traditional counting methodologies. We have . . . ."

"Thank you, Mr. Plano," said Trent cutting him off. "I have no further questions."

Jeremy Haskins on redirect had Plano explain the difficulties of determining mountain lion populations.

"The secretive and isolated character of the species makes an exact census impossible," said Plano.

Plano described the canvassing of elk populations for comparison.

"On a bright day during the winter you can get in a plane and fly over the winter range and see ninety percent of the elk. You will rarely ever even see a mountain lion from the air."

When Haskins finished, Trent made a brief and repetitive cross examination. Alfred Plano was then dismissed.

"Do you have any further witnesses, Mr. Haskins?" asked Judge Russell.

"No, Your Honor," Haskins said. "Our position is fully set forth in our legal memorandum. Briefly, it is our position that the people of Montana, through the legislature, have entrusted the department with the responsibility of managing mountain lions. We have adopted a comprehensive management plan based on a well documented and extensively researched environmental impact statement.

"The actions of the department and the Headwaters County officials were consistent with that management plan. We would, therefore, respectfully request that the restraining order be dismissed and the management of mountain lions be returned to the Department of Fish and Game where it rightfully belongs."

"I understand your argument," said Judge Ross. "Mr. Kirk."

Kirk rose to address the court. Because of the allegations of collusion between himself and the Sharp family, he had not intended to use the testimony of William J. Sharp. The tenor of the hearing made him reconsider and he advised the court, "Your Honor, I would call William J. Sharp."

William J. stood and came forward. He stepped through the narrow gate of the wooden divider that separated the audience from the court officials. The clerk administered the oath and William J. seated himself in the witness chair and looked attentively toward the district attorney.

"Mr. Sharp, how old are you?" asked Kirk.

"I'm seventy-three."

"How many of those years have you resided in Headwaters County?"

"All of them. I was born in the original Sharp homestead cabin on Deep Creek."

"As a boy growing up in Headwaters County, did you have any experience or exposure to mountain lions?" asked Kirk.

"No. I did not."

"Why not?"

"Because there weren't any lions," William J. said.

"When did you first become aware of a lion presence in Headwaters County?"

William J. explained the gradual change which had occurred on the ranch property since his boyhood. Lions were a bountied animal until 1962 he advised the court. In the early seventies, he'd seen an occasional lion track. In the eighties, lion tracks were numerous and he increasingly rode across lion killed deer and elk remains. Now in the nineties, the lions had finally started making cattle and at least one human their prey.

"Mr. Sharp, how many calves have you lost this year to lion attacks?"

"At least six, maybe seven."

"How has this affected you financially?"

"In a normal year, it wouldn't have been a big problem but with calf prices down, it's made things tough. I'm not sure we can make some land payments. It's really got us looking at our hole cards. I don't know what we're going to do."

"During those same years of increasing lion populations were people also beginning to move into that country."

"Yes, we've experienced the Montana Mirage."

"The Montana Mirage?"

"Yeah, city people see the wildlife, the views, the trees and the clear mountain streams. They move to the high country because of those things but when they get there, the wildness and other attractions disappear. Destroyed by their presence. That's the Montana Mirage."

"Do you think we'll see more lion/human attacks because of this movement to the mountains?" Kirk asked.

"It's inevitable," said William J.

"Thank you, Mr. Sharp. Your witness, Mr. Trent."

"Mr. Sharp, isn't it true that in all of your seventy-three years, you've never actually seen a mountain lion?" asked Trent.

"Yes, that is correct."

"Yet, you want this court to believe that the lion numbers have increased to the level that they are threatening people and the financial viability of ranchers?"

"I haven't seen the wind in those same seventy-three years," William J. said. "But let me assure you, Mr. Trent, there is wind in Headwaters County."

"Mr. Sharp, you testified on direct examination that you will experience economic hardship because of the cattle killed by lions. Isn't it true that you've filed a claim with Animals Forever for reimbursement for those losses?"

"Yes, we made a claim."

"And did not a representative from Animals Forever visit the Sharp Ranch and investigate your claim?"

"Yes."

"And didn't he tell you that your claim would be processed and that you would be sent a check for your losses?"

"Yes, he did. But I haven't seen the check."

"Let me assure you that you will get such a payment," said Trent. "Mr. Sharp, if you are fully reimbursed for the cattle losses due to lion attack, how have you been harmed?"

"It wouldn't be nearly as bad as not being reimbursed," William J. said. "It could still mess up your breeding program. For instance,...."

"Excuse me, Mr. Sharp," Judge Russell said. "Gentlemen, I think I've heard enough. I'm ready to make my ruling."

"But your Honor," said Tanner Trent. "I still have some more questions for Mr. Sharp, particularly concerning his relationship with the Headwaters County District Attorney."

"Mr. Trent, I'm about to rule in your favor, don't make me reconsider," Russell said. "It seems to me that everyone's in agreement that the lions responsible for the human victim or victims as the case may be, have been killed. Animals Forever has agreed to fully compensate the ranchers for their cattle losses. I fail to see any harm in continuing the restraining order until a ruling on the underlying action."

"Your Honor," Haskins said scrambling to his feet. "We

273

believe that the absolute jurisdiction in this area lies with the Department of Fish and Game."

"This is a preliminary hearing on the restraining order," Russell said. "I understand your position. But your argument goes to the merits. I will consider it at the proper time and not before."

"Your Honor," said Trent. "We'd like the opportunity to finish our cross examination of Mr. Sharp and the further opportunity to question Sheriff Green about his actions in defiance of the restraining order."

"Mr. Trent, the purpose of this hearing, in case you have forgotten, is not to serve as a forum for the views of Animals Forever. I'm granting the relief you requested and keeping the restraining order in effect until my decision on the underlying action. Court's adjourned."

Judge Russell rose and departed through the small door located behind the witness chair.

Kirk looked over to Haskins and shrugged. Ben was not at all disappointed at the outcome. The restraining order was still in effect but the nervous sheriff had been spared from having to speak in public.

Outside the courtroom, media representatives cornered each of the three attorneys.

"What's your reaction to the judge's ruling?" asked a reporter for the local Helena television station thrusting a microphone in front of Kirk.

"I think the department's argument on the jurisdictional question could have, and should have, been ruled on at this time. But I am glad that the judge didn't allow Tanner Trent to use this proceeding as a forum to publicize Animals Forever's views."

"What do you think will be the ultimate outcome?"

"From what we heard this morning, it's obvious that

Animals Forever has an agenda beyond Headwaters County," said Kirk.

"Could you give us a quick on-camera interview in the courtroom?" asked the reporter grabbing Kirk by the arm and easing him in that direction.

They entered the courtroom just as Heidi walked out.

"Seems like the courtroom is the only place I see you anymore," said Kirk.

"It looks like that's where we're going to meet again," said Heidi holding up the contempt citation.

"This way Mr. Kirk," said the reporter.

After the interview, Kirk hunted up William J. who had been in demand by the reporters.

"Nice job," said Kirk.

"Must've been a hell of a job," said William J. "As soon as I testify, the hearing ends and the judge grants Animals Forever's request. If I'd have talked awhile longer, the court would've probably restrained cattle ranching in Montana altogether."

"You more than held your own. But now that this hearing is out of the way, do you still want me to approach Ray Webster about a conservation easement?"

"I can't see any harm," said William J. "How do you intend to approach him?"

"I haven't quite decided. I'll give it some thought on the drive back to Townsend."

Chapter XIX

Friday, September 19th

Kirk froze in place. The bull elk focused directly on his place of hiding. He hadn't bugled for some time, but still the bull had fixed on his position.

The small five point was a satellite bull to a herd of elk he and Ray Webster had spotted shortly after daylight. They had stalked to their present position and Kirk had positioned Ray Webster about fifty yards in front of him.

The bull had responded immediately to Kirk's bugle and had begun moving in at the mew of his cow call. Unfortunately, the bull had passed to the right of Webster just out of bow range.

The bull eased around Kirk's hiding place trying to get downwind of his adversary and the flirting cow elk. The elk circled around Kirk and began moving back toward Webster's position. Kirk saw Webster rise and the bull turned toward the movement. Kirk chirped once on the cow call and the bull whirled and again fixed his attention in his direction.

The aluminum shafted arrow seemed to shoot from the small juniper bush. It entered the elk behind the front shoulder. The bull turned and crashed off through the timber.

Kirk met an excited Ray Webster at the spot where the bull had stood.

"I hit him," said Webster.

"I saw," said Kirk. "I think it was a good hit, too."

"Let's go after him," said Webster.

"We need to give him some time to die," said Kirk. "We don't want to push a wounded elk. Let's go back and get the horses. By the time we ride back to this spot, we can start tracking."

Kirk tied a red and white ribbon on a fir tree next to where he had discovered a spot of blood. The two men then walked down the ridge to where the horses were tethered.

"I hope Pete doesn't think I'm after his job," said Kirk as they mounted.

"Actually he was really glad you offered to guide," said Webster. "He had some project he wanted to pursue this morning. The cook said he was up and out long before us and heaven knows we got out plenty early ourselves."

They rode out of the stand of quaking aspens where the horses had been tied and on through the lodge pole pine thicket from where they had first called the elk. They returned to the first spot of blood.

The tracking methodology was rudimentary. Kirk would find a blood spot and Webster would join him and tie a piece of the red and white ribbon to the nearest branch or shrub. Webster remained at that site until Kirk moved ahead and located the next bright red splotch.

This technique made for slow progress but after an hour they could determine the trail of the elk by watching the line of ribbon behind them. The bull seemed to be moving due south, but when he reached the bottom of the first drainage, he turned due west and started down the drainage.

"I think this is a good sign," said Kirk. "He doesn't want to go up hill. I think he's hurt bad."

Another two hundred yards down the drainage, they found the elk laying dead in the tall grass.

Kirk extended his hand to Webster and shook it vigorously.

"Congratulations, on your first elk. You'll never forget this moment."

"You're right about that." said Webster. "I finally did it. I was beginning to think it'd never happen."

Webster took off his hat and flung it high into the air and shouted "Yahoo" as loud as he could.

A blood stained but happy Ray Webster and his attorney guide rode back to the chalet. Webster described the events leading up to the kill at least a dozen times.

When they dismounted at the tack shed, Pete Roemer was coming across the horse pasture using a shovel as a walking stick.

"Get ready to go to packin', Pete," said Webster.

"You got one?" asked Roemer.

"It went like clockwork," said Webster who again told the story. This time with much animation and sound effects.

Webster noticed the shovel for the first time and asked, "What ya been doin'? Digging worms?"

"Just playing in the dirt," said Roemer.

"Let's go in," said a jubilant Webster to Kirk. "We can get some lunch and toast our success and you can tell me all about this conservation easement business. Pete and I can pack out the elk this afternoon."

"Sounds good to me," said Kirk.

"You comin', Pete?" asked Webster

"I'll be along in a minute," said Roemer.

Roemer hung the shovel back in the toolshed and then walked across the courtyard to his pickup. He inserted the Winchester .30-.30 into the leather scabbard and shoved the scabbard back under the seat. He hurried back across the courtyard toward the chalet repeatedly tossing and catching an empty cartridge casing.

On the lip of the bluff overlooking the home ranch and

the hay meadows of Deep Creek, John Sharp sat astride his roan gelding. He shaded his eyes against the afternoon sun and watched to see if the mail truck would stop at the lane leading into the Sharp Homestead.

The galvanized metal mailbox gleamed in the sunlight. The blue and white mail truck made a graceful sashay into the pull out, paused briefly and then continued up the drainage.

"Probably just more bills and junk mail," said Sharp as he urged the horse off the bluff.

At the bottom of the slope, Sharp splashed across the creek and loped up the lane to the mailbox. He reined the horse alongside the metal box and leaned over in the saddle to retrieve the stack of mail.

He sorted through several envelopes until he found the one with the logo of Animals Forever. He ripped open the letter and looked past the cover letter to the check itself.

"This has to be a mistake," he said.

He unfolded the cover letter and read the explanation. Sharp grasped firmly onto the stack of mail and galloped up to the ranch buildings in search of William J.

He found him in the shop pounding on a piece of scrap metal balanced on the point of an anvil. The clang of iron striking iron echoed throughout the metal shop building.

"Here's your check from Animals Forever," shouted John above the noise.

Too proud to put on his eye glasses, William J. held the check at arms length in order to read the numbers.

"Two hundred dollars." he said. "How'd they come up with that figure?"

"The letter says that they ruled only one of the six calves a 'documented lion kill'. The others they said were quote

279

unquote 'inconclusive.' They estimated the weight of the calf at 400 pounds and paid 50 cents a pound."

"That calf weighed over 500 pounds easy—probably closer to 600," said William J. "And the cattle market may be down but the lowest price for steer calves that I've heard of has been 65 cents."

"But what are you going to do?" asked John. "It's a voluntary program. You can't sue 'em."

"We're just pawns." said William J. "We've been used and there ain't a damn thing we can do about it."

"They bought themselves a whole lot of advertising for 200 bucks," said John.

"Let's hope Kirk can do better with Ray Webster." William handed the check back to John.

After his lunch with Webster, Kirk drove home and changed from hunting clothes to his trademark navy blue pin striped suit. By the time he arrived at the courthouse, it was almost four o'clock.

Shortly after he arrived, Ben entered Kirk's office carrying a fax.

"I just got a copy of a drug screen on the mountain lions," said Ben. "Did you request it?"

"I did. What's it show?"

"Nothing on the first lion, but the blood of the second lion contained traces of Telazol. What's Telazol?"

"An animal tranquilizer?," asked Kirk. "Let's call Dr. Hanning and find out for sure."

"What's Telazol?" Kirk asked Hanning.

"It's one of the drugs of choice for anesthetizing animals," said Hanning. "It's primary use is in syringe darts for capturing certain game animals. I assume you have an explanation for its presence in the lion's blood."

"I have a theory, but it's still really unsubstantiated," Kirk said. "I'll call you after we check out a couple leads."

Kirk hung up and looked at Ben.

"You know Ben, every once in awhile, a blind pig finds an acorn. I think one of my theories may have panned out."

"God help us," said Ben. "But come on and tell me why you ran the drug screen on the lions."

"When I first read that bacon grease was the foreign substance on the body of Kathy Clay, I knew I'd recently read or heard something dealing with bacon grease in some other context. But for the life of me I just couldn't think of it. It finally came to me one morning while I was running.

"The day we were standing in the parking lot behind the sheriff's office after you came in with the first mountain lion, we were all just shooting the breeze. For some strange reason, you and Slats Smith got on the subject of cures for constipation."

"I remember that," Ben said. "Slats mentioned that he always keeps a coffee can full of bacon grease by his kitchen stove. He related how one time a hound dog of his had lapped up about half of the can. He very descriptively told you that the dog had the runs for a week and that he'd definitely recommend bacon grease as a cure all for constipation."

"What's that got to do with a drug screen on the lions?"

"Nothing, but that's what got me to thinking about Slats, bacon grease and the murder of Kathy Clay. The other thing that's always bothered me about this case ever since we learned of the existence of the knife wound was the timely coincidence of the body being scavenged by a mountain lion.

"I kept trying to think of possible scenarios which would allow for the murder and then the fortuitous baiting of the lion to the body. Nothing seemed logical until I speculated that maybe the lion wasn't baited to the body but maybe a live lion was taken to the body.

"I then had to envision how that could be accomplished by the killer. I assumed that to be captured alive, a mountain lion would have to be snared or darted out of a tree.

A snare would have caused severe injury to the leg caught in the snare. The autopsy report revealed no such trauma on either lion. I figured that if the lion were darted, the blood ought to show the presence of the drug."

"What's the next step?" Ben asked.

"I think we need to proceed carefully," Kirk said. "You may want to check with local veterinarians and drug suppliers to see if anyone recently purchased Telazol."

"That shouldn't take long," said Ben.

"You also may want to check out whether Clay had any veterinary training or related experience that may have familiarized him with tranquilizing animals," Kirk said.

"Maybe all this just means that Slats Smith darted the lion out of the tree instead of shooting him," said Ben.

"But why would he lie about it?" asked Kirk.

"Who knows with Slats?" Ben shrugged. "He'll lie sometimes when tellin' the truth would help him more."

"I need to get going," said Kirk. "I've got several messages to return and then I have a meeting with the Sharps."

"I'll follow up on those leads while you're doing that," said Ben. "Anything else we oughta be concerned about?"

"Let's keep the drug screen results and this investigation between us. I sure don't want to read about Telazol in the morning paper."

By the time Kirk arrived at the Deep Creek Bar, the Sharps were seated in the open beamed dining room.

"Sorry I'm late," Kirk said. "Every time I started to leave the office, the phone rang."

John and William J. looked at him expectantly.

"How'd you make out with Webster?" asked John.

"Went great. I called in a nice little bull and he arrowed him at about fifteen yards."

"I meant with the conservation easement," John said.

"That's about as uninterested in a hunting story as I've ever seen you," said Kirk. "Webster wasn't interested in a conservation easement on the Chappel property. He said it wasn't big enough to waste his time."

"I guess it was worth a try," said William J.

"But he would be interested in a conservation easement if it covered the Chappel property and the rest of your mountain pasture," said Kirk.

"For how much?" asked John.

Kirk told him.

"$250,000." John said. "You've got to be kidding."

"No," Kirk said enjoying the reaction to the revelation. "He wants to meet with you and William J. tomorrow. He's about to head back on tour and he wants to iron out the wrinkles before he leaves."

"How'd you convince him?" asked William J.

"He was an easy sell. For starters, he was in one hellacous good mood after killing that elk. He certainly liked the tax advantages, but more importantly he really liked the idea of having a buffer between himself and the rest of the world.

"He figures that a conservation easement on your property guarantees him all the space he wants without the responsibilities of ownership."

"For that amount of money, I'll be a buffer zone," said William J.

"I never thought I'd say this," said John raising his glass, "but here's to Ray Webster."

"You need to remember that this is a one time shot," Kirk said, "and you'll be forever surrendering the subdivision values of your land."

"I'll drink to that, too," William J. grinned and signaled the waitress for another round of drinks. "The last thing I want to see is that country subdivided."

"A conservation easement won't screw up my next business venture, will it?" asked John.

"What business venture?" Kirk asked.

"Cattle drives." John said. "We'd take guests on one of the spring drives to mountain pasture. Remember how much Heidi enjoyed herding cows the day we weaned the calves? It'd be another source of income apart from the cattle market."

"You mean you'd charge guests to move your cattle?" asked Kirk.

"Exactly," John grinned. "Can't beat having someone pay you to do your work."

"Where is Miss Heidi?" asked Mary Sharp.

"That's a long story," said Kirk.

"You'd better marry that girl," said Mary. "She's a keeper."

The news of Webster's offer made the meal a joyous occasion with much banter and laughter. After dinner, Kirk drove home and called Ben.

"What'd you come up with?" Kirk asked.

"Not much," said Ben. "I checked at Francisco Pharmacy. They carry veterinary supplies but not Telazol. I drove out to the vet clinic, but there was a sign on the door saying that Doc Lewis was out on a call tending to a wire cut horse. It didn't say where. I'll check with him first thing in the morning."

Kirk held onto the receiver and considered calling Heidi. Unable to think of quite what to say or how to say it, he decided against the call. After the contempt hearing on Monday maybe conversation would come easier.

Chapter XX

Saturday, September 20th

At 6:30, Ben called Kirk.

"I told ya I'd get a hold of Doc Lewis first thing in the morning," said Ben. "I'm here at the vet clinic and we just went through Doc's index cards of drug purchases. Slats Smith purchased Telazol on September 4th. That's the date we brought in the first lion. Where do we go from here?"

"Meet me at my office in fifteen minutes," said Kirk.

Ben was waiting for Kirk when he pulled in front of the courthouse.

"What's your plan?" asked Ben handing Kirk the index card reflecting the drug purchase by Slats Smith.

"I think we need to get a search warrant," said Kirk as they walked up the stairs to his office. "I'll start typing out an application. You call the justice of the peace and see if he'll come down and sign the warrant."

Kirk entered his office and went to the computer. He skimmed the police reports for pertinent dates and places while he waited for the computer to do its internal checks and morning warm up. He set forth the facts which supported probable cause for the issuance of a search warrant.

"The judge will be down in about twenty minutes," Ben said.

As they waited for the judge to arrive the sheriff asked, "Do you think Slats really has it in him to kill someone?"

"I don't know," said Kirk. "Slats has always been a rabble rouser and barroom brawler, but I never thought him capable of murder. I've been thinking about his possible motivation. Chasing that first lion gave Slats the most fame of his life. Maybe he enjoyed the limelight and wanted to continue being the hero and the center of attention. If he could catch the mountain lion responsible for the death of Kathy Clay, he'd only add to his renown."

"But is that enough to kill for?" asked Ben.

"Maybe there's some connection between Slats and Clay. Heaven knows Slats loves money and Clay stood to gain handsomely if his wife was killed accidentally by a mountain lion. Maybe Clay purchased Slats' services to make the murder seem like a lion mauling. Or maybe we're just trying to apply rational thought to an irrational individual."

"How are we going to approach Slats' house?" asked Ben. "There's only one lane into there and those hounds of his start barking whenever anyone gets within a half mile of those kennels. We certainly aren't going to sneak up on him."

"I'm also still afraid of the information leaks," Kirk said. "I hate letting anyone else know what we're about."

"Maybe we ought to just drive up to his house in front of God and everybody," Ben said.

"He doesn't know we suspect anything," said Kirk. For all he knows, we've got another lion for him to chase."

"I wouldn't want to go in without some back up," said Ben. "I think I'll call Woods to assist us. He can stay out on the highway as a lookout and provide assistance once we talk to Slats and serve the warrant."

Deputy Woods and Jim Maynes, the justice of the peace, came up the stairs of the courthouse together. Maynes reviewed the sworn application, signed the warrant and handed it to Ben.

Ben and Kirk left in the Wagoneer and Deputy Woods followed in his patrol car. Ben stopped at the convenience store and ran inside for a minute. "I visited with the clerk," said Ben upon getting back in the Wagoneer. "She told me that Slats had been in a time or two with Steven Clay. Seems that Slats did some odd jobs for them."

They left the Mini Mart and headed to the Slats Smith residence. Woods stopped the patrol car on the Canyon Ferry highway at the head of the lane leading into the Smith place.

"There's probably a simple explanation for all this," Kirk said as they bounced down the rutted lane.

"Well, I'd sure like to hear it," said Ben.

As anticipated, the baying of the hounds announced their arrival. Neither Slats nor his truck were in sight.

"This is perfect," said Ben. "Woods can radio us if Slats heads this way. We can search at our leisure."

Ben parked the Wagoneer next to the weathered shop. The howling of the dogs increased as they crossed the cluttered courtyard to the old house.

Ben knocked loudly on the door and then entered. The piles of clothing, old magazines and other items left little doubt that whatever skill Slats enjoyed as a lion hunter, he lacked as a house cleaner.

"Dr. Hanning said that Telazol needs to be kept refrigerated," said Kirk.

Ben opened the door of the old white refrigerator.

"My God, there's mold cultures growing on mold cultures," Ben said as he sorted through the contents.

"No drug bottles?" Kirk asked.

"Bingo." said Ben. He reached in and pulled out a small drug bottle with "Telazol" clearly typed on the label.

A further search produced no other evidence. They left the residence and walked back across the courtyard to the shop. Old tires, scrap iron, nuts, bolts and assorted automobile parts filled every nook and cranny of the old chicken house. But perched on top of an old harness collar lay a syringe dart gun with the syringe still attached. Ben picked up the gun and examined it closely.

"Not the sort of thing you'd find in your average shop," said Ben.

"I'm not sure there's anything you couldn't find in this shop," Kirk said.

The sound of an engine diverted their attention. The motor noise grew louder, coming from the Canyon Ferry Lake side of the old homestead rather than from the lane connecting with the highway.

When Kirk and Ben walked around the corner of the shop, Slats' flatbed pulled to a stop by the Wagoneer. Slats looked at them and then shifted back into gear and accelerated up the lane. Ben sprinted to the Wagoneer and radioed to Woods.

"Slats is coming your way at a high rate of speed. Stop him."

Ben and Kirk scrambled into the Wagoneer and started in pursuit.

"Sheriff," radioed Deputy Woods, "I had the road blocked with my patrol car but he went into the barrow pit and got around me. He's heading south on the Canyon Ferry Highway."

"Follow him. He'll soon have to turn left up Deep Creek or right toward town."

Neither the patrol car nor Slats' flatbed were in sight when Ben turned off the dirt lane onto the pavement, but a cloud of dust still hung in the air where Slats had cut the corner through the barrow pit.

Deputy Woods radioed, "Ben, he's headin' east on the Deep Creek Highway."

"Keep after him," said Ben. "I'll see if there's any assistance in the area."

The voice of the Highway Patrolman stationed in White Sulphur Springs broke in, "Sheriff Green, I'm at the top of the

Deep Creek Canyon heading your way. I'll find a narrow spot where he can't get around me and set up a roadblock."

Ben pushed the accelerator to the floor and climbed the long sand hill which angled out of Townsend before dropping down into the Deep Creek drainage. From the top of this hill, Ben and Kirk had a panoramic view up the Deep Creek valley. The flashing lights of Deputy Woods patrol car were visible far in the distance.

When they passed the Deep Creek Bar and entered the narrow portion of the canyon the highway patrolman radioed, "He's stopped about two hundred yards down the road from me. He's getting out of the vehicle. He's running up the ridge to the south."

"Stay there," Ben said. "We'll be there shortly."

When they rounded a sharp corner in the narrow canyon, they saw Slats' flatbed at the edge of the roadway. The highway patrol vehicle was parked in front of Smith's truck and Deputy Wood's car sat directly behind. The top lights of both vehicles were activated. Both officers stood on the shoulder of the road staring up the steep slope.

"He didn't even hesitate when I told him to stop," said the patrolmen. "He just looked back once and kept on a goin'."

"Is he armed?" asked Ben.

"Not with a rifle," said the patrolman. "All he has with him is a small pack."

"Do you want us to chase after him?" asked Woods.

"No, he'd lose us in that thick timber in a minute," Ben said. "Let me see if I can reach Sergeant Frank in Gallatin County."

Ben ran back to the Wagoneer and talked on the radio for a few minutes before joining the others.

"I caught Sergeant Frank in his vehicle on Interstate 90.

He was taking his dog out for some field training exercises. He'll be here in about forty-five minutes."

"Slats will have a big lead on us by then," Woods said.

"Kirk, what's the country above here like?" asked Ben.

Kirk knelt in the dirt and drew a quick map with a twig.

"He's headin' right into my old stompin' grounds," said Kirk. "If Slats keeps headin' south, he'll cross out of the Forest Service lands onto the Sharp summer range. If he crosses the top of the ridge, he'll drop into Greyson Creek. There's a Forest Service road which switchbacks to the top of Black Butte and connects with the Flathead Indian Trail right about here," he said making an "X" in the dirt. "He'll have to cross one of these roads. If we drive up on top, when the dog gets here we ought to knock off most of the head start we've given him."

"Sounds like a plan to me," said Ben looking anxiously down the road even though the Gallatin County officer wouldn't be in sight for another forty minutes.

Kirk scooped up a handful of dirt from where he'd drawn his sketch and handed it to the sheriff.

"What's this?" asked Ben.

"Thought you might want the map for future references." Kirk laughed.

William J. Sharp leaned against the railing on the deck and looked out over the meadow below the chalet.

"You've got some mighty fine country here," he said to Ray Webster.

"It's that view that sold me on this place," said Webster following William J.'s gaze.

"Now if you'd just get rid of those Longhorns and get some real cattle," said William J.

"You're starting to sound just like Pete," said Webster.

Pete Roemer and John Sharp joined the other two men on the deck.

"Ray, you listen to William J.," Roemer said. "He knows cattle."

"You guys leave my Longhorns alone," said Webster "You may not like 'em but the mountain lions sure do."

"And it looks like Animals Forever is gonna keep us from doing anything about the lion problem for awhile longer," said William J.

"I think the lion problem's behind us," said Roemer.

"What makes you think that?" asked John Sharp.

"Let's just call it a gut feeling," said Roemer.

"I hope you're right," said John. "I don't want to have to use all this conservation easement money feedin' mountain lions."

William J. turned back from the railing and said, "Ray, now that we've got this easement business pretty well hashed out, why don't you and Pete come over to the Dry Creek cabin tonight for dinner and a little card playin'? Doc Adams, Garth Hart and their boys are up for the weekend. We can sure burn up a couple more T-bones."

"I'd like that," Webster said. "Be all right if I bring my guitar along?"

"I guess you could fill in during Garth Hart's breaks," John smiled.

"I don't believe it," said Webster. "I play second fiddle to a 'Garth' in Nashville and now I gotta play second fiddle to a 'Garth' in Montana."

"Don't let it bother you none," said William J. "You just keep practicing and you'll probably go far."

Sergeant Frank held the cotton gloves taken from the cab of Slats' truck to the nose of the German Shepherd.

"Hans, suche."

Frank grasped the leash firmly and began walking along the Flathead Indian Trail. Kirk and Ben followed some distance behind.

"If Slats doubles back or goes west, this ain't gonna work," said Ben.

"I think he'll come straight up one of these ridges," Kirk said. "He won't double back because he can't risk the chance that someone's right behind him. If he goes west, he'd fall into Black Butte Gulch. I'm betting he'll follow the path of least resistance that leads to the south."

A quarter of a mile along the two track trail, Hans lunged sharply off the trail jerking Sergeant Frank with him.

"He's on the scent," Frank said.

They climbed to the top of the ridge and started down a steep, heavily timbered slope into the Greyson Creek drainage. The dog never wavered and kept his nose to the track. At one place, depressions in the thick bed of pine needles revealed the passing of a human foot.

The track crossed the creek bottom and started straight up the opposite incline. The three men and dog followed, their sides heaving from the heavy exertion. They pushed onward allowing themselves a brief breather halfway up the slope.

A hundred yards from the ridgetop, Hans jerked the leash from Sergeant Frank's hand and raced away.

"Damn it." Frank said. "He jerked just as I was gettin' a new wrap on the leash. He'll be hard to find. He was really antsy. I think he was closing in."

The men scrambled to the horizon. They stood on the brow of the hill searching frantically.

Unsure of the route, they crossed a small swale full of jack pines and looked over the vast country beyond. Finding Slats or the dog seemed an overwhelming task.

Suddenly Kirk grabbed Ben's arm and pointed to a ponderosa pine several hundred yards above them. On the first branch, silhouetted against the blue sky, sat Slats. Hans circled the trunk of the large tree looking up and growling.

The three men crossed the open sagebrush park to the tree. Before the sheriff could say anything, Slats called down, "Ben, you gotta know. I didn't plan on doing it. It just happened. It was totally spur of the moment."

"Why don't you tell me about it?" said Ben.

Perched on the single limb, Slats Smith began a rambling disjointed explanation.

"After we brought in the first lion, I took Spike to Doc Lewis to get him patched up. We'd come across another fresh lion track that morning but you said we couldn't kill it because of the court order."

Slats went on to relate that he had obtained some Telazol and gone back after the lion. When it treed, he had darted it and transported it back to his place.

"When I got up on Friday morning and saw her pacing around the kennel, a spittin' and a growlin', I decided that capturing the lion alive was about as smart as the time I roped a cow elk. So that afternoon, I drove up Dry Creek intending to let the lion loose.

"Above the Sharp cabin, I see the Clay woman jogging up a coulee away from her car. I'd worked a few days for her husband. She'd treated me like I was some form of pond scum—wouldn't even talk directly to me. Well, I saw her there, prancing up the road in her pretty little jogging outfit, and it just pops into my head that if the lion'd chase and kill her, I could track the lion down again.

"By the time I got the truck stopped, she'd already went out of sight. Then I got to thinkin', what difference would it make if I killed her or the lion killed her? She'd be just as dead. So, I walked up the gulch and waited for her to come back."

Slats went on to explain that he had left the body on the old logging road and went back for his truck. He had then placed the body in an empty kennel and let the lion in with the body. Slats related that the lion had showed no interest in the body so he had driven home and returned with a can of bacon grease.

"I pulled off the clothes and poured the bacon grease on the body. I set the kennel with the body on the ground and jerked the kennel with the lion off the back of the truck. That really pissed the lion off. She was a snarlin' and a growlin'.

"When I finally get the lion in with the body, she really tears it up. I couldn't stand the noise—the cracking of bones and the lapping of blood. I walked up the gulch to get away from it. When I went back, I shot the lion and threw it on the truck. I dumped the remains of Mrs. Clay out on the road. I drove home and put the lion in my big chest freezer."

"Ben, you gotta believe me. I didn't plan this thing. It just happened."

"Slats, you're under arrest for the murder of Kathy Clay," said Ben. "Now let's get you down."

"Platz," said Sergeant Frank to Hans who at the command pressed himself to the ground.

Slats half slid and half climbed down out of the tree. Ben handcuffed him and radioed to Woods who had driven to a vantage point on the Ridge Road to provide mobile assistance.

Eventually, the group of four men accompanied by Hans, emerged from the dense forest cover and walked across the sagebrush flat to the patrol car.

They drove to the starting point on the Deep Creek Highway. Deputy Woods, with Slats Smith in leg irons, left for Townsend while Ben called for a tow truck to transport Smith's vehicle to the county impound yard.

"Thanks for your help," Ben told Frank as he loaded Hans into the kennel.

"My pleasure," said Frank. "I wanted a training session for Hans. There's nothing like the real thing."

"It's kinda ironic, isn't it?," said Ben. "The great chaser of mountain lions captured by being chased by a dog."

"I can already hear Grover Arlen spouting off about a 'poetic sense of justice,'" said Kirk.

"Not to mention the 'slaughter of the innocent lion'," Ben said.

"Kirk, how about you write up a press release on this case while I tie up a few loose ends?"

"I'll do that right after I draft a Deliberate Homicide complaint," Kirk said.

Late in the afternoon, Kirk appeared before the justice of the peace and swore to a felony complaint charging Slats Smith with the murder of Kathy Clay.

He crossed the alley to Ben's office and handed a stack of press releases to the dispatcher. He turned to leave, but then paused and thought a moment.

"Give me one of those back."

Kirk went to his Blazer and drove to the Mustang Motel. He rapped lightly on the door to room #10. Heidi opened the door.

"Can I come in?" he asked. "I've got a press release that you might find interesting."

She took the document and stepped back, letting him inside.

"What a story." she said. "Who'd have thought?"

"Pretty amazing," Kirk said.

"He always seemed so easy going and friendly. I'd have never guessed."

"You only saw one side of Slats," said Kirk. "He has a dark side. His compass has never pointed true north. But I didn't think him capable of murder."

"But why'd he do it? Not just to drum up lion chasing business, I hope."

"That was apparently a part of it," said Kirk, "but only a small part. Slats told us that he'd worked for the Clays for a few days and that he felt Kathy Clay had slighted him."

"Hardly seems a reason to commit murder."

"You need to understand Slats' background," said Kirk. "He was raised in the hill country of Missouri, the son of a sharecropper. From what I gather, they were poorer than dirt and treated like second class citizens. Slats has always had a chip on his shoulder. He's always gotten along fine with anyone who agreed with him and treated him as an equal. But if anyone ever crossed him or talked down to him, or if he even perceived he was being put down, then watch out.

"There was a hard-of-hearing bartender in town who didn't hear Slats' requests for a drink. After the third call, Slats thought he was being ignored and jumped over the bar, spun the bartender around and went to pounding on him. Another time, a ranch hand called him 'white trash' and Slats went berserk. Spent ten days in the county jail for misdemeanor assault.

"Also, Slats, although I don't understand why, has always thought of himself as somewhat of a ladies man. If he thought Kathy Clay was turning her nose up at him, he had all the more motivation he needed when the opportunity presented itself."

"Do you think there's any possibility of collusion between Slats Smith and Steven Clay?"

"Slats denies it and I tend to believe him. I think our suspicions about Steve Clay were illfounded. I don't think there was any conspiracy whatsoever."

"What about her jogging clothes?" asked Heidi.

"Slats said he'd stuffed them under the seat of his truck and forgot about them until he read the articles in the paper. He drove up the creek one day and tossed them over the creek bank next to where her car was parked."

"So if I understand this correctly, there was one woman-killing lion and one woman-killing man and Animals Forever stirring the pot?"

"That's about the size of it."

"What about the lion that's been killing cattle?" asked Heidi.

"He's apparently still out there, still doing what lions do best. Although Pete Roemer thinks otherwise."

"So, now that this murder case is solved are you still going to have me thrown in jail for contempt?" asked Heidi.

"Of course," Kirk said. "But I will see that you get conjugal visits."

"You only get conjugal visits if you're married," said Heidi.

"I said I'll see that you get conjugal visits," said Kirk smiling broadly.

"Does that mean . . . ?"

"That's about as close to a proposal as you're going to get. Maybe you ought to take it."

As she walked toward him, she said, "You know I never knew and still don't know who gave me those documents. They were just left in the city park and I picked them up."

"Tell it to the judge," said Kirk as he reached out and pulled her to him.

THE END